Engineer's and Manager's Guide to Winning Proposals

Professional Development Library

Engineer's and Manager's Guide to Winning Proposals, Donald V. Helgeson

Global High-Tech Marketing: An Introduction for Technical Managers and Engineers, Jules E. Kadish

Preparing and Delivering Effective Technical Presentations, David L. Adamy

Forthcoming Titles

Total Quality Management in Systems Engineering, Joseph Kasser

Successful Product Strategy for High-Technology Firms, Eric Viardot

Managing Engineers and other Technical Employees, Douglas Soat

For further information on these and other Artech House titles, contact:

Artech House
685 Canton Street
Norwood, MA 02062
617-769-9750
Fax: 617-769-6334
Telex: 951-659
email: artech@world.std.com

Artech House
Portland House, Stag Place
London SWIE 5XA England
+44 (0) 71-973-8077
Fax: +44 (0) 71-630-0166
Telex: 951-659

Engineer's and Manager's Guide to Winning Proposals

Donald V. Helgeson

Artech House
Boston • London

Library of Congress Cataloging-in-Publication Data
Helgeson, Donald V.
Engineer's and manager's guide to winning proposals / Donald V. Helgeson
Includes bibliographical references and index.
ISBN 0-89006-780-5
1. Proposal writing in business. I. Title.
HF5718.5.H45   1994   94-22132
658.15'224.–dc20   CIP

A catalogue record for this book is available from the British Library

ARTECH HOUSE, INC.
685 Canton Street
Norwood, MA 02062

International Standard Book Number: 0-89006-780-5
Library of Congress Catalog Card Number: 94-22132

10 9 8 7 6 5 4 3 2 1

Table of Contents

Foreword

This book tells it like it is, the good and the bad. The government procurement system is not perfect. Our contracting process is not perfect. Nothing is in a democratic society, but it is the best that free-thinking people can devise and will always be subject to improvement. As Winston Churchill once said, "Indeed, it has been said that democracy is the worst form of government except all those other forms that have been tried from time to time." And so it is with our procurement system.

After working on scores of proposals for a number of firms, I became convinced that there just had to be a better way to prepare a proposal than the usual disorganized, often frenetic, always exhausting and frustrating *modus operandi* employed by many companies. This book is the result of trying to bring order out of this chaos by providing managers and proposal writers with a systematic approach to proposal preparation.

This book is the result of many years of experience down in the trenches, writing and managing technical proposals. Its dual purpose is:

- To help engineers, scientists, and technicians to prepare properly written inputs to a proposal by giving them a sensible, systematic procedure for approaching this task and
- To help managers—proposal managers, middle managers, corporate managers, and supervisors—organize and direct a proposal team and provide it the support it needs to function effectively.

If I seem to be a little hard on some of the miscreants one encounters in this business, it is only because I have been exposed to so many of them. Only the insecure who see themselves in the various anecdotes herein will be offended.

The book presumes some exposure by the reader to the business world from the standpoint of the technically-oriented person. It is not concerned with accounting or program costing except insofar as that concerns engineering, scientific, or management personnel. The various chapters are interdependent, and therefore I recommend that you read them in sequence rather than in random fashion.

I firmly believe that if the principles and procedures set forth in this book are faithfully and competently implemented, you are bound to produce a proposal that successfully passes the technical gate. From that point, winning the contract is a matter of cost effectiveness, the competence and reputation of your corporate management, and the integrity of the customer's decision makers.

Acknowledgments

Acknowledgment is hereby gratefully extended to the many kind and generous associates who graciously provided their suggestions and encouragement in the preparation of this book. I especially want to thank the following individuals: Dr. Jeffrey Fitzsimmons of the University of Florida; Ken Marcou, chief systems analyst of Johnson Controls; Dr. Eugene J. Putzer, Vitro Technical Services; William D. Smythe, executive vice president of D P Associates; Don Streitzel, formerly of the Ballistic Missile Defense Systems Command (now with Johnson Controls); Don Thimsen, program manager of the Huntsville division of XonTech, Inc.; Lieutenant General Richard G. Trefry (Ret.) of the Institute of Land Warfare; Gabrielle Wehl, general counsel of D P Associates; and to Lucille for her trenchant observations and critiques.

Introduction

When I first started writing proposals (as an additional duty of my job as an engineer), I looked through the library for a good book on how to write proposals, but in vain. So I had to learn from trial and error—mostly error. I think there were two turning points in my educational process. The first was when I went to a debriefing on why we lost out on a NASA proposal down at Houston. The Source Selection Evaluation Board (SSEB) chairman patiently walked us through our proposal step by step pointing out our mistakes—and there were many—and even using audiovisual aids to show where we did poorly in comparison to some of the other proposals. A very impressive performance for which I was most grateful. I regret to say that I haven't seen the like since. It was almost like a tutorial, not only on proposal preparation, but also on how the SSEB evaluates the proposals. I inferred that the chairman would be using this same debriefing material to justify his decision on award of the contract when he reported to the powers that be in Washington. I'm afraid the procurement process, at least for government services, has gone downhill from there in recent years.

The other turning point was about a year later. An ex-government employee, moonlighting while working on his master's degree, came to us as a consultant. I was managing a large ($100,000,000) proposal even though I had had very little experience in this field. I was trying to write major portions of this proposal as well as manage it. (*Not* a good idea, as you will find out in this book.) This consultant would review and critique each of our inputs, and he even had a scoring system. Well, my inputs started coming back with depressingly low scores, including comments that I was not adequately addressing the request for proposal (RFP). I thought I had addressed the RFP and told him so. He became very agitated and started jumping up and down (literally), and told me that, because my responses were so mixed up with Madison Avenue sales pitches and *themes* and motherhood, it would take a detective to find where I was responding to the RFP.

Suddenly it dawned on me what we had been doing wrong. It was like switching on a light, like walking out from a cave into the daylight, a revelation. Now everything began to fall into place. I had been making it too hard. All they wanted were simple, straightforward responses to the RFP instructions and the statement of work (SOW). Like answering questions on a final exam. I still had a lot to learn, but from that moment on, proposal work was almost fun because I had come out into the light and knew where I was going.

As I look around now some 25 years later, the last nine as a consultant, I still see everywhere I go people groping around in that cave and my heart goes out to them. So that is what this book is all about—a helping hand to guide and lead you out of the darkness.

After working on dozens of proposals for three different companies as an additional duty to my primary job as a systems engineer, I became convinced that there had to be a better way than the disorganized, chaotic, frenzied *modus operandi* I had been enduring. So I set out to bring some order out of this chaos by writing a book (the forerunner of this one) that described a systematic approach to proposal preparation: *Handbook For Writing Technical Proposals That Win Contracts,* published by Prentice-Hall. The new book that you are reading now encompasses everything that was in *Handbook* plus the distillation of about ten years more of diversified experience working for a number of companies, large and small, as a consultant.

Proposal preparation, like any other challenging endeavor, requires: (a) planning; organization; and diligent, systematic preparation; (b) the application of some basic, tried-and-true principles; and finally (c) some thoughtful, focused effort. It does not require interminable, fruitless meetings, 14- to 16-hour days, 7-day weeks, a cast of thousands chasing feverishly around in all directions. All this can be avoided with a little good, enlightened management and some systematic direction, such as this book describes.

I have compiled my own list of reasons why proposals fail to make the grade. And what this book sets out to do is to enable the proposal writer or manager to avoid these pitfalls. I believe there are just six reasons why most proposals fail to make the grade and these are described in this book along with detailed remedies for each.

One day, when I was still working on the staff of a large corporation, the president asked me to have lunch with him. I knew he had something on his mind, because he wasn't the kind who asks you to lunch just to be sociable. We had just been through a horrendous exercise writing a difficult proposal that ended in the usual panic situation compounded by confusion. While I was still unfolding my napkin, he fixed me with his beady eyes and asked, "Don, why does every proposal we do have to be like it was the first one we ever did?"

"For one thing, it's because you never make the decisions that enable your staff and line elements to commence preparation until just before the RFP comes out, and that's too late. Then you appoint a proposal manager who has little experience in the subject matter and no stake whatever in the outcome. Then the proposal manager has to beg, borrow, and steal to get qualified people on his proposal team.

When the proposal team is formed, he or she still has no authority over them, so all deadlines for completing proposal inputs are ignored with impunity."

"But Don, I did tell the proposal manager he could have anyone he wanted."

"Yes, but you neglected to tell the line managers, and so they let all the key proposal people go on vacation during the proposal period. These people saw what was coming and begged off. Nobody likes to work on proposals any more, because they always end up like this one did. And the most qualified people we have for a proposal like this are in the line outfits."

"Well, how about all the people I brought in from our other contracts?", he asked, now with an edge in his voice.

The waiter came by to take our order. "I'll have a martini, hold the olive," I said. I still had a lot more to say before I was in the mood for lunch.

"There were about one or two who did a good job; the rest were more of a drag than a help. All they wanted to do was talk, talk, talk, and carry on with their endless bull sessions. And they ignored all direction from the proposal manager. After all, they don't work for him. In short, there is no operating chain of command when we do a proposal. The proposal manager is in an impossible position; he or she has the responsibility without any authority."

"Well, would you like to tell me what else I've been doing wrong?" Open sarcasm and hostility now.

"Gladly," I said, throwing caution to the winds. (I had already decided I wasn't going to go through another exercise like we just did, anyhow.) "I thought you'd never ask. It would be nice if you would pick a proposal manager who not only has a stake in the outcome, but also with a little training and experience in managing a proposal. This last one was practically invisible; he was actually out on the golf course when the rest of us were putting in 14-hour days.

"The one before that never heard of a proposal plan, so there was no coordinated effort whatsoever, and furthermore, he didn't get around to preparing a proposal outline until three weeks after the RFP came out. I finally made one myself, so we could get started writing. And the organization chart he came up with looked like something an autistic child would construct with a tinker toy set."

"Well, I'm going to put you in charge of the next proposal and we'll see how well you do."

"No, you're not. I've already decided to go into the consulting business, and thanks for the lunch."

What you are going to get in this book is some plain, no-nonsense advice and instruction from someone who has been there. First, my prescription for a well-organized marketing section and an explanation of how it should tie in with the proposal team. Then a chapter on how to organize a proposal team in such a way that it really does function as a *team*.

The underlying philosophy in this, as in all organizations, is that there must be an operating chain of command, coordinated action, and clearly understood incentives for doing the job diligently and in a timely manner. And likewise, potentially unpleasant consequences for a negligent and sloppy performance.

This philosophy is developed further in the second chapter, "Organizational Structures." This chapter will provide you with some of the timeless axioms of leadership and then move on to the criteria that everyone needs to apply in constructing an organization chart.

The next three chapters will get down to the nitty gritty of actually writing the proposal, from analysis of the RFP and preparing the proposal plan and general outline to the actual details of how to write the proposal inputs.

Then we will examine the usual procedures used by the customer for evaluating your proposal, including the "best value" concept. You need to know this in order to have a clear idea of what your objectives in writing the proposal should be and how it will affect your approach.

Then, a chapter on special applications of proposal preparation. While this book generally applies to all types of proposals, there are some types that require unique approaches. Those that I address in the final chapter include: engineering development contracts, R&D contracts, and grants. Although grants are not contracts, I'm including a brief review of the subject here (a) because there are similarities of technique and proposal writers often get drawn into this field, and (b) because the grants world should not be ignored. It is big business in these times, aggregating over $100 billion per year.

And finally, some words of wisdom distilled from my more than 20 years of experience writing, critiquing, and managing technical proposals of all types. Whether you are a proposal manager, writer, or corporate executive, you will get some no-nonsense advice from someone who has seen it all—from laboring in the trenches to jousting with corporate management.

This book is dedicated to the long-suffering engineers who are often dragged unwillingly into this alien environment to stoically endure the long hours of work and frustration and then stand silently aside as the fat cats in corporate management take the credit for any successes. I can identify with you and hope that this book will make your life a little easier and that that you will have the good fortune to work for an enlightened company where management and leadership are not just words.

Chapter 1

The Marketing Function: Where It All Begins

But the Idols of the Market-place are the most troublesome of all idols . . . for men believe that their reason governs words . . . .
—*Francis Bacon*

Introduction

While the main purpose of this book is to help proposal managers and the hapless engineers who are, willingly or not, thrust into the strange milieu of putting together a proposal good enough to win a contract, we must first consider the nature of the environment in which we are going to be working.

The "environment" described in this book is based on the winning of contracts with the government. There is a good reason for this. All contracting with the federal government is controlled and codified by a set of regulations called the "Federal Acquistion Regulations," or FAR. Each state has its own regulations, varying from state to state. And within each state there are various local regulations promulgated by counties, municipalities, and so on and on. Then there is the contracting that goes on within the private sector. There is no codification of procedures here (which is as it should be in a free society). The only controlling factor here is the implementation of statutes in effect in the various jurisdictions and the underlying body of common law (case law) that controls all conduct, civil and criminal, throughout the land and applies equally to local, federal, individual, and corporate conduct.

Now the reason for that brief civics lesson is to set the stage for explaining to you why this book is, of necessity, based on the process of contracting with the federal government. You can readily see that it would be impossible to write a book that would apply the rules of all the 50 states, the thousands of local governments, and the infinite variety of dealings between individuals and companies in the private sector.

But be not dismayed! If you know and understand the methods and processes of contracting with the federal government, you have the basis for understanding

1

and applying this knowledge to all the rest. For one thing, the entire contracting structure is based on a thousand years of jurisprudence that we inherited from England, the common law which governs us all today. The common law is based on the principle of fairness and stability in our personal and commercial activities—a thousand years of trial and error applying what works and rejecting what doesn't work.

So in this book, we are living in an environment that most people would regard as having the *highest* standard of conduct between contractor and customer, because the FAR regulates that conduct under severe penalties if violated. In fact, that is one of the most dramatic differences between contractual relations in the private sector and those with the government. Generally speaking, if Contractor A cheats or lies to Contractor B in securing a contract, then Contractor B might have a cause of action to sue Contractor A, period. But if Contractor A lies or cheats a customer, the government, he or she stands a good chance of going to jail.

Another distinguishing feature that pervades the entire process is that in normal commercial enterprises, you have one or two or some finite number of contractors and 10 or 50 or an infinite number of customers. But in dealing with the government, you have the opposite: a myriad of contractors and only one customer, the government. And that is what you must bear in mind as you read this book. Most of the instruction you will be exposed to herein applies to commercial contracting and marketing as well as government contracting. The principles are generally the same. But in selling to the government, it doesn't do much good to run expensive ads in the paper or engage in hard-sell used-car-salesman techniques. Instead you must write a good proposal that responds to the customer's needs. You are generally dealing with professionals, experts in their field, wary of any Madison Avenue gimmickry. Your reputation must be impeccable, because among that one customer's hierarchy, they all talk to one another, and you will soon be found out if you engage in shady deals or are guilty of gross incompetence. And of course, honesty is important if you want to stay out of trouble, and I mean *real* trouble.

And so the exceptions noted here will affect your approach in coping with the one or the other (commercial or government). So then, with these caveats in mind, we address ourselves to the place where it all begins, the organization and implementation of an effective marketing capability. Like they used to say in the paratroopers school, "It don't mean a thing if you don't pull that string." Well, all the rest of this book "don't mean a thing" if you don't have an effective marketing capability.

The starting point for any company's growth is its marketing organization. If this organization is poorly organized or poorly managed, virtually everything that follows will come to naught. For it is the marketing group that must seek out and identify the viable sales opportunities, create a favorable image of your company, and make the one-on-one contacts in the customer community that provide the fertile ground for future growth. After many years as a *proposal* manager and *proposal* consultant, I have reluctantly come to the conclusion that the effectiveness of the marketing organization is just as important as writing good proposals and indispensable to company growth. The reasons for this will become clear as we get further into this book, but for now let us focus on the concept for organizing this most important function.

First however, a word about the marketeers themselves. These are a special breed of people. They should have a technical background in most cases, so that they can clearly understand and articulate the engineering, scientific, or mathematical concepts upon which your technical proposal will be based. They should have some business background, certainly enough to distinguish between viable business opportunities and the pie in the sky. A working knowledge of contract law would be useful, and also a well-developed knowledge of the laws upon which the FAR (Federal Acquisition Regulations) is based and the rules of ethics involved if dealing with the Government.

But successful marketeers need something more. They must have charm, poise, initiative, empathy, and good judgment. They must have the good sense to know when to talk and when to listen. They must always remember that their primary mission is to gather accurate and reliable information on the one hand and, on the other, to project a favorable image of their company. Some of the marketeers I have known focus too much on the charm and image and never seem to know when to shut up and listen. You can't learn anything when you are doing all the talking. You can find out whatever you need to know just by keeping the other person talking.

The Marketing Organization

In the broadest sense, marketing begins with the identification and tracking of potential contracts and ends with the delivery of a proposal and award of a contract. Right now, however, we are talking about the specialists who identify and track an opportunity and make the customer one-on-one contacts. These are the people who comprise your marketing organization. Once the RFP is issued, their role is reduced to an advisory capacity and the proposal manager assumes full responsibility for the remainder of the effort. I have seen it tried in other ways. Like having the marketeers try to write the proposal. It doesn't work. Besides not being cost effective, it is unrealistic to expect the marketeers to have the in-depth knowledge and experience to prepare technical proposals covering a broad range of disciplines. Also, marketeers must be good talkers, and it is unusual to find a good talker who is also a good writer.

So how to organize the efforts of these talented and diverse individuals so that they are all singing off the same sheet of music and so that their activities are coordinated with the other key players in the process? The organizational *concepts* involved in forming a good marketing organization are like Newton's laws, immutable. That is because they are based on two fundamental imperatives: (a) the absolute necessity to fix responsibility for well-defined goals in a specific, discrete, identified individual; and (b) the requirement to provide a recognizable incentive for

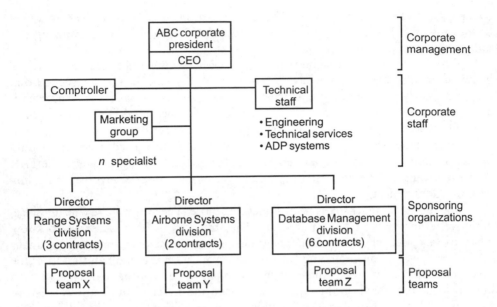

Figure 1.1 Levels of responsibility for proposal support in a typical corporate organization.

that individual to achieve that goal or else to suffer a potentially unpleasant experience for not achieving it.

Therefore, a successful marketing and proposal effort should be based on the management doctrine outlined in the next chapter. But first, take a look at Figure 1.1, where I have shown the various levels of proposal responsibility in a typical corporate organization.

Note the four levels of management involved in proposal preparation: corporate management, corporate staff, operating divisions (or "sponsoring organizations"), and, finally, the proposal teams. Now this is a medium-size company doing, say, $100 million gross per year in the business of providing government services and employing, say, about 1,000 employees. This organization is patterned roughly after a fast-growing company for whom I once worked which had a marvelously successful marketing organization. That's why it is now no longer a medium-size company but is instead a large company doing some $2 billion a year with about 30,000 employees.

As this corporation grew, it added a Commercial Products Group and an Engineering Development Group in addition to the Government Services Group. So it had to decentralize the marketing function down to the group level because of the wide diversity of expertise now required to fulfill the corporate objectives.

My reason for presenting this organization chart is to show the hierarchy of all the people involved in the marketing effort and to identify the roles of each level in the process. Which is what I'm going to talk about in the discussion that follows. What follows is the doctrine upon which allocation of marketing responsibilities should be based. The following rules apply to *any* organization, whether large or small, high tech or low tech, so long as the organization depends on proposals to win competitive contracts.

1. Assignment of marketing responsibility to dedicated specialists (at the corporate or group level) *who have a stake in winning the contract* as well as a *responsibility for the money expended in the effort.* This is the marketing group that is the main subject of this chapter.
2. Assignment of proposal preparation responsibility to an organization (call it the "sponsoring organization") whose charter and capabilities most closely reflect the technical requirements of the targeted contract, and that will be the organization ultimately responsible for successful performance of the contract after it is won.
3. Assignment of cost proposal responsibility to an experienced accountant with a proven track record for costing proposals of *the type represented by the target contract.* He or she must coordinate closely with the proposal manager and the manager of the organization responsible for the proposal effort (the "sponsoring organization") and with the corporate office having the final decision-making authority for funding the proposal effort. This is the CEO, or if so delegated, the comptroller.
4. Assignment to the proposal team of the same key personnel who will have comparable responsibilities for the performance of the contract if it is won. These key personnel will be the proposal manager and the team leaders of the proposal effort.
5. Assignment of *responsibility for proposal support* to a *specific corporate officer* at the corporate (or group) level. This includes the responsibility to respond to requests for specialized equipment (e.g., computers or communications equipment), negotiations with subcontractors, specialized personnel (such as those needed to address a specialized RFP requirement), interdivision support, special transportation needs, and so forth.
6. And, finally, (a corollary of rule 2): delegation to the *head of the sponsoring organization* (the person to whom the proposal manager reports) authority commensurate with his or her responsibility for the success of the proposal effort and with the ultimate performance of the contract. This person is in the best position to make the day-to-day proposal judgments and decisions (in concert with the proposal manager). Corporate management should stay out of the mechanics of the proposal preparation. However well meaning such intervention may be, it soon becomes micromanagement, kibbitzing, second guessing, counterproductive, and demoralizing and incentive-destroying to the proposal team.

Now you have the underlying principles that control the structuring of an effective and responsive marketing organization. Referring again to Figure 1.1, note that the "sponsoring organization" is the organization that has direct responsibility for ongoing operational contracts. That is where the hands-on technical expertise resides. The corporate proposal support responsibility would be assigned to an individual in the group or corporate staffs, depending on which level has the resources and authority to provide the proposal manager with whatever help he or she needs. So now let us examine in more detail each of the organizational rules set out previously.

Dedicated Specialists at the Corporate Level

Remember, we are talking about the up-front marketing people here: the image makers, the customer contact, the intelligence gathering people.

One of the best marketing organizations I have ever seen is in the computer sciences business. Starting from scratch about 30 years ago, it is now a multibillion dollar company with over 30,000 employees and still growing. The corporation is broken down into functional groups such as Government Services, Commercial, and Advanced Programs. As is evident from these titles, each group has a discrete mission that differs markedly from that of the other groups. Obviously there is a different *modus operandi* and different philosophy involved in performing in the commercial world from that in the government services environment.

For this reason, each Group has an autonomous marketing organization dedicated to finding and initiating the capture of contracts unique to the mission of each respective group. Now let's take the Government Services Group. The mission of this group involves the Department of Defense (DOD, including the Army, Navy, and Air Force), the Department of Commerce (DOC), the Environmental Protective Agency (EPA), the Department of Energy (DOE), the State Department, the Treasury Department, and so forth. The Group Headquarters Marketing Section then has an extensive staff of dedicated professionals—specialists in each of the major fields represented in the Group mission. For example, one individual with significant active duty in the Navy might be responsible for all Navy programs, and likewise for the Army, Air Force, and so on. Other individuals with civil service experience in the EPA or the DOE would go after those programs.

Each of these people is charged with the responsibility to track any and all opportunities that may arise in his or her respective field. This includes maintaining personal contact with the movers and shakers in that field, wherever they may be. Once they have targeted a viable opportunity, they coordinate with the organization that would most likely be involved with the proposal process. (The same organization that would be responsible for performance of the contract—the "sponsoring organization.") If the manager of the sponsoring organization agrees that this is a desirable and viable target, both the head of that organization and the marketeer would sell the corporate management on the advisability of bidding. Remember, they hold the purse strings. (See Figure 1.2). In order to do this, they have to present

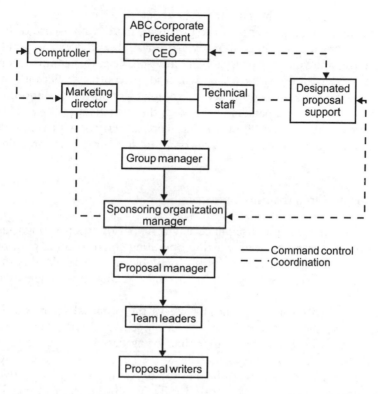

Figure 1.2 Chain of command—a typical corporate organization for a proposal effort.

facts, not conjecture, on the likelihood of success, the nature of the competition, the estimated dollar value, and especially their estimate of the proposal cost.

The keys to the success of this system are:

- The marketeer has to go out on a limb by convincing the group president and/or the chief executive officer (CEO) of the viability of this opportunity and of the probable cost of pursuing it. This precludes any half-baked, frivolous pursuits of pie-in-the-sky will o' the wisps and puts the marketeer on record as to how much money the effort is supposed to cost.
- The marketeer is generously rewarded with a fat bonus if the proposal wins. This provides the incentive for the marketeers (who by the nature of their work must be virtually unsupervised) to keep hustling for new business.

The poor, unappreciated proposal writers have to take it from there and do the really hard work of putting in long tedious hours actually writing the proposal with little guidance and even less recognition or appreciation. And that is where this particular company's system often falls apart. Because there is little incentive for proposal writers to do a professional, conscientious job. The proposal writers are brought in from all over the country. They put in a couple of weeks (or even months) writing various segments of the proposal; there is no "sense of belonging" to a team or having a common goal or reward for a job well done. So you treat people like garbage, and you get garbage. Generally speaking, this company's proposals are just not very good. So why do they win a lot of contracts? Because of the outstanding work the marketeers do in their tracking of opportunities and the political fence mending they do on a personal basis with the customers.

Solution to the problem: Reward the proposal writers with recognition—not just a form letter, but companywide approbation and something tangible for their efforts.

The Sponsoring Organization Concept

The proposal team needs the disciplined environment of an operating, businesslike office. It needs the presence of an existing operating chain of command, because of both the existing physical resources readily available and the availability of management assistance and counsel, and, finally, for the channeling of requests for corporate assistance.

I have worked on many proposals where the proposal team was located in leased space near the customer's site (e.g., Lompoc for Vandenberg AFB, Cocoa Beach for Kennedy Space Center) rather than being based at an existing corporate, group, or division office. I contend that the small benefit gained (access to the customer's technical library, access to the site for observation visits) is outweighed by the disadvantages: greatly increased costs for TDY, office lease cost, increased security risks, lack of management control, nonavailability of physical resources and management resources, and so forth. Why do I emphasize management control, chain of command, and so forth? Because proposal teams have such a tendency to indulge in aimless, pointless, fruitless, and endless bull sessions instead of closing their respective mouths, rolling up their sleeves, and doing some solitary creative and innovative thinking, analyzing, organizing, and studying. Instead they will grab a piece of paper every time and give you a brain dump without doing any of these things first, so that they can get back to their open-ended bull session. Of course there must be brainstorming sessions where various approaches can be aired and examined and input from various disciplines integrated into the proposal. But these sessions must be structured. They must have a beginning, an objective, and an end.

People don't like to hear this, but I'll say it again: Proposal preparation must be a disciplined effort. And that is why I insist it should be based on an existing organization with the head of that organization responsible for its outcome. The best and most successful proposals I have worked on were done in this manner: that is, in a proposal site physically separated, but in close proximity to an existing operating office (of the sponsoring organization).

Some of the worst experiences I've had (for whom, I'd best not say) were located "near the customer blah, blah." After four months, virtually nothing had been accomplished except much sound and fury signifying nothing—a collection of leaderless dilettantes cast adrift in a sea of confusion.

Cost Proposal Responsibility

A delicate balance must be reached here. If the contract award goes on price only, and you bid a *realistic* cost with emphasis on performance or quality, you lose.

Whose fault is it? If the costing specialists (commonly referred to affectionately by most engineers as bean counters) were unaware of this, it is the fault of the marketeer, who should have known it would go on cost and should have so informed the bean counters. If the marketeer did inform the bean counter, then it is the bean counter's fault. What about the proposal manager? The proposal manager is not about to tell the bean counters that their bid is probably too high, because he or she is the one who will have the impossible job of managing this contract under an unreasonably low bid.

The delicate balance lies in the fact that we have several conflicting motives involved here. The costing specialists, above all, do not want to bid a contract that loses money for the company. And on a cost plus contract, an overrun can also be a reflection on their competence. The marketeers want to win the contract at all costs (literally). They want their bonuses and they don't care if the contract makes money or not. While the poor beleaguered program manager is trying to cope with the low bid contract, the marketeers will have pocketed their bonuses and basked in the adoration of the marketing director. "It's not their fault if the bean counter was too inept to price the job correctly."

Then there is the proposal manager, who also wants very badly to win the contract (because there is probably a promotion in it for him or her), *but not at all costs*. Because the proposal manager will be charged with performing the contract at the bid cost and would prefer not to win the contract at all than to win it at an unrealistically low cost. (One of the many reasons why I insist that if at all possible, the proposal manager should be the proposed project/program manager). So how do you, the sponsoring organization director (manager, chief, president, or whatever) designated to be responsible for the outcome of this proposal, balance these conflicting interests? You force these three people to coordinate the bidding effort and try to reach a consensus. If a consensus cannot be reached, then each should present their case to the president of the group or the corporation for resolution. It's their money. Furthermore, these people are less likely to try to pull a snow job at this level. Often times, this may turn out to be a good time to fall back and regroup and consider no bidding this thing.

Assignment of Key Contract Personnel to the Proposal Team

This subject will be discussed in detail in Chapter 9, which is concerned with managing the proposal, so I will not belabor the point here. Suffice it to say that, once again, the purpose of this rule is discipline and incentive. Problem is, too many proposal managers succumb to the caterwauling whines and pitiful cries of subordinate managers who insist the world would just come to an end if you took dear old Joe Schlimiel away from him for a few weeks to work on a proposal.

Assignment of a Specific Corporate Officer for Proposal Support

Military doctrine holds that "if responsibility is divided, then no one is responsible." Divided responsibility is the absence of responsibility. But it doesn't take a military genius to conclude that this doctrine governs all phases and aspects of our lives, whether it is the raising of children or the management of a corporation or playing second base for the Dodgers. We will get into this subject in depth in the next chapter. But for now we are talking about the corporate responsibility for supporting the proposal effort. Most places I have worked, it is simply *assumed* that corporate management will see to it that this very important activity, the proposal effort, will get whatever it needs from wherever in the corporation the capability exists. Nothing could be further from the truth. Here we have an example of not just *divided* responsibility, but instead *diffuse* responsibility. Even within your own group or division, it is next to impossible to get assistance for the proposal effort from anyone who has not been directly charged. As for getting assistance from another division or group—forget it, Charlie Brown. I have found in my experience that it is actually easier to get assistance from *another corporation* than it is to get assistance within your own company! And this is why it is absolutely imperative that the highest level of corporate management, the president or CEO, designate in writing a high-level corporate officer with the *specific* responsibility for the corporate support of the proposal team.

On any large, complex effort there are almost always some areas in which you lack experience and in-depth knowledge and therefore need help. The requisite capability exists somewhere within the corporation. But unless a specific individual at the *corporate* level is specifically charged by corporate management with the duty to support this specific proposal effort, the poor hapless proposal manager is going to encounter nothing but frustration in getting the help he or she so desperately needs.

Authority of the Head of the Sponsoring Organization

Presumably the head of the sponsoring organization will be providing most of the people who do the nuts and bolts work of actually writing the proposal. This is because that organization was chosen for this job because of its expertise in performing the requirements of the RFP. The head of the sponsoring organization will also be responsible for providing the facilities to be used in the proposal effort, and for this reason should be the management contact for the proposal manager in getting support, both physical and intellectual, for conducting the proposal effort. The sponsor organization manager must have commensurate authority to make the decisions and resolve the problems of the proposal manager on the spot, without recourse to the corporate management.

The Role of the Marketing Director

The marketing director certainly has a right and a duty to maintain an interest in the progress of the proposal and the *marketing* aspects thereof. And he or she has a duty to respond to requests for intelligence on the customer's intentions, desires, technical requirements, idiosyncrasies, and so forth. Essential Elements of Information (EEI), I call it, borrowing a term from the intelligence community. (More on that later.)

But the marketing director and his or her subordinates should not try to intervene in the mechanics or techniques or any aspect of the proposal preparation. This is solely the proposal manager's duty and prerogative. The point of contact for the marketing people should be the head of the sponsoring organization. Since it is this person's facility and responsibility, he or she should not have to tolerate an uncontrolled mob of corporate people—marketeers, consultants, observers, spies, nitpickers, and kibbitzers—looking over the shoulders of the proposal team while they work. And when the head of the sponsoring organization requests support from the designated individual at corporate, he or she should get the undivided attention of that individual until that support is provided.

In summarizing the structuring of an effective marketing organization, I would say that the up-front marketing should be a corporate (or group) function, depending on the corporate structure). Proposal preparation should be the overall responsibility of the sponsoring organization. The criterion for selection of the sponsoring organization should be which corporate element has the technical expertise and experience to perform the contract. Proposal management should be the responsibility of the proposed program manager. Direct proposal support should be the responsibility of the sponsoring organization, and all proposal support, corporate management review, proposal status inquiries, and corporate assistance should be coordinated through the head of the sponsoring organization. Responsibility for *corporate* support of the proposal should be assigned in writing to a specific named individual on the corporate management staff.

Customer Relations

A complete description of the methods by which the marketing group accomplishes its mission would be the subject of another book. Since this is a book about proposal preparation, I will limit this discussion to marketing as it relates to the proposal preparation process. As we will find later, in Chapter 6, your proposal will be evaluated against three criteria: (1) the RFP evaluation criteria (Section M of the RFP), which everyone sees; (2) the government standards (which only the government evaluators see); and (3) the criteria that no one sees: your company's image—good or bad impressions, biases, prejudices, and perceptions. The latter is primarily the mission of the marketing people: to create a favorable image, good impressions, and a perception of competence and reliability in the minds of the customer's community. If they haven't done their job well, then the proposal manager has an uphill battle.

Creating a Favorable Image

Generally speaking, the marketeers should project an image of confidence, knowledge of their customer's environment and of their needs, possess a very thorough knowledge of their own company's capabilities, and, finally, demonstrate a desire to provide customers with any information they need to fulfill their requirements. In short, they must know their customers, must know their company's capabilities, and must be adept at showing how their company can meet the customer's needs.

Gathering Information—Where and How to Find It

So the first part of the marketeers' mission is to create a favorable impression of your company in the customer's environment. What is the second part? To gather information. The information-gathering stage for any given proposal begins as much as years before the RFP hits the streets and continues until the proposal has been delivered and even beyond then until an award is made. In order to gather this information, the marketeer has to live in the customer's environment, maintain a constant presence in the field, establish an informal rapport with the key people (the decision-making people in the technical area), and be prepared to answer questions, render assistance, and present briefings ("dog and pony shows").

The gathering of information by the marketing group can make all the difference between success and failure for the proposal manager. Proposal managers will virtually never be involved in the proposal effort until about the time the announcement is made in the Commerce Business Daily (CBD). After all, they have another job to do—program manager of another contract, an engineering department head, and so forth, because they have to have the unique technical training and experience that will be required to manage the targeted program. But the marketeers have been tracking this opportunity for months or even years—literally. So if they have been doing their job right and earning their keep, they should have been able to gather a wealth of information to put at the disposal of the proposal manager.

The gathering of information is analogous to the mission of an intelligence agency—the CIA, for instance, or the G-2 of an army division. First the agents must project themselves into the enemy's (the customer's) environment. It's not nearly as risky for the marketeer as for military intelligence personnel *as long as you play by the rules, if you know what I mean.* But there are some analogies. In government procurement, the customer is prohibited by law from revealing anything to you that he or she doesn't tell all your competitors. So you have to gather scraps of information wherever you can get them and piece them all together to get the whole picture. A good G-2 will find out everything there is to know about the enemy—all the enemy's strengths and weaknesses, leaders, methods of operation, objectives, plans, aspirations, and decision-making apparatus. Once the G-2 has learned all these things, he or she must disseminate all this knowledge to the troops in time to be useful for the next phase of operations.

I once had the good fortune to manage a proposal—for the same company I cited above for having such a good marketing organization. When I arrived on the scene, I was presented with a folder about ten inches thick that had the answers to almost every question I could think of, plus more. It had a summary of the political situation, an analysis of the potential competitors, the old RFP (this was an operations and maintenance (O&M) contract), incumbent brochures, clippings from trade and professional journals, briefings by consultants, organization charts, an analysis of the incumbent's performance ratings, his contract cost history (contract modifications, overruns, even an accurate estimate of the incumbent's cost per man-hour), government organization charts, and personality profiles of the government's key personnel. What a rare pleasure for a proposal manager to begin work with this kind of prior preparation! Needless to say, we won that contract.

Lest any of you think any of this information was obtained illegally or even unethically, let me put your mind at ease. This information is all available to the alert and resourceful competent marketeer. It can all be deduced from freely available government documents, from commercial publications such as Frost & Sullivan reports, and from just keeping your eyes and ears open. And if all else fails, there is a wealth of information that can be obtained through the Freedom of Information Act (FOIA). This is the kind of work your marketing group should be able to do. And if they don't, the wise executive should find out why. Is it lack of training, armchair paralysis, lack of incentive, or just plain lethargy? If the latter, fire them all and start over, because you are headed for zero growth and stagnation. The most pervasive problem I've experienced is that so many marketeers hate to take notes or write memos or roll up their sleeves and do some analytical thinking. As I said before, too much talk and not enough listen.

There are too many marketeers out there today who subscribe to the charm school approach. Who actually thinks you can secure multimillion dollar contracts by wining and dining the customer, plying them with gratuities, winning them over with sweet talk and gentle persuasion and so on. There used to be a lot of that in the old days. There also used to be a lot of sub-rosa tricks and subterfuges: bugging offices, going through a competitor's garbage sifting through the egg shells and coffee grounds looking for company confidential data on costs, strategies, and personnel; infiltrating the organization with moles, and so on and on. And if you have been reading the papers, you know that worse things have happened.

This kind of fun and games led to Ill Wind[1] and indictments, and a reign of terror for some of the people who practiced this sort of thing as a way of life. The whole procurement system has become more sophisticated now and somewhat more honest, thank goodness. It still has a long way to go (especially in some procurement districts and field offices)—not in the procurement of hardware but of services. But that is another story.

The Bid/No Bid Decision

This is the single most important decision that any company's management will have to make in the entire process, because so much money is riding on it. You can easily spend $100,000 bidding on a $10 million contract. If you decided to No Bid because you suspect the procurement was rigged in favor of the ABC Corporation and events prove you right, you saved your company $100,000. If however, the contract is instead awarded to the XYZ Corporation,you are going to look like a fool, because you lost out on a chance at $10 million of new business for your company. I'm sure there are at least hundreds of CEOs out there who periodically spend some sleepless nights over these decisions. The best general advice I can give on this subject is this: Don't make multimillion dollar decisions in haste, and don't make them in a vacuum. Gather all the information you can get your hands on; process it, brainstorm it, get all the expert opinion you can, and, lastly, remember that the decision once made is irrevocable. I remember one time we got cold feet after spending a lot of money and decided to drop out of a $400 million contract, because the incumbent appeared to have it locked up. Well, two weeks later some 25 FBI men showed up on the incumbent's doorstep because of allegations of fraud and embezzlement. It is prudent to stay in the game until your cost curve begins its steep rise, which would be after the bidders' conference.

From my observations, the biggest flaw in the Bid/No Bid decision process is that all too often it is made solely on intuition and emotion and too seldom according to any sensible criteria. This is not the way to make sound business decisions of any kind. Every manager should develop a set of objective criteria upon which to base marketing decisions. I believe that if an independent survey were made of the reasons why heads sometimes begin to roll in the executive suites, you would find that the main reason is the lack of a sensible and objective decision-making process by the victims.

So in order to help business executives to keep their heads, I have devised a set of criteria to apply in making Bid/No Bid decisions. If you are not an executive, you might show this list to your boss. He might invite you out to lunch some day.

---

1. Ill Wind was the code name given to an FBI probe into procurement fraud which resulted in the conviction of some 50 defense industry and Pentagon officials.

Note: These criteria have been devised mainly on the basis of experience on O&M-type contracts. Some of them apply to any type of contract. For specific contract-type applications, such as engineering development or research and development, the criteria unique to these efforts will be addressed in Chapter 8, "Special Applications."

List of Bid/No Bid Criteria

The following is a list of Bid/No Bid criteria:

1. Incumbent's performance ratings over the last five years
2. Incumbent's program manager
   a. Qualifications, general reputation
   b. Performance history on current program
   c. Program manager turnover
3. Changes in key personnel in *customer's* organization
4. Contract and procurement history
5. Reputation of the procurement agency
6. High-level political factors
7. Cost factors
   a. Analysis of competitor's costs versus your costs
   b. Competitors' history on cost competition
   c. Profit potential. Is it worth winning?
   d. Estimated cost of preparing the proposal
8. Long-range benefits to your company
9. Can you secure qualified subcontractors?
10. Do you have sufficient resources: talent, time, money, and have you done your homework well enough?

Now let's take a look at each of these criteria. If you have already worked on at least 50 proposals, you may already know some of what follows. But if I've learned anything in the last ten years as a consultant, it is that people very seldom know as much about proposal writing as they think they do, and there is no greater impediment to learning than thinking you already know everything there is to know on a given subject.

Incumbent's Performance Ratings

This should be the starting point for any marketing evaluation of an award fee-type contract, because you can obtain documentary proof of the contractor's performance history. And, I might add, most contracts for services these days are of the award fee variety, and the trend is inexorably in this direction, especially in high tech, engineering development, research and development, study contracts, and so forth. If it's a hardware contract, you can find out about prior performance by your other competitors through your marketeers' contact with the hardware community.

Through the Freedom of Information Act (FOIA), you can demand a copy of any government contract (subject to security classification and, to a limited extent, company proprietary information). Or, as I said before, you can obtain these contracts and all contract modifications from such commercial services as the Frost & Sullivan reports. A smart marketeer can usually deduce such information as the number of people on the contract, the cost to the government of each man-hour of labor performed, and the contractor's performance ratings. Now if you find that the incumbent contractor's ratings have been above 90% and climbing the past few years, forget it. Unless you find something else in your analysis—a recent scandalous situation, or solid information the contract will go on cost and you know you can beat him there, for example—don't waste your money.

If on the other hand, you find his ratings have steadily declined over the past year or two, you must look further, examine other criteria. Do these ratings coincide with a change in program managers or maybe in their corporate structure? Have they screwed up on some important projects? These are the questions your marketeers are supposed to answer. If they don't have the answers, tell them to get busy and find the answers.

Of course, even when you get the answers, it would behoove the careful executive to take them with a grain of salt. I know of one blatant case where the government fooled everybody. Remember, the government is required by law to use the competitive bidding process in awarding contracts. This is regulated by the FAR (Federal Acquisition Regulations), and maximum application of the competitive bidding process is the expressed desire of both Congress and the Executive Branch. So it is imperative that the people who administer our government procurement process maintain the perception, at least, of honest competition.

But after all, the government is made up of people—or rather bureaucrats. And people have a tendency to keep their old friends around with whom they feel comfortable. After 30 years, their kids have intermarried with the contractors' kids, and so forth; in short, an incestuous relationship develops. Then too, who wants to go through the hassle of phasing in a new contractor and break up the comfortable routine established over a 30-year period just to save a few million government dollars?

Well, in this particular case, they had perfunctorily recompeted this contract for some 30 years, always retaining the same contractor, even though he was usually underbid by millions of dollars. So here we go again! But this time is different. The incumbent contractor had been getting poor performance ratings, sometimes even down in the 70s. Rumors spread that some of the key people on the government side were not even speaking to some of the key people on the contractor team and, further, that there had been some significant personnel changes.

So all the big companies who had wasted their money bidding before came rushing headlong to take advantage of the new situation. After all, the contract was now up in the $700 million range. At last it's going to be an honest competition! But wait. What's going on here? Just as the proposals were submitted, the incumbent's performance ratings soared—not to %80, not to %90, but (gasp!) to 100%! Well, you know the rest. The contract was yet again awarded to the miraculously born-again incumbent even though three other contractors turned in lower bids. As I said to one of my colleagues at the time, "Not even Jesus Christ, Himself, could have improved their performance that much in two or three months." So all the competing contractors docilely took their lumps once again, went home to lick their wounds and total up their multimillions of wasted dollars one more time. What else could they do? This is the nature of the game when there is one customer—the government—and a multitude of contractors.

It will be interesting to watch this scenario unfold yet another time. Will the government throw a party to which no one will come?

The Incumbent's Program Manager

Without a doubt, the most influential persona involved in this scenario is the incumbent's program manager—or better or worse. Sometimes a dynamic and personable manager can develop such close personal ties with the customer that he or she can make the contract performance look better than it is. In most cases, this influence will be limited to just a few of the customer's top brass. So turn your marketing people loose on these people to project an equally good impression of your own company. Or you might pray for their early retirement, because such people often turn up on the customer's Source Selection Evaluation Board (SSEB) or the Source Selection Advisory Committee (SSAC).

Another thing to look for is the history of the management of this contract; not just the current program manager but his or her predecessors, if any. And not just the program manager but also certain sensitive department heads: the finance and administration manager or the engineering manager, for example. I once persuaded my management, against their better judgment, to bid on a contract that they were sure was wired for the incumbent. But I had noted that the incumbent (let's call him XYZ) had changed engineering managers three times in the past two years. After a little snooping around, talking to some of the disgruntled current employees (and there were many), I determined that not only was morale in a deplorable state, but also that the incumbent had promoted a number of engineers to their level of incompetence as supervisors and managers, that engineering projects seldom got off the ground, that there was little coordination between engineering and the operations and maintenance people, and so on and on. This convinced me that XYZ's contract just *had* to be up for grabs. And so it was, and so we won it.

We did our homework; the competitors didn't. They simply assumed that since the incumbent had been there a long time, it was no use bidding. As a consequence, there was only one other (poorly prepared) nonincumbent bidding.

So here are some other things to look for: Did the incumbent actually provide the same program manager whose resume was provided in bidding the contract? Sometimes a company will pull the old bait and switch act, giving the customer a different manager than they proposed, pleading some last minute "emergency." Or they will put the proposed manager in for just a month or two and then find some more important place to reassign him or her. Needless to say, this sort of thing infuriates the customer, who feels cheated and will forever more doubt your honesty and reliability.

Has the current manager been there for less than a year? What happened to his or her predecessor? Put out to pasture? Kicked upstairs? Sent off to some ignominious lesser assignment? Or actually promoted to a more responsible assignment? The answer to these questions can be a very significant clue to whether and where the incumbent has some weaknesses. You might apply the same questions to the incumbent's most significant personnel also. You can almost always be sure that program managers and key personnel will not be replaced during the year before a program is recompeted unless something is wrong somewhere.

Procurement Office History on Recompetitions

All government agencies (DOD, Commerce, FAA, Interior, whatever) are governed by the same set of regulations (the FAR), which are admirably designed to ensure real competition, and fair competition between all qualified contractors. Only trouble is, regulations no matter how drawn are administered by people: people with all their frailties, biases, idiosyncrasies, built-in incompetence, avarice, ignorance, arrogance, and all the other "ills which flesh is heir to," as Shakespeare might have said. So you should not be surprised to find that there is a vast amount of difference in the manner in which the various procurement offices around the country comply with the regulations designed to ensure fair and honest competition.

As a general observation, I would say that within DOD, the Air Force is the most meticulous in carrying out the *mechanics* of the procurement function. I emphasize "mechanics," because after the proposals are in, they start playing games just like the rest. That is to say that their RFPs are thorough, demanding, and well organized. There is always—as it should be—a strong emphasis on management techniques: reporting procedures, organizational structure, job control, maintenance procedures, documentation, and quality assurance. All the pieces fit neatly together with paper trails, staff surveillance, and feedback systems coming together in a coherent, integrated document. I think NASA goes even a step beyond this in meticulousness. And NASA is the most progressive of all the agencies I've experienced in continually trying to improve the system. For example, it was NASA that finally saw the nonsense and waste involved in sticking to the standard five-year contract (i.e., 3 + 2 or 1 + 4, etc.) and introduced the nine-year contract. This on the basis that if a contractor was not performing satisfactorily, there were other cheaper ways of terminating him than recompeting the contract periodically whether he was doing a good job or not. Also NASA is getting away from the inane, fixed-price contract for technical services such as R&D, engineering development, and so forth that are so dear to the hearts of some misguided bureaucrats.

But there is also a marked difference in the methodology employed by different procurement offices in the same agency of government or even within the same department. Some will play everything strictly by the book, some will play games (like the one I cited above), some will blithely ignore almost all the rules, some will almost always go for the low bidder no matter how unrealistic such a bid may be, and far too many will simply ignore all the ingenious apparatus by which a fair and realistic selection is supposed to be achieved.

This is made possible by one flaw in the regulations: the provision that the Source Selection Authority can vitiate the whole system by simply ignoring the recommendations and findings of the SSEB and make his or her own personal selection without even having to give any reason. And even though this opens the door to potential fraud and collusion, it happens all the time. And it is high time the government closed this loop hole instead of periodically whining about "unscrupulous contractors."

The most challenging job for the marketeer, then, is knowing how to gather and analyze all the facts that can enable you to evaluate these situations, the personalities involved, the idiosyncrasies, the motivations, the weaknesses, strengths, and biases, the intuition that will lead to the right Bid/No Bid recommendation. Nobody can prescribe a formula for this. It is a rare talent and an art. And that is why a *good* marketeer is usually an affluent one.

Changes in Key Personnel in the Customer's Organization

The alert marketeer will look for significance behind changes in key personnel in the customer's organization. Often times such changes will signal profound changes in the direction of policy for that particular agency or department. For example, the replacement of Richard Truly as head of NASA signaled far reaching changes in the direction of NASA's space program. Sometimes a management change will signal a change in philosophy from an R&D environment to an operations environment, or from a free spending to a penny-pinching mode. Sometimes you'll see a switch from an engineering-oriented leadership of a program to a bean-counter management. (This is what happened to the Detroit auto industry in the 1970s and led them to the brink of disaster.)

What you must look for are the underlying reasons for the change: perhaps allegations of fraud, waste, or mismanagement; or perhaps charges of favoritism, nepotism, or other unethical practices. Whatever the reason may be, it will seldom be announced in the news media. You have to look beyond the stated reasons to the real reasons. What are the most striking differences between the old manager and his replacement? You can be sure of one thing. If the old manager left under a cloud, there will be a change of direction under the new management.

Significant Changes in the Contract

You can be pretty sure there is going to be a change in contractors when you see a really significant change in the contract, whether it be in the scope, the mission, the funding, or administration. Don't ask me why. There could be any number of reasons, but experience points to this conclusion. I've seen it happen over and over again. One of the most dramatic cases in my experience was a case where my company had a very nice contract performing database management involving the operation and maintenance of a large computer center—about 400 employees. We had an excellent rapport with our counterparts in the government, excellent performance ratings, an outstanding program manager, and a high state of morale among both employees and management. But on our next competition, the government changed from a work-order–type operation to a mission-type contract. No one knew why, but we felt we could easily adapt to this since we had several other mission-type contracts and were performing well on them too. So, no big deal.

Well, one of our competitors came from out of nowhere and grabbed the contract right from under our noses. I read the government's review of the proposals and rationale announcing the award decision and right up to the last paragraph, you would conclude we won the contract, because our proposal was outstanding. Obviously the document was written by the SSEB chairman, who had evaluated our proposal and had recommended award of the contract to us. Then came the last paragraph that contended that we did not sufficiently understand mission-type contracts. We all concluded this part of the document was written in Washington. We had all wondered why our one competitor came on like gangbusters right from the beginning, like they knew something we didn't. Now it was obvious. They did know something we didn't: that the government in Washington was going to award the contract to this competitor, and changing to a mission-type contract was how they would justify it.

Here are some other examples of what to look for: Changing from an ordinary contract to a small business set-aside. If you are the incumbent and are a big business, this is probably a subtle hint that they want to get rid of you. If you are not the incumbent and are a big business, you should assess the feasibility of small businesses being capable of handling this contract without some big help. Look at the disciplines involved. If they are multiple and complex, it is unlikely that a small business can handle it. In that case, you should approach the small companies most likely to be credible competitors and offer your services as a subcontractor. Don't let petty pride get in your way. The money you get as a sub is still the same color. And every big business started out as a small business. Small businesses have proven to be more innovative and creative than large businesses. So you might learn something from them.

Significant Changes in the Scope of the Contract

The usual case here is either the consolidation of two or more small contracts into a larger one or the opposite: the segmentation of a large contract into two or more smaller contracts. This is illustrated by NASA's favorite cycle game. I wouldn't presume to fathom the NASA mentality. I once worked on the same NASA project for three different contractors in one year. Same job, same program, just three different contractors. But I suspect they save a lot of money this way, because it does engender competition between contractors.

This is how it works. Contractor A has been the incumbent for eight years. Contractor B (and maybe C and D) come to NASA (and/or their representatives in Congress) and whine, "We would like to bid on this contract, but it has grown so big and complex that it is hard for any company to bid on it. The incumbent has an unfair advantage."

So NASA says, "Not to worry; we are going to break this contract up into 'more manageable segments' to encourage more open competition." They then break Contractor A's piece of the pie into three parts, one of which is a small business set aside (good politics). So then all the qualified contractors (and some unqualified) come rushing forth to *buy in* to this contract, cutting salaries to the bone, sacrificing profit, paring their G&A costs, in order to get a piece of the action now and figuring to make it up in future years. So about that time (ten years later), NASA decides it is time to consolidate some of these contracts into one large one, and the bidding starts all over again in an endless cycle. Yes, it probably does save the government money. Never mind that the poor engineers and technicians on some of these NASA programs end up working for five different companies over their careers. And until the Service Contract Act was passed, every time a new contractor came in he or she took a pay cut to enable the new contractor to get the low bid, and corporate executives got a promotion for winning new business.

In any case, this book is not concerned with what should be, but what is. Just remember, when you see a really significant change in a contract coming along, you can be sure there is an opportunity there for someone. You can bet on it.

Cost Factors

Analysis of Your Estimated Costs. For a services-type contract, a good marketeer should be able to get you all the information you need to make some fairly accurate cost estimates. You should be able to determine the number of people actually employed on the contract and, with a little extrapolation, the average cost per man-hour based on the total contract cost. Now figure up what it will cost your company to perform this contract. If you and your staff know your business well enough to perform the contract, then you should be able to come up with a rough estimate of the staffing requirements. Then multiply this by the average cost per man year that you experience on similar contracts or on other factors that your bean counters should be able to provide you. Add in your G&A and fee and an intelligent estimate of other direct charges (ODC) and you have a good rough estimate of what you should bid on the contract. If you are not in the ball park with the actual current cost, forget it. Maybe your cost structure just isn't competitive with this incumbent on this type contract. Maybe corporate management should look into the reasons why. Some companies can and will perform more cheaply than others.

If you are almost in the ballpark, then consider the various means of getting more competitive. There are always perfectly practical ways of cutting costs in any operation, and the longer the operation has been in effect, the easier it is to find ways of doing the job cheaper. Every contractor, every business inevitably puts on a little fat over the years by hiring a few more people than they actually need: adding frills that are nice to have, making life a little easier, especially for the upper management people, by hiring people to do some of the mundane, boring jobs they could do themselves—like bringing them coffee in the morning; making out their expense reports, a private secretary for each department head as a status symbol rather than sharing secretaries. Almost any organization I have ever seen could take a 10% cut in staffing without any degradation of performance. And that should be your *minimum* goal—to bid *at least* ten percent under what you think the incumbent will bid. If you don't underbid him by at least ten per cent, it is not cost effective for the government to make the transition of contractors. If you are in the ball park now, then consider some other cost factors.

G&A and Fee. G&A comprises the general and administrative costs of doing business—that is, lease costs, personnel administration, office supplies, and so forth. The fee is the flat rate charged for performing the contract, over and above G&A costs. Say you are looking at a large, complex, and technically challenging contract that could not only expand your business base, but also extend your technical base and open the doors to new technologies down the road. If you feel you really have the capability to perform this contract, then go for it. My advice in a case like this is: be prepared to make some sacrifices to gain the benefits that will surely inure to your company in the long run. Trim your G&A, bid zero fee. If it is a five-year contract and you know you can do a good job, then look at it as a potential ten- or 20-year contract. So in order to win the contract, bid on the basis of breaking even the first five years. If you are doing a good job, the customer is not about to make a change of contractors and go through the hassle of phasing in a new contractor after that short a period. So in the ensuing five or ten years or 20 years, you will have ample time to make up for the lack of profit the first five years. I regret to say this advice has usually gone over like a lead balloon, but I think this is because thinking more than five years ahead is anathema to most American businessmen these days. Probably one of the reasons the Japanese have been eating our lunch in a variety of manufacturing businesses for so long.

Just one more caveat on this subject. If the contract is for anything other than making 10,000 widgets, don't bid on a firm, fixed-price contract. If it is for operation of large, state-of-the-art facilities with unpredictable technical problems or for engineering development, software development, R&D—anything that you don't have total control of—don't touch it. Let the suckers who don't know any better have it.

Cost of Preparing a Proposal

Most people new to this business or experienced only in responding to RFQs or IFBs are appalled at the high cost of preparing a *good* proposal. (Of course, you can save a lot of money by preparing dumb proposals. And one would be surprised at the number of people out there with that mentality.) It is hard to understand how you can go through some $200K just to prepare a 200- or 400-page document. But here are some of the things you have to consider:

- Travel and per diem (for people you have to bring in to help write the proposal).
- Overtime (for nonexempt employees).
- Printing and publishing costs.
- Consultant costs.
- Travel and per diem for bidders' conference, bidders' tour, Q&A conference, best and final offer (BAFO) and negotiations
- Marketing costs. The up-front people who make the customer contacts and gather data on the contract
- Lease costs. Usually you have to lease separate facilities for writing the proposal. You cannot use space the government provides for you to perform an ongoing contract.
- Advertising. You need to advertise for certain special skills required by the contract which you can not make available from your own current resources. It's best to advertise in the local paper where the contract will be performed. Two reasons: (a) This will often turn up some people who have retired from the contract or else current disgruntled employees, either of whom can be a gold mine of information on the current contract, and (b) it is somewhat demoralizing to the incumbent employees to see that there is someone out there who is seriously going after their contract.

This should give you some idea of why the costs run so high and also give you some idea of why a proposal effort has to be carefully planned, meticulously organized, and managed in a disciplined, orderly manner.

How can you make a quick estimate of these costs for planning purposes? I have found that you can make a pretty reliable estimate for services type contracts by taking 1% of the gross value of the contract for one year. For example, say you have a five-year contract whose total value is $100,000,000. Assuming a straight line cost (not always true), you have gross value of $20,000,000 for the first year. So you estimate the bid and proposal (B&P) cost of this contract to be $200,000. You, the marketeer and your corporate management should keep accurate experience data on such costs. Some will run higher, some lower, but I would hazard the guess that if you find you consistently run substantially higher, you are not managing your proposals efficiently. If you run consistently lower and you are not winning your share of contracts, chances are you are not investing the time, talent, and management to write winning proposals.

On the other hand, the costs of preparing a proposal for a hardware contract may run much higher—that is, from 1% to 3% *of the total contract value.* The reason is that such contracts may require some applied research such as component testing, breadboarding, and so forth.

Writing a proposal is expensive even if done efficiently. That is why I emphasize management. If a proposal is poorly planned and inefficiently managed, the costs can skyrocket, and the end product will be a disaster and an embarrassment to your company.

A final observation. The trend is now toward shorter proposals with severe page limitations. I think this is a welcome development. It gives the evaluators a chance to focus on what is really important without having to wade through reams of garbage to get there. Most proposals I've seen are replete with self-serving sales pitches sprinkled throughout, all of which is totally irrelevant to what the evaluator is looking for, i.e., your response to the RFP with facts and data and solutions to problems.

And sometimes because of the detail spelled out in the RFP, you are almost forced to regurgitate a large part of it in order to be fully responsive. For example, why should you have to explain how to perform first echelon maintenance on a truck, or how to maintain an airplane taxiway, or how to operate and maintain a telemetry station, for that matter? Any damn fool knows how to do these things or they wouldn't be in the business. And the evaluator can ascertain that by checking out the company's work experience and references (required in every RFP). So severe page limitations would obviate the necessity for this kind of nonsense. What the evaluator does want to know is: do you know how to organize this contract effort, and how, when, and by whom do you make things happen.

The fact that proposals are getting shorter does not mean, however, that they are getting easier. On the contrary, this presents an even greater challenge to the proposal manager. Now you must make every word count; you must rely more and more on graphics to tell your story. (You know, a picture is worth a thousand words.) Proposals must now be planned with greater care, and proposal writers will need greater skill than what I have been accustomed to seeing.

Availability of Subcontractors or Partners

In general, I would recommend avoiding the subcontract route if you have the capability and experience to perform 80% of the RFP requirements *except* when the other 20% constitutes a very sensitive portion of the contract. Such would be the case, for instance, if you were bidding on a missile development contract and you lacked the experience in the particular type of guidance subsystem involved.

That is the general rule. However, for large, complex contracts it is not only necessary to use subcontractors to fill certain gaps where you are lacking, but also because such contracts these days always have small business or minority set-asides included as a mandatory requirement. So good marketeers will start doing their homework early on this matter, because the proposal manager won't have the time to go searching, negotiating, and then orienting subs on what they are supposed to contribute to the proposal and to the contract. You must not only validate their technical qualifications, but also their financial viability, their performance reputation, and their perceived acceptability to the customer. This is important, because the customers are aware that they can exercise virtually no direct control over subcontractors, since there is no privity of contract between them and your subcontractor. They can exercise control only through you, the prime.

For large, complex contracts ($100 million and up), it is often necessary to form a teaming arrangement. If you can prove successful, related experience in less than 75% of the RFP requirement, then this is probably the way to go. Even large corporations frequently go this route by jointly forming a new corporation using an agreed-upon formula for sharing any profits from the venture.

But the point of all this is that you have to get your homework done early. Such arrangements take time: the search for the right one, the negotiations, the drawing up of an agreement, the review by the legal eagles. And the larger the companies involved, the longer it will take. You can bet on it.

Do You Have the Resources of Time, Money, and Talent?

First, an axiom: Proposal expense is inversely proportional to the amount of time and talent available.

$$E = 1/(t_1 + t_2)$$

Or, since good management is a multiplier of talent, you might say:

$$E = 1/(t_1 + k \cdot M \cdot t_2),$$

where E = expense; $t1$ = time; M = management; and $t2$ = talent. k is a figure of merit for the quality of management.

Some places I've worked tried to shotgun everything in sight with the result that they turned out a vast amount of dumb proposals and seldom won anything. They either had to spread their talent too thin or churn out proposals without sufficient time to plan or analyze what they were doing. If they had had some good management, they might have had a chance of making up for some of the other deficiencies. The only ones they won were the auctions, the ones that went on price alone. So they spent a lot of money to win contracts that didn't make any money. It doesn't take a rocket scientist to see that all these Pyrrhic victories would eventually doom them to bankruptcy. (Some other company finally bought them out and replaced their marketing group—lock. stock, and barrel.)

Since there is always a limited availability of these resources, especially talent, they need to be controlled in a sensible manner by someone who can plan ahead more than a few weeks—like a few years. This has to be done at the corporate level, because that is the only place that controls *all* the resources required for an integrated marketing effort. This has to be the CEO (or president) acting in coordination with the marketing director, because they are the only ones in a position to make these decisions on B&P (bid and proposal) money. Not, repeat not, the comptrollers, because their only concern is to guard the company's money. And don't knock them for that, because that is their job. You will never get anything out of them without some arm twisting by the CEO.

So the bottom line is: The CEO, in coordination with the marketing director, must do the long-range planning in the allocation of B&P money, which controls all other proposal activity. The long-range planning must be based on the identification of marketing opportunities by the marketing director taking into account the time frames involved, the expertise and proposal talent available, and the estimated costs of each bid effort.

What we've covered so far are the practical nitty-gritty of making the Bid/No Bid decision. There are other broader and more subjective factors involved, and sometimes one or more of these factors might even override the above practical criteria under special circumstances, because they constitute long-range benefits to your company. Here are some of these factors. Each must be analyzed on a case-by-case basis, taking into account the special situation in which your company finds itself at the time with regard to the resources available.

Would the contract:

- Broaden your business base?
- Open the doors to a new technology?
- Enhance the reputation of your company?
- Give you an entry into a new geographic area?
- Eliminate competitors from your area?

The Role of Marketing in Proposal Preparation

The Development of Themes

Now we are in the proposal preparation stage and the responsibility has shifted to the proposal manager. The marketeer's responsibility from now on is merely to support the proposal manager by obtaining whatever additional information may be needed to proceed with the proposal. And to assist him or her in the development of the themes that will permeate the finished proposal. In my opinion, there is far too much emphasis placed on this theme thing, especially by most of the amateur managers I have had the misfortune to encounter. I think they get this from attending some of these whiz-bang seminars where you learn everything there is to know about proposals in a twelve-hour weekend from instructors who have a 99.7% success record in writing winning proposals, of course. I suppose they must teach them something else, but *themes* seems to be the only thing they carry away for that $950 of the B&P money they spent on the course. I once had a boss who probably never said anything else intelligent in his life. But that one thing made him memorable. And that was, "Forget about themes. Everybody spends so much time trying to think up clever themes that they never get down to what we are here for, and that is to respond to an RFP with some plain, common-sense, simple declarative sentences." Amen.

When you have become proficient at writing those simple declarative (and one would hope, coherent) sentences, then you can start worrying about themes and other advanced proposal writing matters.

One reason I'm inclined to down play the themes bit is that this sort of thing gets in the way of what the evaluator of your proposal is really looking for—an objective, common sense, pragmatic response to the specific items in the RFP which are crying out for answers. We will get into the details of how the evaluator really does his job when we get to Chapter 6. Then you will see why I feel so strongly about this subject.

Well, back to the subject at hand. An essential part of the marketeer's job is to gather data on the competition's weaknesses, the customer's concerns (the hot buttons), and the strong points which will most effectively influence the customer to select you as their contractor. The essence of themes is their effect as a sales pitch, and the best source is the marketeer who has been tracking this contract, talking to the customer, pulsing the technical community, and digging up information on the competition. This forms the basis of the themes that proposal managers then weave into their proposal in a subtle fashion, always in a positive way, never denigrating the competition, but pointing out how your company can best respond to the customer's hot buttons. And a good marketeer should be able to provide proposal managers with all the input they need to take it from there. And that is all I'm going to say about themes. At least until I get to Chapter 5.

Gathering of Real-Time Information

The final phase of the marketeer's duty is to gather any real-time information requested by the proposal manager. This is the kind of information that can be acquired directly from the customer or the technical community involved in the contract. This is where the marketeer has been living for the past several months or years, so no one should expect the proposal manager to obtain it. It's true that the marketeers' main interest in life now is to track other opportunities farther down the road, but this does not preclude them nor excuse them from performing this duty. And if necessary, this is a good place for the corporate designated support individual to step in and see that they do. I'm not talking about the research that the proposal team must do in the technical library. I'm talking about the critical bits of information that are accessible only to marketeers and indispensable to the program manager. An example would be the customer's perception of the desirability of substituting your proprietary software for the inferior but established software currently being used by the customer on this contract.

Although this is primarily a book about proposal preparation, I have taken pains to provide a thorough description of the organization and mission of the marketing group. The reason for this is to show the importance of this group—indeed, how absolutely essential an effective marketing group is to successful growth. And furthermore, to show the intricate way that the marketing organization must fit into the overall corporate organization and interface effectively in order to accomplish the corporate objective.

In the next chapter, we will set forth the principles upon which any endeavor must be organized in order to function efficiently and in an orderly manner to achieve its objective.

Chapter 2

Organizational Structures

Worthy chieftains accept full responsibility for all assignments—even those they have delegated to their subordinates.
—Attila the Hun

The Appalling Truth

The Disastrous Consequences

A bright, sunny morning, unusually cold for Cape Canaveral.

The countdown 5 . . . 4 . . . 3 . . . 2 . . . 1 . . . lift off! The space shuttle lifts slowly off the launch pad and soars majestically into the heavens. And suddenly— disaster! Challenger has exploded in a gut-wrenching burst of smoke and flame. In seconds, it is all over, and America mourns its worst disaster in the history of space exploration. A Congressional investigation finds that engineers had warned of a dangerous condition existing under such launch conditions. What went wrong? Why wasn't this information acted upon by those responsible? A failure of the chain of command to function properly. A failure of the decision-making process at a crucial time.

Superbly trained American paratroopers, Rangers, and Marines, supported by Navy Seals, land on a small island in the Caribbean—Granada—in a well-planned operation of combined land, sea, and air combat elements. After three days of confused fighting, seven battalions of U.S. troops defeated the small garrison of Cubans and rag-tag elements of Granadians on the island. Not exactly a textbook operation. Here is what one consultant to the House and Senate Armed Services Committees had to say: "Navy air strikes were delivered against Army positions on at least one occasion. Army ground units and Marine units are not able to talk directly to each other even though they may be deployed in the same area, because their radio frequencies are different. Nor can Army units talk directly to Marine or Navy aircraft which may be called upon to deliver air strikes in support of ground operations. It is ridiculous for each of the four services to have different radio frequencies for controlling air-to-ground strikes. During the initial days of the Grenada operation, Army ground units had to send calls for air strikes back to their headquarters in Fort Bragg, North Carolina. The messages would then be relayed via satellite to the Navy commander, who passed the requests on to the air controller aboard the aircraft carriers."[1] What's wrong here?

The axiom that says, "A commander (read manager, supervisor, leader, whatever) must have direct control of all resources needed to perform his or her mission" has been violated.

Organizational structure is the vital factor in the success of any operation, large or small, military or civilian, governmental or commercial. Failure of the chain of command or of the staff and line functions to coordinate properly can invariably be traced to a faulty command structure, a defective organizational concept. Organizational structure is as vital to the viability of any enterprise as the skeleton is to the human body. Faulty organization leads to sloppy performance, confusion, chaos, and finally disaster.

Yet I have often seen proposal efforts muddling along halfway through to the completion deadline without an established organization chart. How on earth does a writer address the titles for describing who does what? Or describe intraorganizational interfaces? Or delineate responsibilities for accomplishing the contract objectives? I have watched in awe and amazement as some proposal managers drifted along blithely oblivious to the consternation and frustration they are causing by this procrastination. Some "managers" seem to thrive on chaos, and this is what you get if you delay this most important step more than one week after the RFP comes out.

One of the reasons for this procrastination, I believe, is that most proposal managers simply do not have any set of criteria upon which to base an organizational concept. Thing I hear most often is, "We gotta have an organization that mirrors the customer's organization." Nonsense. The customer's organization normally is based on different objectives than a contract organization. Your contract organization has primarily an operational objective—and a limited one at that—within the customer's overall mission. Sure, you have to have an organization that facilitates the interfaces between your key personnel and their counterparts in the customer's organization; but to try to organize your contract to mirror the customer's is asinine.

Some Examples of Organizational Ignorance

I am appalled at the ignorance of even experienced managers, even some career officers coming out of the military, in the principles of organizational structures. And

---

1. "Military Incompetence," Richard A. Gabriel, Hill & Wang, 1985.

that is why I am devoting a separate chapter to this subject, hoping that we can bring some order out of the chaos I've seen everywhere I go in my capacity as a consultant. In fact, the most vexing problem I have encountered as a consultant is the agonizing process of reaching agreement with the proposal manager (or more often, some self-appointed expert from management) on a mutually acceptable contract organization. The problem usually stems from the fact that almost everyone, no matter how unqualified, thinks he or she is an expert on organization charts. Let me give some examples.

Example 1

Col. Blimp (Ret.), now senior staff to the CEO, says, "Never mind staffing for this intermittent requirement in the RFP. When we need to perform this function, I'll just grab some people from this other contract."

Me: "Like hell you will. Suppose I am Mr. GS-15 on that other contract. These people belong to me. They are my assets. Touch them and you die."

Example 2

Proposal manager: "Okay, I concede that supervisor Able doesn't have all the resources under his control to perform his total mission. But he can borrow people from time to time from Supervisor Baker to help out."

Me: "What if Supervisor Baker doesn't want to lend his resources to Mr. Able?"

"Oh, that's no problem. Able and Baker are good friends and they will cooperate."

Me: "You idiot. Able and Baker could both be somewhere else six months from now, or dead for that matter."

Example 3

Me to Mr. V.P.: "Why, if I may be so bold to ask, have you got the 'future planning' function down here in a line section?"

V.P.: "Because that is where it is in the customer's organization."

Me: "The customer's organization is an Army Headquarters. There are no line organizations, only staff sections. Can't you see that their Future Planning Section is part of another staff section reporting directly to the Army Commander?"

V.P.: "So-o-o what's the difference?"

Me: "The difference is that a line function is performed by an operational unit having a discrete operational, parochial objective, headed by a manager or supervisor whose authority is limited to the function of that unit only and nowhere else. The future planning function here pertains to the contract as a whole. The future planning manager would be reporting to a line organization manager who has no interest in, responsibility for, or qualifications for reviewing future plans for the contract effort. Future planning, as with any other function that affects the contract as a whole, must be a staff section reporting to the program manager. Furthermore, a line manager has no more authority than any other line manager, so how would he or she be able to implement any of his plans that affect other line units?"

V.P.: "Duh-h-h."

Example 4

Me to company president: "Forgive me if I seem to question your infallibility, sir, but why are you proposing a program management office in Honolulu when the government program manager is in California and the contract is to be performed on Kauai?"

President: "Because the program manager wants to live in Honolulu. Besides, Mr. GS-15 in California likes to be entertained when he stops in Honolulu on his way to Kauai."

Me: "Well, I hope you won't think I'm being presumptuous when I suggest that you find another program manager and that you or one of your staff take care of Mr. GS-15's entertainment needs. Mr. GS-15 would probably like to have someone within a thousand miles or so from his office when he wants to discuss our contract performance."

Example 5

V.P., (proudly): " I have directed that the quality control manager report directly to me on this program. That way, the program manager can not cover up any problems."

Me: "If you don't trust your program manager to fulfill his management duties, why don't you get another program manager?"

V. P.: "Oh, it isn't that; it's to impress the customer with our determination and commitment to implement a rigorous QC effort."

Me: "It's more likely to impress him with the suspicion that you can't trust the honesty and integrity of your proposed program manager. And another thing, who is going to be responsible for carrying out the mechanics of the QC function?"

V.P.: "Oh, the supervisors of each operating element, of course."

Me: "But they report to the program manager, and the QC manager, under your organizational concept, reports to the vice president. So how can the QC manager know what's going on? Nobody reports to him. He's out of the loop."

V.P.: "Oh, ah, well, er, uh . . ."

Example 6

Me: "What's this? You've got the program manager reporting to two people: the company operations vice president here on the right of the organization chart and to the government contracting officer on the left side."

Self-appointed expert: "Yes, that's to show our understanding of the government's role in directing the contract effort."

Me: "On the contrary, it shows your confusion and ignorance of government contracting or of any contracting, for that matter. (a) You are creating an illegal personal services contract, and (b) it is axiomatic that no man can serve two bosses."

These are all real-life examples that I have encountered, and I could go on and on, but I think you get the idea of some of the problems and some of the stupid solutions that otherwise intelligent managers come up with. Why? Because they do not have a set of criteria, a logical rationale upon which to base these organizational decisions. And that is what this chapter sets out to provide.

Organization charts are the most important single factor in any proposal effort, because everything else in the proposal flows therefrom. No one can begin to write any part of the proposal without an agreed-upon organizational structure to write to. It is the structure upon which the proposal is built, the structure upon which the entire programmatic effort will stand or fall.

Most rational people would heartily agree with the previous characterization of the importance of contract organizational structures. But alas! There is a paucity of rational people who know how to take it from there.

Axioms of Attila the Hun *et al.*

First let us review some axioms. These axioms of leadership, management, organization have been in existence for more than 2,000 years, first (at least in our culture) by the ancient Greeks (Alexander the Great), then the Romans (Julius Caesar), then the conqueror of Rome (Attila the Hun) and so on down to the present. Why are these simple truths as valid today as they were a thousand years ago? Not because of historical precedent, but because of the pragmatic application of lessons learned by great leaders down through the ages, through the ineluctable conclusions drawn from what worked and what didn't.

Axiom 1: *No man can serve two bosses. (Except perhaps a certified schizophrenic.)*

Surely this is such a well-accepted truism that it needs no discussion. A corollary of this is that management cannot be shared; that is, "co-managers" is a nit-wit idea.

Axiom 2: *Divided responsibility is no responsibility.*

The reason for this is that when something goes wrong, blame cannot be assigned and corrective action taken. The finger pointing can go on interminably.

Axiom 3: *Responsibility cannot be delegated.*

The responsibility must remain with the delegator; however the delegatee is responsible to the delegator. Otherwise, managers could always get themselves off the hook by telling their bosses, "Hey it's not my fault, I told so-and-so to do it."

Axiom 4: *Authority must be delegated and always must be commensurate with responsibility.*

Here is where inexperienced, insecure managers often go wrong. They assign a mission to be accomplished by a subordinate, but retain the authority for getting it done. This puts subordinates in an impossible situation. They have the responsibility, but their hands are tied. What is worse, it forces subordinates to let the manager do their thinking for them. When this happens, subordinates cease to think.

Axiom 5: *Managers must have direct control of all resources required to perform their mission.*

If a manager must depend on the good will, "cooperation," sense of duty, or the like from parallel organizations to get the personnel or other resources required to complete his or her mission, that mission, sooner or later is doomed to failure. I get some vehement argument sometimes about this from people citing company loyalty, the common good, and all that. Baloney. It just doesn't work that way in the real world.

Axiom 6: *Nothing will happen or be prevented from happening unless there is incentive for someone, somewhere, to make it happen or prevent it from happening.*

This is analogous to Newton's laws of motion and just as inexorable. Take for instance, the marketing organization described in Chapter 1. You could have the best marketing organization in the world, but nothing is going to happen without (a) rewards for acquiring new business and (b) unpleasant consequences for not getting new business.

Axiom 7: *A manager's staff exists for the sole purpose of assisting managers in carrying out their command responsibilities. The program manager's staff supports the entire program, thus cutting across all parochial aspects of the program.*

Although staff section leaders have no direct authority over other sections, they do have derivative authority. That is, when acting within the scope of their responsibility, *they speak with the authority* of the program manager. The program manager's staff generally serves the entire contract, rarely any severable portion of it. For example: personnel administration, payroll and accounting, quality assurance, safety, security, contract administration, future planning, and so forth. Obviously they do not serve only the Field Operations Department or only the Transportation Department, but the entire contract.

Axiom 8: *A line organization has a limited operational function that is a well-defined segment of the contract objective (or end product).*

Line organizations produce an identifiable portion of the end product of the contract and because of span-of-control limitations are generally organized into clusters of related disciplines. Examples: O&M of a radar system, or a group of radar systems, or even a group of electronic systems that include radars, telemetry, and communications. (But not optics. Optics is essentially a separate discipline.) There has to be a rational grouping of related disciplines to satisfy span-of-control limitations. You can't expect anyone to provide hands-on management of a broad spectrum of unrelated disciplines.

Line organization managers (or supervisors) must have direct control of all resources that are needed to fulfill their operational mission. They must have ready access to all resources required for the performance of their mission. They do not (and must not) have control over any other line elements. Coordination and control of all line elements is the responsibility of the program manager functioning either directly or through his or her staff.

These are the axioms that govern the structure and functioning of any organization large or small. The failure to apply these axioms is guaranteed to result in chaos, recrimination, and ultimate disaster for all concerned.

Organizational Structure Criteria

Now let's take a look at the criteria that should govern the structure of any program (or project) organization. These criteria are: chain of command, management staff, interfaces, span of control, and resource control.

Chain of Command

The organizational structure should clearly delineate a chain of command from the program manager down to the operating elements. Each operating element (or line organization) must have a clear fixed responsibility for performance of a specific segment of the SOW. A line organization performs an operational objective (e.g., fabrication of widgets; software development; facility maintenance; field installations; etc.) In other words, an end product of the program. A line function is comprised of one discipline or a set of related disciplines, providing a discreet segment of the program mission. The coordination and support of the line functions are the responsibility of the program manager.

Management Staff

The staff exists for the sole purpose of assisting the program manager in fulfilling his or her management responsibilities. Its function is to coordinate, control, and support the operational objectives of the line organizations. The functions of all staff sections are:

Preparing plans and directives. Staff sections assist the program manager by drawing up plans for carrying out his or her various management responsibilities: safety, quality control, personnel administration, security, accounting, and so on. The program manager sets out the broad guidelines and objectives to be realized, and the staff sections prepare detailed plans that spell out all the procedures for accomplishing these objectives. Upon approval by the program manager (and, where stipulated in the RFP, the customer), the plans then become a directive for accomplishing the program objectives for the respective areas (safety, security, and so forth).

That is why RFPs so often want you to come up with so many of these plans. They want to see if you know how to run this program.

Providing information to the program manager. The function of staff personnel is also to keep the program manager informed. First, he or she must be kept informed of technical and administrative matters: the arcane ramifications of a radiation hazard, for instance, by the safety engineer, or the possible legal effects involved in a subcontract, by the legal counsel. But there is a far more pervasive duty of staff personnel.And that is to function as the eyes and ears of the program manager in supervising the performance of the contract. This is known as "staff surveillance." And that is the next function of staff personnel.

Monitoring and supervising the execution of plans and directives. Staff personnel have the duty to exercise staff surveillance over all contract activities within the scope of their respective staff responsibilities. For example, quality assurance managers, after having drawn up the quality assurance plan, will, upon approval of the plan, be responsible for ensuring the implementation thereof by all elements of the contract. When acting within the scope of their responsibility, they act with the authority of the program manager. In this way, they becomes a part of the chain of command. And the wise program manager will make it clear to all concerned that (a) he or she does have this authority and (b) that the exercise of this authority is strictly limited to the scope of the staff person's responsibility. (Implicit in this relationship is the line manager's prerogative to appeal to the program manager if he or she thinks the staff person lacks jurisdiction for a particular request or that it is inconsistent with the program manager's guidelines).

Of course, all other staff supervisors operate the same way. The personnel administrator issues directives implementing the personnel plan, the safety officer issues directives covering safety procedures, and then they must see that these directives are carried out properly. There is no way that program managers can be everywhere at once performing these functions, and that is why they need well-trained staffs. And that is why the QC manager in Example 5 must report to the program manager. He can't carry out the program manager's directives exercising staff surveillance over the program manager's line elements unless he is part of the program manager's staff, a part of the chain of command, reporting to the program manager.

Providing technical and administrative services in support of the contract. Payroll and accounting, personnel administration, and supply and logistics serve the entire contract: all line elements as well as other staff personnel. This is characteristic of all staff functions: that they serve the entire contract not just a segment thereof. These services, like morale and welfare of employees, configuration management, discipline in the work place, safety, and so on, are management responsibilities—inherent in the scope of management—or as they are termed in the military, they are a function of command, an implied responsibility in any venture, whether spelled out in the RFP or not. And that is why they are performed by the manager's staff.

And now, continuing with the criteria for organizational structures:

Interfaces

The organizational structure should be such as to facilitate interface and coordination both within the organization and between the contract organization and the customer and, where necessary, with other agencies. This means that each of the key personnel in your organization should have a logical interface responsibility with a corresponding key person in the customer organization. Inherent in this responsibility is the duty to keep his counterpart informed and to coordinate the activities of his office with that of his counterpart.

Span of Control

Neither line section supervisors nor staff section managers can be expected to control a multitude of diverse, unrelated disciplines. Moreover, it is generally considered that no more than eight subordinate managers should report to each manager. This is for the same reason that a juggler shouldn't try to keep more than eight glass balls in the air at once. The wise program manager will find ways of consolidating some of the functions of his subordinates to stay within this rule.

Resource Control

All managers, department heads, and supervisors must have all the resources directly at their disposal that are required to fulfill their mission. Whether personnel, funding, supplies, facilities, or equipment, they can't be expected to do the job if they have to depend on the cooperation, good will, or generosity of others not under their control. If ever there was a place for the invariable application of Murphy's law, it is here. Because sooner or later, when the chips are down and you absolutely, positively have to rely on these other people for immediate assistance, they are going to have a higher priority of their own, (or at least they will think so) and besides, there is no compelling reason for them to help you.

We have now presented the basic criteria upon which to build an organizational structure. These criteria, along with the judicious application of the axioms presented, should go a long way toward the goal of program organization in a sensible manner.

Some History and How To Overcome It

How We Let Foreign Competitors Eat Our Lunch

There has been a plethora of foolishness in the media lately by self-appointed experts trying to tell us what happened at IBM and General Motors, *et. al* to bring about their need for reorganization and the reasons for their recent problems and how they are accomplishing it. They tell us that "in the old vertical structure, a chairman presided over a large corporate bureaucracy. Orders were passed down the chain of command and decisions were passed up, slowing the process." Really? Decisions were passed up? These are direct quotes from the newspapers.

And here is another one: The news media say, ". . . as troubles intensify, companies dismantle hierarchies . . . companies are abandoning the old command and control approach [after all, who needs command and control]. . . companies are eliminating layers of management, and [get this] *authorizing workers to make decisions.*" Horrors! What a revolutionary idea! And the "in thing" now is the new "horizontal" structure, where specialized workers work in teams (presumably without any command and control), and we have so much to learn from the Japanese and so on and on. In other words, take anything you read in the papers with a generous grain (or should I say, dose) of salt.

As I said before, management doctrine has evolved through the ages based on what worked and what didn't, and you won't find any revolutionary changes unless some one repeals the laws of human nature. The Japanese themselves admit that everything they know about management they learned from us. They came to the conclusion they had a few things to learn from us after our well-managed armed forces annihilated them in World War II while at the same time (thanks in large measure to the help of the indomitable British) destroying Hitler's invincible Wehrmacht. And I might also point out that American workers are still the most productive workers in the world. This is fact. Check it out.

Of course, we can improve our management methods, and this is what is going on right now. The problems we are having in industry today are largely attributable to the fact that for some 20 or 25 years after World War II, we enjoyed a virtual monopoly in steel, autos, machine tools, oil drilling equipment, commercial aircraft, pharmaceuticals, and many other products. When the competition is weak, the fat cats start coming out of their holes.

Our corporate managers went into the same mode that any incumbent on a government contract gets into when they have had the contract too long. They get careless and sloppy. The corporate structure evolves through a long series of decisions based on the expediency of the moment rather than a rational, deliberate plan for achieving the most cost-effective and soundly managed program. So after 20 years or so you acquire offices and facilities that are not really necessary but are nice to have. Everyone improves on the perks: company-provided limousines, a private secretary more as a status symbol than a necessity, corporate "management meetings" at plush resorts; good old boys promoted to their level of incompetence (because of their loyalty to the company), and then of course there is the corporate jet and the golden parachutes. You get the idea. This is the part that the Japanese wisely haven't learned from us—yet. Give them time. They will.

So along with all this came the pressure of labor union bosses aided and abetted by their benevolent political allies in Washington, which forced our corporate leadership to cave in to exorbitant demands. Inflation spiraled, sloppy work habits developed, discipline in the workplace declined, and the modern European steel plants that we financed with the Marshall Plan were now able to export steel to this country cheaper than we could make it ourselves.

Add to this the fact that corporate managers, now under siege by the stockholders, had to give up long-range planning in favor of immediate profits in order to make the stock attractive. This led to a mentality of planning only as far as the next quarterly report. And along with that came an every-man-for-himself mentality. And so here we are. And corporate restructuring is beginning. The United States is still the most productive country in the world; our GDP is still about two and a half times that of Japan, and so no "revolutionary" changes are necessary in our management methods notwithstanding what the nitwits of the news media may be telling us.

What the big corporations are doing now is eliminating some of this fat; consolidating functions, facilities, and equipment for greater cost effectiveness; instituting tighter cost control; selling off losing divisions; decentralizing management (delegating authority commensurate with responsibility to middle managers); contracting out functions that can be done more cheaply by specialists (subcontractors)—in other words, doing things they would have done long ago if they had not enjoyed a monopoly situation. Now they are reorganizing according to the principles of management I have just described and according to the organizational criteria outlined previously. There is, was, and always will be an absolute requirement for *focused direction* (a chain of command), *coordination* (a management staff), a *limit* to the breadth and complexity of effort that one mind can direct (the span of control), and the expedient and reliable *availability of resources* to perform the mission (resource control). We've all read about the saga of Steve Jobs, the undeniably brilliant entrepreneur who built Apple Computer and then got eased out of his company. So much for the brave new world of unstructured management. Need I say more?

How To Recognize a Screwed-Up Program

So now let's get down to cases by constructing an organization chart based upon what I've been saying. For the sake of brevity and simplicity, I think the best way to do this would be to show you a real-life, horrible example of an organization for which I once worked (another depressing experience of my life) and show you how this organization needed to be restructured.

In Figure 2.1 we have an illustration of just about everything you could do wrong. This is an example of what the government gets when it awards a contract without competition to a small, disadvantaged company. (Known as an "8a contract award.")

Well, when I came along to manage the program, they had just received word that the gravy train was over—no more sole sourcing under the 8a (small, disadvantaged) status. The contract was now about to be competed. This meant we had to streamline the organization, trim our personnel staffing, and in other ways get serious about cost effectiveness.

I still wince with the recollection of seeing this organization chart for the first time. Let's start at the top and work down. The first two things to go were the deputy and the secretary. This was a contract of about 200 people. Why should I have the exclusive use of a secretary whose services would be needed about two to four hours a day? I'll wager that even the CEO of General Motors doesn't keep a private secretary busy eight hours a day. All the typing and filing I need can be provided by

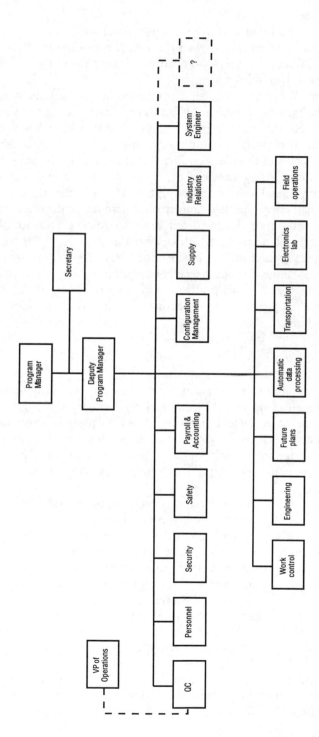

Figure 2.1 Wombat Company's organization chart.

secretaries in the personnel administration section—and they can answer the telephone for me, too, and take messages when I'm out. If it worked for Robert Townsend, chairman and CEO of the Avis Corporation, (as described in his book, *Up the Organization*), I figured it could work for me.

And what of the "deputy"? I can't for the life of me understand what anyone needs with a deputy. Even the President of the United States doesn't have a deputy. Sure, he has a Vice President, and it is a well known fact that Vice Presidents are always unhappy people, because they don't have anything to do. I know deputies are common in combat outfits in the military, but that is because of the very real possibility of the No. 1 man getting knocked off by enemy action and a replacement must always be handy. But I wasn't expecting that kind of attrition here, so inasmuch as my deputy had considerable administrative management experience and no engineering background at all, I designated him the finance and administration (F&A) manager of my organization, which is what I'll get to next. Of course, having an engineering background for the position of F&A manager wouldn't hurt. (I once worked for a very large computer services corporation that made an engineering background mandatory for this position, and it worked very well.) But I sure didn't want this guy trying to run the operating elements, the line elements of my organization in my absence.

Staff Procedure

Now take another look at this organization chart. In its original form, there were 19 people reporting to me (count 'em). No way can my ordinary-size brain cope with 19 people's problems. Management doctrine generally prescribes no more than eight. And what is even worse, is the fact that we have 19 people here all protecting their turf, their perks, trying to look useful, trying to expand their little empires, generating paper work, and getting paid as supervisors without having much of anything to supervise.

So I combined the functions of personnel, security, industrial relations, payroll and accounting, and supply into the F&A section headed by my erstwhile deputy. And now, woops! What's this, work control down here as a line function? That goes into the F&A section, too. *Anything* that controls the whole contract must be a staff function. Otherwise, where do work control supervisors derive their authority to tell line supervisors how to fill out their unit's time cards? As a line supervisor, he or she would have no authority whatsoever over a parallel organization. So at one fell swoop I was able to eliminate six supervisors and at the same time make the organization run more efficiently, because I had eliminated six turf and perk defenders. And also improved the morale of my deputy, because now he had something to do, and busy hands are happy hands, right?

So now let's take a look at the rest of the staff. Uh, oh. What's this, a block with a ??? Well, it wasn't really a question mark. There was a man's name in it. So I asked, "What does he do?" "Well, uh, he is sort of liaison to the Air Force." (Our customer.) "Who needs that? That is my job at the top level, and of my key personnel at the technical and administrative levels." Well, it turns out this individual was a sort of sacred cow. An ex-pilot, he was a little dingy, had an attention span of about 40 milliseconds. Maybe he flew a little too high too many times without enough oxygen or something. But he was an Air Force hero and, therefore, untouchable. So what to do?

Nobody can write a book that answers all questions of judgment. But the politics being what it was in this particular case, I put him to work under one of my most experienced, mature, patient, and reliable supervisors and it actually worked out fairly well. In any case, I certainly wasn't going to leave him hanging out for all to see at the end of a dotted line. (As a matter of fact, I emphatically hate dotted lines in an organization chart. It usually indicates nothing but confusion and indecision on the part of the program manager.)

The next move was to consolidate the technical staff functions under one person, as I had done with the administrative functions. This I called the Technical Support Staff section, to be managed by a senior engineer. I considered the QC supervisor first but concluded he was nothing but a deskbound paper shuffler, mindlessly making out his perfunctory little reports periodically as prescribed by the Air Force. So I picked the senior engineer out of the Field Engineering section (not without a bit of reluctance by the section supervisor). But, as I told him, good supervisors take care of their people and want to see them get ahead; also, good supervisors are constantly grooming their subordinates to take on more responsibility, aren't they?

In any case, I needed a competent and mature leader for this staff section, because he or she would be responsible for a variety of critical functions: QC, safety, configuration management, technical publications, future planning (which, inexplicably, some moron had put down among the line functions), and, last, systems engineering. The latter encompassed the function of conceptual design and procurement of new sensor systems or major modification of existing systems to meet new Air Force operational requirements. As such, it is very closely related to the future planning function. In fact, it is so closely related that the two functions overlap. Therefore, I merged the future planning function into the systems engineering function under one supervisor. Up to now, the deputy program manager, working with the supply supervisor, had been going through the motions of supervising these functions, with predictably disastrous results.

So now I had my staff sections organized. Oh yes, about that dotted line from the QC Supervisor to the company V.P. I had fortuitously seen a copy of this organization chart before I agreed to take this job. That's when the dotted line was removed. I made it clear the QC man either worked for them or me, not both. If they wanted to send auditing teams down to my organization and inspect my records or methods and make constructive suggestions, fine, but there could be only one person running this program, the person responsible for its success or failure, and that would be I, myself. And I would strongly advise every other program manager to get a clear understanding on this sort of thing *before* he or she accepts the position.

Next let's take a look at the line elements of this contract. We've already removed Work Control and Future Plans. What about this Transportation? In this case, Transportation is not an end product of the contract. It is incidental to the fulfillment of the contract objective. You could have a contract to operate a fleet of buses. Then transportation would be an end product and therefore, a line element of the contract. But here, in my organization, it would be a staff function. Here we had a motor pool complete with minor repair and maintenance functions. This was not directed by the RFP. It was a decision by management. Not a very good decision, I decided after a little analysis of costs. So we sold the vehicles, disbanded the motor pool and eliminated three jobs. The contract elements like Supply, which required constant use of vehicles, were assigned leased vehicles and were to be the responsibility of the respective supervisors. Two additional leased vehicles were assigned to the program management office under the control of the F&A manager to be available for all personnel for official use on a sign-out basis.

What is left is the Engineering section, the Automatic Data Processing Section, the Field Operations Section, and the Electronics Lab. The latter was essentially a shop for repair and fabrication of electronic and electrical equipment. The Electronics Lab supervisor was up in years and getting ready to retire, so I consolidated this element into the Engineering section, so that when he retired, we could do with one less supervisor here. (The shop foreman took over the supervisory duties.) Besides, the Engineering section functions were so closely associated with the E-Lab functions that they should never have been separated in the first place.

So we end up with three line organizations and two major staff sections. I now have five people reporting to me instead of 19! How do you suppose anyone in his right mind ever came up with an organization chart with 19 sections reporting to the program manager? I'll tell you one way. When amateur managers and proposal writers go through an RFP, every time they see a *function* listed, they think you have to have an organizational element, separate and discrete, to perform each function. One has to decide, based on his or her experience and common sense, which functions can and should be combined and performed by one organizational element. Are the skills related? Can these two (or three) functions be performed adequately by one person expending just one man-year? Can this group of functions reasonably be within the span of control of one supervisor? Or manager?

Another important point. After consolidating the various functions under, say, the F&A manager, I told him to organize it however he wanted it. Just as you see it in Figure 2.2. It was up to him. Then submit his plan to me for approval. This is just to make sure he doesn't do something really stupid or try to gold plate or overstaff his section. Those are my concerns. How he organizes it and sets up his operation are his concern. He is the one who has to live with it. Of course, he knows if he does the job too ineptly and starts to screw up my contract, he's out of here. But I am not going to do his thinking for him. And this is the weakness of nine out of ten

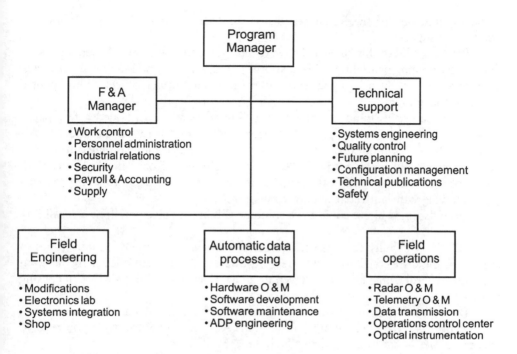

Figure 2.2 Organization chart of an enlightened manager.

managers I've known: trying to micromanage, trying to do everyone's thinking for them. And without fail, they eventually fall on their face, because first of all nobody is that smart and second because they destroy initiative, enthusiasm, and self-esteem of their subordinates.

Now take a look at Figure 2.2. This is the clean, streamlined organization I ended up with—now lean, efficient, capable of immediate response to customer requirements, and higher morale (for those who are left) because everyone knows what is expected of him or her, no more no less. And instead of expending their time defending their turf and expanding their perks, they are all busy trying to keep up with all the constructive work they now have.

One more minor point—and you can take it for what it is worth. I have used the terms "supervisor" and "manager" somewhat interchangeably here, but there is a distinct difference, in my opinion. I think much confusion and uncertainty could be avoided if everyone would adopt this rule of thumb: Supervisors are responsible for a one discipline operation; they supervise a hands-on operation in which they themselves have some experience and expertise. Managers are responsible for a multi-discipline operation; they manage. They are not responsible for hands-on supervision of a one-discipline operation, but, instead, they have to bring together a many-faceted effort and therefore have a more complex job and are somewhat higher in the hierarchy than supervisors. The head of the Technical Support staff, then, would be a manager; the head of the Field Engineering section would be a manager; the head of the Radar section or the Optics section in Field Operations would be a supervisor.

Before we leave this subject, I have to provide you a few well-chosen words on the subject of staff procedure. This is another area where I find an almost total lack of understanding, even by experienced managers and former officers who spent a career in the military.

What comes to mind at once is that "sacred cow" I mentioned a few pages back. Remember, he was supposed to provide "liaison" between me and the Air Force. Well he just about drove me nuts before I reassigned him, coming into my office with some half-baked idea like, "Don, we ought to approach the Air Force with a proposal to use the XYZ technology to improve the data compression problems we are having with our radar data transmission."

Don: "Sounds like it could have some possibilities. Have you done a feasibility study on it.?"

SC: "A feasibility study? No, but I had a discussion with Lt. Cmdr. Jones in the bar at the Officers Club, and he seemed interested. So I sent a letter to the commanding general of the base, and haven't had an answer yet. That's why I'm coming to you."

Don: "You WHAT? You sent a letter to the CG recommending a new engineering project? Well, why don't you write to Ann Landers, too, while you're at it. Have you ever heard of going through channels?"

S C: "Well, yeah, but I talked it over with Mr. Half Track, the vice president, and he thought it was a good idea. So here is the follow-up letter he told me to send them over your signature. He thought it would get more results if *you signed it.*"

So after throwing him out of my office and taking a handful of aspirins, I tried to compose myself for what was sure to follow. Well, sure enough about a week later, I get a letter from Mr. Half Track complaining bitterly that I haven't yet pursued this brilliant idea and why hadn't I approved the letter SC had prepared for the Air Force?. So here in effect, is the letter I sent him:

"I can't approve this letter in its present form. First of all, I can't even tell what it is we are asking for, and if I can't, I know they can't. It says, we are seeking 'informal recommendation of initial development of the XYZ . . . .' If you were the Air Force, would you sign a blank check like that? They want to see specific, finite recommendations to accomplish specific development, modification, or procurement of real-world hardware/software systems with specific target dates for accomplishment of various phases of completion, etc., etc.

"We have simply got to develop a more professional methodology for submitting recommendations to our customers for engineering development projects. Such recommendations should be based on an engineering study that sets out the design concepts, alternative approaches, trade-off analyses, block diagrams, cost estimates, target dates, milestone charts, systems parameters, performance specifications, identification of uncertainties, risk assessment, identification of CI/CPCIs, etc., etc. Specific off-the-shelf hardware components must be identified, specific software development tasks defined (and whether it can be accomplished in house), and estimated man-hours for completion set out.

"Making proposals to our customer without first having completed a thorough engineering study of the problem and specific recommendations is simply tossing a problem in their lap. They are paying us to *solve* problems, not present more problems for them to solve.

"I suggest that it would be better for all concerned, save time in the long run, and avoid confusion if in the future, engineering projects involving this contract were coordinated through me from the inception."

So here we have a pretty good example of what happens when people (through some bizarre twist of fate) wind up in responsible executive or staff positions without having the faintest idea of command channels, staff procedure, completed staff action, or even the most primitive concept of the word "coordination." How could I possibly manage a program when a subordinate and a superior were collaborating with my customer on a project completely without my knowledge? Chaos, anarchy, confusion . . . .

That is why we have a chain of command, staffs, and line organizations. The project, program, contract, venture, enterprise—whatever—must have one leader who can provide direction and integrated effort to achieve an established, defined goal. A leader who alone must make the major decisions that affect the outcome of the project after consultation with his or her staff.

Such decisions must be the result of coordinated effort by the staff in gathering the necessary information, making studies, evaluating courses of action, coordinating inputs from the line organizations and all other elements to be affected by the decision, including outside agencies: government, vendors, subcontractors. This is the job of the staff. It's called "staff coordination."

Coordinated staff action means that before a recommendation is presented to the manager, it has been staffed through every element that could have the slightest interest in the outcome of the decision. Each supervisor or manager of every concerned line element or staff section has had a chance to register his or her concurrence or nonconcurrence or make suggested modifications or exceptions (or forever hold your peace). This way everyone will be singing off the same sheet of music.

It's best to point out here that this doesn't mean that the program manager is obliged to have a consensus on every decision, as some I have known seemed to think. (That's why nothing ever got done or decided.) Good managers weigh all the comments of their staff and then make their own decisions based on their experience and good judgment, which presumably were the reasons they were selected to be chiefs and not Indians. For those of their staff who have an adverse view to their decisions, they tell them, "Your objections are noted, but there are other overriding factors that require me to take a different course of action, so be prepared to mitigate your problems with it the best you can."

Completed staff action means that when recommendations are presented to managers, all they have to do is sign it or reject it. If they sign it, the wheels are automatically set in motion to implement their decision. What they sign usually is either an order to implement the decision or else an approval for the staff to begin preparation of detailed plans for implementing the decision.

Summary

I have presented in this chapter some of the axioms of leadership that have been distilled from thousands of years of human endeavor. These have survived the test of time, based on what worked and what didn't. These are not all the axioms of leadership, just the ones which pertain to the concept of organizational structures.

Then we have examined the criteria, upon which organizational structures are based, that govern the construction of a workable, efficient organization. Without these axioms and criteria to guide them, managers or proposal writers are drifting on a sea of confusion without an anchor.

Then I have walked you through an (ugh) horrible example of an organization chart, through a morass of confusion, divided responsibility and misguided mismanagement and out into the enlightenment and beautiful symmetry of a properly devised organizational structure. Here is a happy place where everyone knows who is responsible for what, everyone has a full day's work to do, and neither the company's nor the customer's money is being wasted on duplication of effort, sloppy work, and frustration. Ah! Verily, a consummation devoutly to be wished.

Chapter 3

How Proposals Are Organized

A proposal is not the same as a proposition.
—*Helgeson*

Before we get into the details of preparing a proposal, we need to get an overview of just what a proposal consists of, so that we have an idea of where we are heading and what our goal is. In other words, we are going to take a look at the big picture here before we get into the details of how the picture is put together.

Elements of a Contract

Offer, Acceptance, and Consideration

Since the whole idea is to secure a contract, let's examine the concept of contracting and define what a contract is. Basically, a contract requires three elements: an offer, an acceptance, and a consideration (money or a promise to do or not to do something). The RFP (request for proposal) is neither an offer nor an acceptance. It is a request by the customer for you to make an offer. If the customer accepts your offer (your proposal), you have a contract, provided there is full agreement on the consideration. You may go to an enormous amount of effort writing a proposal, but remember, this is just an offer by you; the customer is not obligated to accept it and, under common law rules, does not even have to give you a reason why. In governmental contracting, however, the FAR (Federal Acquisition Regulations) require the government to give you a debriefing on demand, if the potential contract is for more than a stipulated amount of money (depending on the type of contract).

Those are the very basic elements involved. Of course, there are all sorts of things that can complicate the whole process and even make a completed contract null and void—things like fraud, collusion, misrepresentations, not negotiating in good faith, mental incompetence, and so on. I bring this subject up here because of the confusion that exists among many people regarding the status of the RFP. Strictly speaking, the RFP is not a contractual document; it is simply a request by the customer for someone to make an offer.

Your offer (proposal) is an integral part of any contract that may result, and that is why precision of language is of paramount importance in writing proposals. Anything you say you will do in the proposal constitutes a binding promise to perform specifically as stated, and the offeree (customer) can take you to court and nail you for damages in the event of your failure to perform as stated. By the way, the only excuses accepted are those attributable to an act of God. If you can't perform, you had better pray for a fortuitous hurricane, or a well-placed bolt of lightning.

Verbal Contracts

While we are on the subject of contract law, there is one other aspect that is worthy of note, and that is the verbal contract. Of course I'm not talking about the contract resulting from an RFP. I am talking about modifications thereto that have the same legal status as a contract. Generally speaking, verbal contracts are not enforceable. There are of course exceptions, notably when a court applying rules of equity will, under certain circumstances, enforce a verbal agreement where one side of the agreement has in good faith been fully and unilaterally performed. That is one reason why government contract officers get very nervous about subordinates or field managers telling the contractor what to do or how to do it, or in any way even implying that contractors are authorized to perform something different from what they were contracted to do. (The other reason is that this could lead to charges against the government of engaging in a "personal services" contractual relationship, as we will see later.) The boilerplate in virtually all RFPs specifically forbids the contractor from departing from the terms of the written contract without the specific written authorization of the contracting officer.

Even that does not necessarily guarantee against problems arising from misunderstandings, misinterpretations, and excessive "supervision" by the customer. And that is why I emphasize that the language of your proposal must be carefully written, with precision and specificity. And that is why an otherwise good proposal might be thrown in the wastebasket by the customer if it is sloppily written or carelessly organized. When writing or reviewing a proposal, my practice is when in doubt about any passage, imagine this passage being read in court and that the judge's decision could turn on the interpretation of it.

Personal Services Contracts

The mention of "excessive supervision" brings me to the last item on contract law: personal service contracts. The botttom line on this subject is to the effect that in government contracting, personal service contracts are illegal. There are certain exceptions to this general rule which are specifically and narrowly defined in the (Federal Acquisition Regulations). The FAR and other government regulations severely limit the authority of contracting officers to negotiate personal services contracts. And the courts and Congress have wisely upheld this restriction. The philosophy is that the government (that is, bureaucrats) should manage *contracts*, not people. The rule is intended to keep bureaucrats out of the business of supervising the contractor's employees, but instead force them to deal only with contractor management according to well-established contract management procedures.

One of the basic reasons for this is that otherwise the bureaucracy could circumvent civil service personnel ceilings by augmenting their little empires with contractor personnel as a mere extension of the bureaucracy. But a more important reason is that the basic function of government should be to govern, not to perform services that can and should be performed by contractors who have learned to survive in the competitive world by performing these services more reliably and cost effectively.

In the past, NASA in particular has had a difficult time with this rule. In my experience, they have often had an overlay of monitors looking over the shoulders of contractor personnel, even down to technicians monitoring technicians. This kind of micromanaging is bound to lead to trouble, and that is what NASA got. I am convinced that some of the NASA disasters are directly attributable to the diffusion of responsibility, confused lines of authority, and failures of the decision-making process caused by micromanagement policies.

This kind of monitoring led to situations that were tantamount to personal services contracts giving rise to the establishment of the famous Pellerzi Criteria, Pellerzi being the judge who tried to set up some guidelines for government managers (in the course of a lawsuit against NASA) to help them stay out of "personal services" trouble. Since this is not a book on industrial relations, I won't list these criteria here, but if you are interested, you could ask any NASA administrator. I'm sure they are all well read on the subject.

Now let us get on to the overview of how proposals are organized. The first section of any proposal will be the executive summary.

The Executive Summary

Purpose

The executive summary should be prepared by the proposal manager working in close collaboration with the cognizant marketeer who presumably has been tracking this program. The proposal manager should write it, because this is where he or she must set the tone for the proposal, set forth the major decisions embodied therein, and summarize the manner in which the proposal is organized.

The marketeer should collaborate, because he is the person who at the inception knows more about the program or project than anyone else. He knows (or should know) all the buzz words, the hot buttons, the discriminators, the customer's idiosyncracies, the funding ramifications, the background, the history, and a thousand other things that good marketeers are supposed to find out while enjoying those generous expense accounts.

Elements

The executive summary has evolved in recent years into an integral part of every proposal. It used to be a sort of cover letter where the company president sneaked in a sales pitch; then it became a blatant sales pitch and nothing more. It was an opportunity for contractor management to bypass the Source Selection Evaluation Board (SSEB) and go directly to the Source Selection Authority (SSA) to convince that individual that the award should go to them, regardless of what the SSEB said. This is logical, since it is unlikely the SSA will have time to read any of the proposals but probably will read the executive summaries, provided they are just a few pages each. And in this respect they served a useful purpose.

Trouble is, too many windbags got into the act; the sales pitches became too blatant and too long, which completely defeated the purpose. So now, the government, probably impelled by an environmentalist desire to cut down on the paper waste, started regulating things by prescribing what goes into the executive summary, how many pages, and so on. For once, we see a welcome move by the government to regulate.

The purpose of the executive summary should be to introduce your company *in a few brief, well-chosen words*. Then go on to summarize the highlights of the proposal, the approaches taken, the major management and technical decisions made and why, and any innovative ideas you have come up with that you think will set your proposal apart from the rest. Then a brief summary of how the proposal is organized and you have it.

The executive summary will be the shortest section of any proposal, but will require the most skillful writing by far. All too often this section is written by a vice president or someone else high in the hierarchy who knows nothing about the program, but worse yet, doesn't know how to write. Somebody whose writing experience is limited to preparing memos to stick on the bulletin board about excessive use of the copying machines. Somebody with the attitude, "I'll have to write this because it is very important, and I'm the most important person around here."

I have a cover letter in my files written by one of these that contains nine obvious errors in grammar, punctuation, and sloppy writing in one page! Things like: words that don't exist, like "ourself;" singular verb form with a plural subject; hyphens between verbs and their objects, and just plain sloppy sentences. My advice to all proposal managers and executives: If you are not a skillful writer with a thorough knowledge of the English language, hire a consultant to review your cover letter and your executive summary (or better yet, have them write it for you), because these documents are most likely to be read by the powers that be in selection of the contract. And sloppy documents imply sloppy contractors.

The executive summary should be dynamic, terse, and designed to capture and hold the interest of the nontechnical reader. Do not get bogged down in detail. Skip the busy charts, graphs, tables, complicated mathematics. If you feel a need to back up your statements, refer the reader to the body of the proposal where this backup is provided. Use words that have impact. Keep the sentences short and to the point. The executive summary must have focus; that is, a limited number of central themes should come through loud and clear.

The tendency of many people, especially engineers, is to try to put down everything they know. No one is going to absorb more than two or three central themes or impressions from reading anyone's executive summary. Putting down any more simply diffuses and vitiates the important things you wanted to say.

The executive summary should be brief, never more than ten pages. I would recommend less than five in the great majority of procurements, even if the RFP should stipulate ten. Remember whom you are addressing: Maybe a general with a command of 100,000 service personnel and a 100-billion-dollar budget. Do you think he is going to read and absorb the contents of five executive summaries from five bidders each ten pages long? No way. He is human and he is busy. He will read the short, dynamic ones and toss the long, tedious ones aside. So get your message up front and make it short.

A word about those themes. I find an inordinate amount of time spent by proposal managers on this subject. If the proposal manager and the responsible marketeer would sit down together and talk about the matter for about 45 minutes, they should be able to come up with all the themes they need (three or less, never more than that; any more than that, they are no longer themes). I would define a theme as: (a) a factor (a quality, characteristic, capability, or feature) that distinguishes your company from all the other bidders, or (b) a recognition of a serious concern (i.e., a hot button) that your company recognizes and is uniquely prepared to satisfy. As such, a theme can recur over and over in a proposal in various forms in such a way as to define and distinguish your proposal from the others. A theme should be something you can weave throughout your proposal. A theme should be comparable to the aria "La Donna E Mobile" in the opera *Rigoletto* or like the haunting melody ("Lara's Theme") that recurs throughout the movie *Dr. Zhivago*.

What my brethren in the proposal business usually come up with purporting to be themes are in reality just motherhood statements 90% of the time. "We have great engineers and an experienced management team" is a motherhood statement. (Don't you think everyone is going to say that they have great engineers and an experienced management team)? "We are the only organization capable of providing the ABC technology in support of the program's communication problems" is a theme. "We have a long history of support to environmental programs" is a motherhood statement. "Our environmental research lab was designed with the purpose of solving problems directly related to this program" is a theme.

Sometimes you have the opportunity to shoot one or more of your competitors down in the executive summary. Let's say you are bidding on an engineering development contract for a state-of-the-art system. You know that your most formidable competitor bombed out not so long ago on a somewhat similar system. A huge cost overrun, a technical approach that was only marginally successful, inadequate quality control, poor configuration management—whatever. You get those marketeers of yours busy and find out the details. (Usually it soon becomes common knowledge within the community what caused a failure or even a less-than-hoped-for success.) So in your executive summary, you focus in on the cause, whatever it may be, and then proceed to outline what measures are built in to your proposal to avoid this sort of thing in your performance of this program. You never, never mention the failed program specifically or the name of the competitor. Let the readers make their own connections. They will get the message without you hitting them over the head with it. After all, maybe they or their friends in the bureaucracy were partly responsible for the foul-up.

In summary:

- The executive summary is a job for skilled writers.
- It should be brief, terse, and designed to hold the reader's attention.
- It is a sales pitch based on the presentation of provable facts.
- It should focus on the salient features of your proposal and of your company.
- It provides the reader with:

An introduction to your company;

The highlights of your proposal, the major decisions, innovative features, and benefits to the customer;

Themes (what distinguishes your proposal from the rest); and

The organization of your proposal.

The Technical Proposal

I keep six honest serving men,
(They taught me all I knew;)
Their names are What and Why and When
And How and Where and When and Who.
—Kipling

The Three Basic Requirements

This is where you get down to the real core of the proposal. All the rest plays a supporting role to this section, because this is where you tell customers *how* you are going to provide the services, hardware systems, or data that they are contracting to obtain. This section is usually the most heavily weighted section in the evaluation criteria of a proposal, with the management section being next. This is the section that the engineers and scientists on the Source Selection Evaluation Board (SSEB) zero in on and examine with a fine-tooth comb.

So you must adopt a radically different approach here than in writing executive summaries. Always bear in mind that, in the technical proposal, you are addressing engineers and scientists with in-depth technical backgrounds. Don't for one minute think you can snow them with techno-babble. They are looking for solutions to technical problems and the proof that your solution is feasible and practicable.

The most pervasive thing I find in all proposals is the use of bare, unsupported statements. Like, "We will provide a configuration management system that will ensure conformance with MIL STD 483A." And that is supposed to suffice. On the contrary, this is merely a statement of a goal, not a solution to a problem. You must show how the configuration management system works, who is responsible for implementing it, how it functions, what are its mechanics, whether there will be a configuration control board, what the criteria upon which it was established are, and then show just how your configuration management concept actually does implement MIL STD 483A.

The Elements of Technical Response

The content and format of the technical proposal will be dictated by (a) the RFP—primarily the statement of work (SOW), (b) the proposal instructions, and (c) the evaluation criteria. The general outline, your roadmap for addressing these factors, will be provided by the proposal manager. We will get into all that in the next chapter, but for now we are just looking at the overall content of the technical proposal. The content may include a myriad of items, from technical approaches to cost tradeoffs, from engineering design concept to work flow to life cycle cost considerations, from task organization to interfaces. But the sum and substance of your technical proposal, when finished, should address three major entities: the nature of the problem, your understanding of the problem, and your solution of the problem.

The success of any major section of the technical proposal will be a measure of the success with which you treat these three fundamentals, the three essential entities. Note that when I speak of "the problem" in this context, the word is interchangeable with "the requirement."

Nature of the Problem. A good way to start out any major subsection of the technical proposal is to restate the mission, the goal, or the objective of this subsection. Do not regurgitate the RFP, but restate the requirement in such a way that it illuminates, clarifies, or defines what you are about to describe in this section. This way, evaluators have a bench mark to reassure themselves that they are looking at the section of the proposal that they have been assigned to evaluate. RFPs are often sloppily written, and this is an opportunity for you to clarify the language of the requirement and define the parameters of what you are going to address, thus avoiding any misunderstandings between you and the reader, and possibly future misunderstandings between your company and the contracting officer when your proposal becomes a contract. Again, the implications for care and precision in preparing this statment are clear. Of course, it must be emphasized that this statement must *not* change the substance of the requirement, but clarify it. Any substantive departure from the RFP requirement would be an exception to the terms of the RFP and would require approval of corporate management.

Understanding the Problem. Many RFPs require the bidders to state what they believe to be the critical areas for successfully performing the contract. Their purpose is to ascertain whether you really understand the requirement and all its ramifications. And although there may be other ways to show your understanding, I think this is the best. You can't really understand what the critical areas are without some in-depth analysis and some wise judgement based on experience with similar requirements. I would advise that you, the proposal writer, have some brainstorming sessions with colleagues on this subject well before you put pencil to paper. You can be sure that the evaluators' impression of how well you understand the requirement will be heavily weighted on how they score your proposal. After all how can you solve any problem if you don't understand the problem ?

Solution of the Problem. The "problem" is the requirement set out in the RFP: what the customer wants to buy. All the problems are listed in the SOW, and your general outline should provide you the roadmap to follow in addressing these problems or requirements. What you must do is respond to each of these requirements in turn, as you would answer the questions on an exam paper. You must interpret the requirement literally, describing how, when, and where this requirement is going to be provided and by whom. Simply saying you will provide this and that is not adequate. Many proposal writers (I should say most) think they can get away with simply stating a *goal*. You've got to convince the readers that you know how to achieve that goal. Give them a step-by-step description of who does what to whom and when and where . . . and, sometimes, why.

An example: "XYZ Corp. will provide emergency construction and rehabilitation support of facilities on the remote islands." Wait a minute. Where are the construction crews coming from? How are they going to get to the remote islands? What construction equipment can be made available? Who in the XYZ Corp. will be responsible for this requirement? What type of construction will you be prepared to provide? Well, you get the idea.

And another thing. Give them exactly what they ask for and nothing more.[1] Engineers have a tendency to propose the latest state-of-the-art equipment without regard to what the customer asked for. This is natural and understandable. That is why they are engineers. But you will never win new contracts that way, because you will price yourself out of the competition. Proposing something nice to have is all right only if it does not raise your cost. Nice to have won't raise your score in the evaluation, because everyone is evaluated solely on the requirements set out in the RFP, nothing more nothing less.

I once worked on an engineering development proposal for an engineering firm that was really uptight over having lost their last bid even though they felt they were the best qualified of those bidding. After about a week, we had a meeting to discuss the preliminary design review that we were going to propose. Since this was one of those outfits that seemed to think consultants are to be seen and not heard, I listened patiently for about an hour while each engineering section leader proposed his version of what they were going to propose. "We can do better here than what they called for; they probably don't know that there is a better computer for this job. And they should have nine workstations instead of three. And they'll need more redundancy here." And so on and on. I finally couldn't stand it any longer and stood up, "I can't believe what I'm hearing. It's little wonder you lost the last bid opportunity. You probably priced it out of the ballpark. What we have here is a customer who has requested bids on a pickup truck, and you guys are proposing a Cadillac convertible with white sidewalls! If the customer wanted a state-of-the-art system, he would have said so. Forget about state of the art. Go back to your drawing boards and come up with a pickup truck, or else we are all just wasting our time here." Fortunately, they had a chief executive officer there who had the good sense to agree with me, and consequently they won the contract.

My point is, *do not* think you know better than the customer what he wants. Don't read into the RFP anything that isn't there. Interpret everything literally. What *you* think he should have is totally irrelevant. If you give him more, it will raise your cost; if you give him something less, you are nonresponsive.

How should you, the proposal writer address a technical proposal requirement? That is, what aspects should you address in convincing the reader that you know how to provide the services or thing of value that constitutes the requirement? There may not be a universal answer to this question, but this will probably suffice for 99% of the cases you encounter. The order in which you address these aspects or elements of the requirement will depend on the context—perhaps the proposal instructions, or perhaps the nature of the subject of the requirement.

But generally you should start out by telling them who is responsible for performing this function and just where that person is located in the organization. Then a statement of the mission; a restatement of the requirement. Then the most

---

1. This is the general rule. For a description of a major exception for negotiated contracts, see "The 'Best Value' Concept" in Chapter 6, "How the Customer Evaluates Your Proposal."

salient feature or critical area or biggest problem you perceive in accomplishing the mission. (If any. Don't try to manufacture one if there isn't one. Many mundane items don't require this.)

Now you are ready to describe your technical approach. Tell them how you are going to organize your resources to perform the mission. Who is going to manage it and what are that person's primary interfaces in performing the mission? Then provide an organization chart showing staffing numbers and functions of each subordinate element.

Describe the duties and responsibilities of each of the key personnel. Explain your rationale for the staffing levels and how the organization will function in a coordinated manner to perform the SOW requirements. Weave in the applicable contract data requirements list(CDRL)/data item description (DID) requirements that have been referenced in the RFP. Not just that you will comply, but *how*. Use the MIL STDs (and standards adopted by various professional societies such as IEEE, SMPTE, IRIG, if applicable) and the various regulations referenced in the RFP—not just by acknowledging them but by using them in your response. They are there to help you—to tell you how the customer wants you to perform the mission. Moreover, the customer had a reason for referencing them, so it behooves you to demonstrate that you have read, understand, and know how to comply with them.

You must tell the evaluator how you are going to perform this mission. But you must do it with an economy of words. Nearly all RFPs stipulate page limitations these days. So how best to do this in the shortest space? In short, you tell how the flagpole gets painted, not how to paint the flagpole.

You keep it at the level of how you make things happen. You tell how you direct, guide, prioritize, supervise, monitor, plan, coordinate, and organize the successful performance of the task. *Do not* get bogged down in procedural details. "Solar calibrations will be performed by so-and-so at T-2 hours for the purpose of ____." But you don't have to tell them *how* you perform a solar calibration. You are not writing an operations manual or an SOP. You have to provide work-flow diagrams, interface charts, milestone charts, and any other graphics that help to illuminate or clarify your presentation.

Now a word about those graphics. They should be designed to make the reader's work easier, not harder. They should help to make the text more understandable and save time. Therefore, they should be kept simple and clean. Evaluators usually don't enjoy working puzzles. If they have to spend more than three minutes figuring them out, they will probably just say, "The hell with it." Much better to use two graphics that are simple and easy to follow than one that takes five or ten minutes to figure out.

Of course, there are a myriad of things that go into a technical proposal, far too many to cover in detail here. But they will always be directed by the RFP, either in the proposal instructions or in the SOW. Some of the things you will be called upon to provide in the technical proposal: system concepts, design reviews, acceptance tests, risk management, quality assurance, life cycle cost criteria, cost controls, engineering trade-offs, work control, work breakdown structure, schedules, task organization, training, spare parts, maintenance, technical publications, flight safety, configuration management, and so on, *ad infinitum*.

In summrary, the technical proposal is the core of the proposal. In effect, all the rest plays a supporting role. A good technical proposal should be your response to three basic entities: the nature of the problem, your understanding of the problem, and your solution of the problem or technical approach. The technical approach should set the stage by telling who is responsible for this function and where that person is in the organization. It should describe the duties and responsibilities of key personnel, what their interfaces are, and how resources are coordinated to perform the function. It should describe how things are made to happen, not the procedural details. And, finally, it should include ample graphics to illuminate and clarify the text and to make the reader's comprehension easier, not harder.

The Management Proposal

Objective

The objective of the management proposal is to convince the customer that your company's management techniques, quality of personnel, organization logic, and related experience enables you to provide the best planning, quality control, task supervision, skill, and contract support required to perform effectively within schedule and budget.

This is where you put into practice what you learned in Chapter 2, because organization is the essence of a good management plan. Organizational structure is what makes everything else work: coordination, planning and execution, support systems, feedback systems, work control, cost control, quality control, and even such subjective factors as motivation, morale, and the "can do" spirit that differentiates the outstanding contractor from the rest.

General Approach

The best general approach I can give for preparing the management proposal is the same I would give for the technical proposal: Set out to provide the reader with the three basic entities, the nature of the problem, your understanding of the problem, and the solution of the problem. It doesn't matter what you call them, just so you respond to these underlying factors, the *sine qua non* to a complete response to an RFP requirement.

Management Concept—Who Is Responsible? The RFP proposal instructions will of course override anything I say here, but in general I would say the best way to start out the management proposal (or plan) would be to open with an introduction that first summarizes your concept of the management mission in performing this contract. Then introduce by name the person who is going to manage it. Then, a one- or two-sentence summary of this person's background, emphasizing, of course, the relationship of his or her background to the unique aspects of this contract.

Set the Stage. Next you should discuss what you regard as the most critical areas to be addressed in successfully managing this contract. These critical areas should be researched in collaboration with the marketeer who has been tracking this opportunity, because in most cases, the critical areas will be the hot buttons, the areas of most concern to the customer. And these are the areas the marketeer should know best. For example, if this is an O&M contract, your critical area might be resource control and accountability. You have an existing, proven, effective system for tracking of supplies, materiel, man-hours, equipment, subcontractors, and spare parts, so that there is *zero* delay or disruption of operations caused by red-lined equipment. (You know that the customer has sometimes been tearing his hair out over work stoppages due to late delivery of materiel or spare parts, which the incumbent blames on vendors and subcontractors.) If you have any additional comments or observations that indicate a commendable insight into the unique features of this contract, this is the place to state them, because this is your best chance to demonstrate your understanding of the contract right at the outset.

Having thus set the stage for a favorable impression of your company by showing you have an in-depth understanding of the contract and that you have just the right person to manage it, you get down to the most important things the customer wants to know. Like where the program management office is to be located, who and what office in the corporate structure that the program manager will report to, and the extent of authority or autonomy that will be granted to your program manager.

Then you briefly summarize the salient features of the management proposal. For example, if you have developed an MIS system that is especially adapted to this program that enables you to reduce administrative overhead while at the same time, enhancing incentives, efficiency, and interfacing, you mention it here and reference the paragraph where it is detailed in the management plan.

In other words, for an introduction, give them a mini-executive summary that sets the stage for what is to follow and gives the customer an initially favorable impression of your company.

The Necessary Ingredients of a Management Proposal

Proposal instructions and RFPs may differ, but I can't imagine a complete management proposal without the following main features. (In fact, I would include all these sections whether the RFP instructions call for them or not.)

- An organizational chart showing the overall corporate structure. If you are part of an element of one of the corporate divisions, then the corporate organization chart should show its subordinate elements down to divisions, including your own. In most corporate structures, the name of the division indicates its function (e.g., Commercial Products Division). If the name does not so indicate, then you should use bullets under the block for each division showing its primary functions. Show how your organization (the parent of the proposed contract) fits into the division, so that the reader can ascertain exactly where your contract fits into the overall corporate structure. (See Figure 3.1.)
- An organization chart showing the overall contract structure. Usually the RFP instructions are very explicit about this, but if not, you should use your own judgment on how much of the following information to include on this chart, the criteria being how much can you include on one chart without cluttering it up to the point where it becomes confusing. As I said before, if a chart begins to get too cluttered, use two simple charts instead.

First, show your organizational structure down to and including those headed by a supervisor. Applying my definition of a supervisor from Chapter 2, this would be all line elements incorporating essentially one discipline for accomplishing its mission. (For example, the telemetry section, or the ADP section.) Under each block,

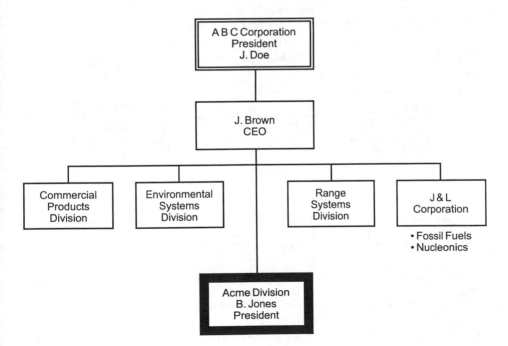

Figure 3.1 Example of a corporate organization chart.

show with bullets what functions are performed by each of these sections *as directly related to the SOW.* Then when you address that section in the body of your management plan—say, the ADP section—you can provide a breakdown of the organization of that section there. (For example, the ADP Section could have several subsections such as maintenance, software, operations, and so forth.) Now take a look at Figure 3.2. Here we have an example of an organization/function chart incorporating the corresponding work breakdown structure (WBS) sections that show which of the organizational units performs which function. (For example, "Administration" comprises WBS 1.1. If you want more information on WBS, see Chapter 9.)

- An interface chart showing the primary interfaces for your program manager on down. Include all the key personnel, not only the interfaces with the customer organization, but also with your corporate and other supporting and parallel organizations as shown in Figure 3.3. After all, no man is an island, right? The customer wants to know if you understand that successful accomplishment of your mission involves the cultivation of a variety of supporting and parallel elements as well as keeping the respective key personnel in the customer organization informed and advised of your plans and progress.

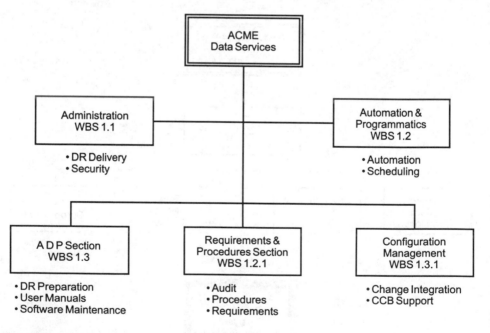

Figure 3.2 Functional organization chart, data services program.

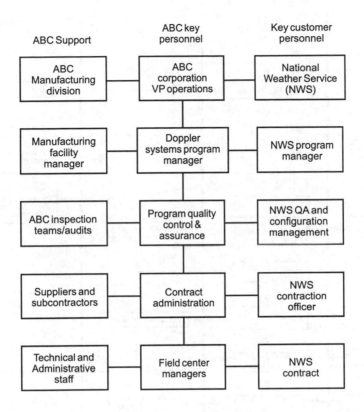

Figure 3.3 Milestone chart for ABC contract.

Figure 3.4 shows a somewhat different kind of interface chart that shows the interfaces involved in a process. The chart shown shows the systems engineering process.

- *A chart listing key personnel.* Okay, so now you have laid out the structure of your organization and how it functions, you must then show how things get done. What better way than to describe just what all these high-paid managers and supervisors do to earn their money? So you outline their duties and responsibilities, starting with the program manager and working on down to the supervisors. Be careful to associate duties with responsibilities. Don't get bogged down in irrelevant details. Signing time cards may be a duty, but you wouldn't describe that among their responsibilities, would you? So skip the mundane details and focus on how these key people make things happen. They assign and prioritize tasks; they control work flow, they monitor task performance for quality and timeliness, they supervise training and task

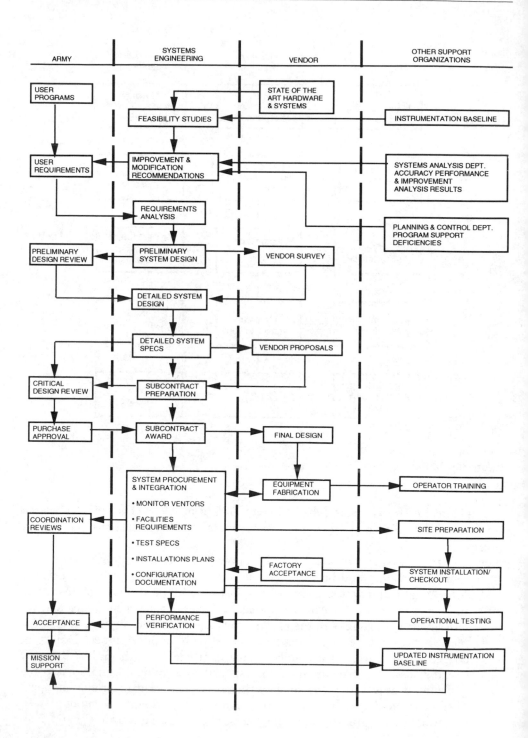

Figure 3.4 Chart showing the interfaces involved in the systems engineering process.

progress. Who cares about time cards? Who cares about making out requisitions for spare parts? The supervisor's job is to see that these things get done; never mind the details.

Management Planning

Next, as I indicated in Chapter 2, you will always have essentially two staff sections. If you want to break them down further than I did there, that's up to you. But nevertheless, there are two main staff functions that will always be there on almost any contract. One is concerned with all the administrative details of managing the contract and is headed by an administrator. The other is headed by an engineer or other technical person and is concerned only with the technical aspects of the contract. The former is known by such names as the Administrative section, F&A (Finance and Administrative) section, Business Management section—take your pick. The latter is referred to as the Technical Support section, Engineering Section—whatever fits.

Under the administrative section, your proposal will address such things as all project or program management controls (schedule management, cost/schedule status reports, work control, contract work breakdown structure (CWBS)), as well as personnel administration, security, industrial safety, payroll and accounting, program staffing tables, recreation, work incentives, program management reviews and reports, supply and procurement, and just about anything else that is not technical.

The technical staff section will comprise systems engineering, maintenance, configuration management, safety (such as flight safety, as distinguished from industrial safety), quality assurance, technical reviews, technical publications, value engineering, human factors engineering, project planning, and scientific investigations.

The RFP will frequently require that all or most of the above items be presented in the form of a plan: a maintenance plan, a quality assurance plan, configuration management plan, and so forth. Most proposal writers will respond to such a requirement by dusting off one of the company's existing plans and changing the titles. *Voilà*—a brand-new maintenance plan. In my opinion, this is a deplorable practice, because every contract is unique and requires unique approaches. Use the existing plan as a model format, if you like, but you must apply some thought to each RFP independent of what you have done before. If I were an evaluator, I could spot this subterfuge in a minute and would conclude, "You lazy bums; you don't deserve this contract." And I would do everything I could to see that you didn't get it.

There are two more items I have to cover before we leave the subject of management proposals, and they both have to do with operations- and maintenance-type contracts where there is an ongoing contract performed by a contractor using government furnished facilities and/or equipment. These contracts are recompeted periodically—usually every five years—although there is a trend now to extend this period to nine or ten years, which makes good sense to me. These contracts include the government owned, contractor operated (GOCO) facilities, like munitions plants or critical materials plants such as the synthetic rubber plants established during World War II, and government operated, contractor supported facilities, like missile ranges, some military bases, and NASA centers such as the Johnson Space Center.

The first item is my advice to incumbent contractors who are preparing for a recompetition after some ten years on the contract. The second item concerns those who are trying to win such a contract and have to write a phase-in plan as part of the management proposal.

When someone is an incumbent over a long period of time, an organizational structure evolves through a long series of decisions based on the expediency of the moment rather than a rational, deliberate plan for achieving the most cost-effective and soundly managed program. So after ten or 20 years, you may have developed somewhat confused lines of authority, divided responsibility, complex interfaces, illogical grouping of functions and missions, organizational elements working at cross-purposes, duplication of effort and insufficient cost-accounting methods. Some of this may have resulted from compromises dictated by personalities involved at the time, temporary emergencies long forgotten, resistance to changes in technology, hubris, and just plain negligence. It happens to every organization unless some outside force (competition) intervenes.

So my recommendation to you is to get someone with experience both in management and the disciplines involved in this contract—someone who has not been directly involved with this contract, if possible. Have him or her team up with an experienced cost accountant (bean counter) and come up with their own version of a work breakdown structure and an organizational structure to go with it—without any input from anyone currently working on the contract. Tell them to use the draft RFP if available (or else the old RFP), to ignore everything they may know about the current contract, and to apply only two criteria in this process: cost effeciveness and sound management principles. Chances are they will come up with something significantly different from what you currently have. Now consider this a straw man and let the burden of proof be on your current contract management to improve on it or accept it as the basis for your next proposal.

This way you will have taken a fresh, objective look at your operation from a different perspective. It is mandatory that you get this fresh look at it, because that is what your competition is going to do. And if you don't do it, there is a very good chance that the competition is going to come up with some practical economies, some streamlining, and some innovations that will enable them to underbid you and still match you technically.

The Phase-In Plan

Phase-in plans are always required in the type of contracts that we've been talking about. And because the phase-in plans I've seen are consistently the sorriest part of these proposals, I'm going to devote a section exclusively to this part of the management plan.

I've noticed that proposal managers often assign the phase-in plan to some dud almost as an afterthought as though the phase-in was of little importance. This is attributable to the fact that so many managers lack one of the basic ingredients of leadership—empathy. Put yourself in the customer's shoes. Suppose you are the program manager's counterpart in the government. The contractor's management is far from perfect, but you tolerate their occasional incompetence because at least this contractor is a known quantity. A different contractor might be even worse. You are on the SSEB and you've read Contractor's X's technical proposal and are quite impressed with his know-how and are favorably disposed to recommend awarding the contract to him.

So now let's take a look at his phase-in plan. Well, he jumps right in and says he will have the program manager and technical director report on Day 1 for a meeting with the contracting officer. But wait. Where does it say anything about recruiting and processing the incumbent personnel or how this will be done? Surely the program manager and technical director can't process these 125 people in the incumbent's workforce.

Then he says he will bring his key personnel on board. But for what? To have a party? To inspect their new offices? What about transfer of property accountability? Orientation of key personnel in their new duties? Arranging for security clearances? And then he launches into a sales pitch about his company's phase-in experience and how important they think phase-in is and blah, blah, blah. At this point you don't give a hoot about his past history. There is no way you are going to let him have this contract and screw up your whole operation for months on end.

Of course, what the customer wants are some specifics like what is your plan for transfer of operational control, transfer of classified documents, orientation and coordination between incoming and outgoing key personnel, criteria for incumbent personnel retention, your sources for replacement of existing personnel, logistical and administrative support requirements during the phase-in period, and so on.

As with any time-phased activity, the phase-in plan must be illustrated with a milestone chart showing the sequence, duration, and schedule of all major events involved in the phase-in cycle. See Figure 3.5 for an example of a milestone chart for a 60-day phase-in.

In this example, we have a contract award notice just two days before the beginning of phase-in (tight, but not all that unusual). The program manager does not run off half-cocked and unprepared to meet the customer's management and contracting people immediately. He telephones the customer and arranges a meeting four days hence. This gives him an opportunity to convene his phase-in team and review the proposal phase-in plan. (It may have been turned in months ago.) Specific dates and schedules will be set up for accomplishing specific goals during this meeting; travel reservations will be made; appointments will be set up with counterparts of the various members of the phase-in team; there will be review of the

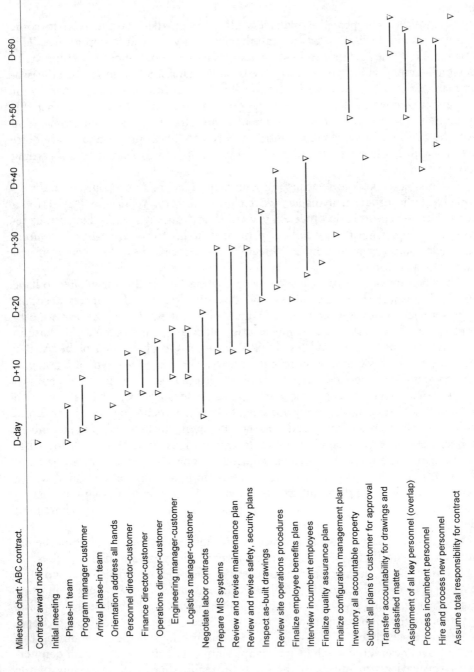

Figure 3.5 Milestone chart for a 60-day, phase-in contract.

proposal, dissemination of information to key personnel who will be assigned to the contract, and on and on with a myriad of details that must be planned and coordinated before reporting to the customer's facility.

While the details of these activities are being finalized, the program manager travels to the customer facility and meets with his counterparts in the customer organization. He goes over the phase-in schedule he submitted in the proposal and gets approval or makes necessary changes recommended by the customer. He gathers all the useful information he can during the next two days: ground rules, security requirements, availability of transportation, arrangements to orient incumbent personnel on what to expect, peculiarities of the local community and so forth.

On arrival of his phase-in team (five days after contract award date), the program manager is fully prepared to brief the team on the current situation, give them a firm schedule for achieving their goals, and introduce them to their counterparts in the customer organization.

While his staff is coordinating with their counterparts on the detailed plans for phase-in of the various elements of the contract, the program manager has plenty of other things to keep him busy. He should take his operations director with him and make a complete tour of the sites or facilities involved in the contract, establish working relations with supporting sites or facilities and with parallel organizations whose support and cooperation he needs for fulfilling his responsibilities on the contract.

Concurrently, he schedules meetings between the key members of his phase-in team and the *incumbent* key personnel for the purpose of establishing a general modus operandi for the phase-in period. In particular he must establish a tentative agreement for phase-over of property accountability, overlap of key personnel, transfer of software and all other contractor developed documentation (O&M procedures, plant-in-place drawings, schematics and configuration management documentation), and coordination of replacement of MIS (management information systems). This can be a particularly delicate and crucial stage in the phase-in and in fact often results in very serious consequences where you have a disgruntled outgoing contractor coupled with a careless and/or tactless incoming contractor.

As you can see from Figure 3.5, there are many activities going on, both in sequence and concurrently. To integrate all of these interrelated functions into a coherent effort to create a cohesive labor force takes *organization* and *planning* on the part of the contractor. And that is what the customer is looking for in the way you present your phase-in plan: *organization and planning*.

In all cases I can conceive of, you should take over all of the operational responsibility on a given day, not in phases or segments. The reason: It complicates matters for the customer by dividing responsibility if you don't. The customer wants either one contractor or the other in complete charge at all times.

To keep costs down, you should assign only the minimum number of your key personnel to overlap with the incumbent's key personnel, and for the minimum time necessary. More than two weeks is usually counterproductive. It is not uncommon for the bidder to propose absorbing the phase-in costs in order to be more competitive with the incumbent (who has no phase-in costs). This really gives the program manager incentive to hold down costs in preparing his phase-in plan.

In furtherance of my crusade to improve the quality of phase-in plans, I am presenting herewith a model phase-in outline, which, like the sample milestone chart I have provided, is to be regarded as a guide only and not a panacea for *every* phase-in requirement that may confront you.

Model Phase-In Plan Outline

Introduction

General statement of your company's policy and experience on phase-in, addressing incumbent retention on a selective basis, replacement of incumbent key personnel in policy-making positions, and the program manager's role in creating a dynamic new workforce in your company's image. *Keep it short.*

1.0 Policy and Criteria Governing the Phase-In

1.1 Management

Replacement of key personnel
Replacement of existing systems
Property accountability transfer
Orientation of incumbent workforce
Role of program manager

1.2 Technical

Familiarization of your key personnel
Transfer of technical control of operations
Preparations for assumption of control

2.0 Staffing Plan

2.1 Sources of Contract Staffing

Estimate the number of incumbent personnel retained, your company's personnel transferred, and new hires in three categories: management, technical, support.

2.2 Time Phasing

Plot the contract staffing numbers versus time on a matrix, broken down by job classification.

2.3 Critical Skills

Identify and describe how you will provide a contingency plan for responding to the possibility of certain portions of the workforce not being available by contract start time.

3.0 Phase-in Preparation

3.1 Organization of Phase-In Team (or Cadre)

Provide an organization chart

Provide a milestone chart of phase-in assignments

3.2 Duties and Responsibilities of the Phase-In Team

3.2.1 Program Manager

List the individuals he or she will contact and the specific matters he will discuss with each. For example, the program manager will visit the customer's contract manager and discuss his policy in regard to interfacing with contractors, any potential problems or uncertainties regarding logistic (or other) support, and critical time periods anticipated by the customer during the period.

3.2.2 Operations Manager

Similar to the program manager description.

3.2.3 Other Managers

The list of items to be discussed should collectively address every detail that needs to be resolved and every item of information that is needed in order to effect a smooth and orderly takeover of contract responsibility by a thoroughly-oriented, fully-informed, qualified phase-in team. For example, the program supply manager (among others) and the incumbent logistics manager will discuss specific plans for inventory of GFP and the mechanics of assuming responsibility for property accountability. This kind of detailed list of people to contact and what specific items are discussed must be accomplished for each key member of the phase-in team.

4.0 Policy on Interfacing with Incumbent

Include an interface chart here to show who interfaces with whom. Outline procedures for resolving disputes, with resolution by the customer being only the last resort. Describe how phase-in team will work out interface details during initial conferences with incumbent (see above). The program manager discusses incumbent's phase-out obligations in his initial meeting with the contracting office.

5.0 Assumption of Transferable Personnel Liabilities

Continuation of fringe benefits for retained incumbents. This is where you describe procedures for processing transfer of incumbent hires.) Your personnel and finance departments provide this.

6.0 Security Clearances and Assumption of Accountability for Classified Documents and Other Documentation

Briefly describe the procedures and objectives you propose to employ for this purpose.

7.0 Phase-In Procedure

7.1 Detailed Method for Transfer of Responsibilities

    7.1.1 *Work Performance*
        Task acceptance and accomplishment

    7.1.2 *Work Documentation*
        Task control (method of assigning tasks during phase-in)

    7.1.3 *Status and Cost Reporting*

    7.1.4 *Engineering, Fabrication and Installation, Drafting, and Technical Literature*

    7.1.5 *Configuration Control Documentation (O&M Manuals, etc.)*

    7.1.6 *Operations Control*

    7.1.7 *Project Management*

    7.1.8 *Project Administration*
        Include property inventory and signover; payroll and accounting procedures; personnel records, including clearances; transfer of responsibility for existing subcontracts, if any; initiation of commercial relationships with suppliers (of spare parts, matériel, transportation, and the like).

8.0 Conclusion

A short sales pitch to reassure evaluators you understand the magnitude and complexity of the problem of phasing into this specific contract (skip the generalities, the platitudes, and the clichés cut and pasted from old proposals) and convince them that you are well-prepared and experienced enough to handle it without any interruptions of ongoing activities.

In summary, you should start out your management proposal with a mini-executive summary that introduces your company. Then identify the critical areas involved in managing the contract and how you propose to meet these challenges, discuss your innovative approaches or other salient features of your management plan, and provide a summary of what it contains.

The body of your management proposal should contain a minimum of four ingredients: organization charts showing your parent organization and where this contract fits in, the organization chart for this contract, an interface chart, and, finally, description of the duties and responsibilities of each of the key personnel. Most of the management proposal will concern the function of the program manager and his or her staff in planning, coordinating, directing and supporting the activities of fulfilling contract requirements as set out in the SOW.

In the next chapter we will get into the step-by-step procedure and the techniques for analyzing the RFP and translating your decisions and responses into an articulate, well-organized, and persuasive proposal.

Chapter 4

A Systematic Approach to Getting Started
(or How to Avoid Proposal Paralysis)

"He that lies down with dogs riseth with fleas."
—Herbert

The purpose of this chapter is to provide all proposal personnel (proposal writers and proposal managers) with a *modus operandi*, a step-by-step method for proceeding in an orderly and systematic manner in the preparation of responses to the RFP. For many of you readers, this may be the most important chapter in this book, because it is a serious attempt to bring some order out of the chaos that characterizes most proposal efforts. "Why," I am often asked, "do all of our proposals have to be like each one is the first one we have ever done?" Well, it doesn't *have* to be that way. The reason it is that way in most organizations is because the engineers and technicians who are expected to do the writing have been given no guidance or direction whatever in how to go about their tasks. The result is frustration and inaction followed by panic and paralysis, and then disaster, which is followed by a search for the guilty and punishment of the innocent—usually the poor beleaguered engineers and technicians instead of the real culprits, the people in management who should have provided them some help and guidance.

We will start with the RFP. This is the basic document from which all else flows. You don't address anything that is not contained therein. You respond to this document and nothing else; not to your preconceived opinions of what the customer ought to have, not to extraneous material gleaned from other sources, not to anyone's assumptions. The requirements stated in this document are what the customer wants you (and all other bidders) to bid on—no more, no less. And the information included therein, whatever it may be (data, drawings, specifications, and reference material provided as part of the RFP), constitutes all of the raw material with which you must work in constructing your responses to the RFP. If it isn't in the RFP, it doesn't exist as far as you are concerned. If more information or clarification is needed, it must be requested in the form of written questions to the contracting officer. Such questions will be answered in writing and published to all bidders simultaneously to ensure equal treatment for all concerned.

When I first started working on proposals, I was just horrified at the bulk of the RFP when they carried it in to my office. How was I ever going to wade through all that stuff in the time available? Well, as I soon found out, you don't have to. Most of the bulk is the information and reference material referred to above. Sometimes such material is so voluminous that the customer provides a library for the use of all bidders throughout the course of the proposal. What you do have to do is analyze the RFP to determine exactly which parts of this information you need in order for you to write an adequate, informed response to your portion of the RFP requirements.

Speaking of voluminous RFPs, take a look at Figure 4.1, which was the original RFP that launched the multitrillion dollar aerospace business. They didn't beat around the bush much in those days. We've come a long way since then, but sometimes I'm not sure in which direction.

Form No. 18.

Signal Corps, United States Army.

These Articles of Agreement entered into this -------tenth--------- day of February---, nineteen hundred and-eight--, between ----Chas. S. Wallace----, Captain-----------------, Signal Corps, United States Army, of the first part, and

Wilbur and Orville Wright, trading as Wright Brothers, of 1127 West Third Street, Dayton,

in the county of--------Montgomery----------, State of------Ohio----------- of the second part, WITNESSETH, that in conformity with copy of the advertisement, specifications, and proposal hereunto attached, and which, in so far as they relate to this contract, form a part of it, the said --------------------Chas. S. Wallace, Captain,--------------- Signal Corps, United States Army, for and in behalf of the United States of America, and the said --------------------------Wright Brothers------------------------- (hereinafter designated as the contractor) do covenant and agree, to and with each other, as follows, viz:

ARTICLE I. That the said contractor shall manufacture for and deliver to the United States of America,

One (1) heavier-than-air flying machine, in accordance with Signal Corps Specification No. 486, dated December 23, 1907.

Figure 4.1 The 1908 agreement between the U.S. Army and the Wright Brothers.

So how to analyze the RFP? As a proposal writer, you need concern yourself basically with just three sections[1]: Section C, the SOW; Section L, the proposal instructions; and Section M, the evaluation criteria. The SOW states the requirement that the customer wants you to provide; Section L tells you how he wants you to provide the response (the format, which areas deserve emphasis, the sequence in which you should present your response, pertinent details, etc.); and Section M tells you how he is going to evaluate your response (which items are considered most important, least important, comparative weights, etc.). There are certain other sections of the RFP with which you will be concerned from time to time, but we will get to that later.

Fools rush in where angels fear to tread. And that's what most neophyte proposal writers do as soon as they get their hands on an RFP. Even after I have spent hours preparing detailed instructions for making the necessary preparations and talked myself blue in the face trying to get them started off right, they will still grab a pencil and start writing off the top of their head. Especially those who have worked on two or three proposals before and therefore have the idea they are experts. I assure you, nobody can even think about being an expert until he or she has played a significant role in at least 50 proposals. Nobody, not even Isaac Newton, could write an adequate proposal off the top of his or her head.

What I'm going to provide you in the following pages is a step-by-step procedure that anyone anywhere should follow in preparing a proposal about anything. This procedure has no gimmicks or shortcuts or whiz-bang panaceas or revelations of deep, dark secrets. (There are none.) It is simply a pragmatic practical approach for completing a writing project the same way you would or should complete any other project. The only secret involved is that it is so obvious that most people miss it. I have seen several manuals on proposal preparation that try to reduce the whole procedure to a fill-in-the-blanks exercise. They have a form for this and another form for that; you put your narrative on the left side of the page and your graphics on the right side; they worship the story board technique; and so on, *ad nauseum*. In other words, someone is trying to do everyone's thinking for them by straitjacketing them into being proposal robots. This is another example of micromanagement, and I find it deplorable. I have worked for companies that tried to impose these stultifying techniques. We all tried to go along with it, but it just drove everybody nuts, and management finally gave up in despair.

So here is my pragmatic, step-by-step procedure for writing your input to a proposal.

---

1. For federal government procurements.

Step 1. Preliminary Preparations

Read All of the Proposal Plan

The proposal plan is a document that your proposal manager should have prepared and given to you before the RFP was released. This document should provide all the background you will need in order to know what you are bidding on and why, where, when, and who the players are. If your company is on the ball, they will have started work on this document well before RFP release, outlining the program as best they can with the knowledge then available. The document should start out with some well-founded assumptions upon which you can make prior plans, such as what you should be boning up on to get ready. (Incidentally, this is a good place for management to find out whether they have been getting their money's worth out of those marketeers, because these are the people who should be able to provide most of this information.) For example, the propsal plan should provide you with an overview of the kind of requirements that the customer will include, the type of contract (e.g., cost plus incentive fee (CPIF), firm fixed price (FFP)), the geographic location, and so forth.

Another thing that should be in the document is a list of what I call Essential Elements of Information (EEI). This would be all the information we still need in order to prepare an intelligent proposal or the things we need to know more about than we currently do. Other things that should be addressed in this document are suggested themes to weave into the proposal, tentative subcontract decisions or teaming arrangements, and any ground rules on customer contacts or plans for briefing the customer on company capabilities, if permitted. (Usually at some specified time before RFP release, the customer muzzles his personnel so that they cannot discuss anything relating to the contract with anybody.)

As more information is acquired, addenda will be issued; this will continue on through to the end of the proposal period. In this way, there is just one living document covering everything anyone needs to know concerning proposal instructions and related information. This precludes a blizzard of piecemeal instructions and information floating around the place to the confusion of everyone concerned. Organizing and directing a proposal team for a complex contract has enough inherent opportunity for confusion and frustration without leaving any doors open for the application of Murphy's Law. Trust me.

One of the other things that should be included in the proposal plan before RFP release is a tentative organization chart for the proposal team. How the proposal team is organized will be covered in Chapter 9.

There are many other things that can be addressed in the proposal plan at the discretion of the proposal manager. Depending on the experience of his team, he might want to include some instructions to writers or maybe a style guide or some ground rules concerning logistical or administrative support. But there is a caveat: the document should be strictly limited to need to know information directly related to *this* proposal. The last proposal I worked on had a proposal plan of over 200 pages! (90% cut and pasted, of course.) No one has the time or inclination to wade through all that stuff, so everyone just tossed it aside, trusting instead to a process of osmosis to find out what was going on.

Before we move on to the next step, there are two items that the proposal manager absolutely, positively must publish in the proposal plan, and he or she *must* do it within five days maximum after the RFP comes out. I'm referring to the general outline and the organization chart. Nobody can or should try to start writing anything until they have these two documents in front of them. We have rigorously described organization charts in Chapter 2, and we will provide some words of wisdom on general outlines in Chapter 7; which brings me to the next item.

Read All of the General Outline

And after you've read it, reread the part of it that you are assigned to address with your proposal contribution. The idea is to ascertain just how your segment of the proposal fits into the overall program, what interface responsibilities are entailed in the SOW function you were assigned, what supporting elements are available, and so on. If the general outline isn't ready yet, go on to the next step. There are plenty of other things to do before you should even think of writing your part of the proposal.

Read the Proposal Instructions

The proposal instructions can be found in Section L of any Federal program. These instructions are very explicit, and you are not to vary in any respect from the literal interpretation and detailed compliance with these instructions. The issues addressed in much of this section (e.g., the size and pitch of type) may not apply to you *per se,* but the instructions regarding proposal input are to be interpreted very seriously. If there is any doubt in your mind about the interpretation, seek help. Often there are unintended ambiguities or room for misunderstanding because of sloppy writing, and it is not at all unusual for such uncertainties to require clarification through written questions submitted at the bidders conference. But the bottom line is: If you fail to follow these instructions in any particular, your proposal will be ruled nonresponsive.

Step 2. Preparations Prior to Writing

Read All of the SOW

Read all of the SOW, and then reread the section(s) you are supposed to address. Be absolutely sure you understand exactly what they want. By all means, discuss the requirement with some knowledgeable colleague. Very often the wording of a requirement will mean different things to different people. The people who write RFPs are not infallible, either; they often are sloppy, imprecise writers and what they say sometimes isn't exactly what they mean to say. If in doubt about the meaning of any requirement, ask your team leader or proposal manager for help. It may require the submission of a question at the bidders conference. Above all, do not take a chance and *assume* you understand, because if you are wrong your response will be nonresponsive and your proposal will be penalized accordingly.

Gather All Reference Material

If there are any references listed in your SOW section, take immediate action to secure copies of them. If they are not immediately available, see to it that the responsible parties get on the ball and get them. And no excuses! If you have to start pounding on some desks to get action, do it, because you cannot proceed intelligently without them. The customer didn't reference those items just to demonstrate his erudition. I'm referring to such things as MIL-STDs, AFRs, ARs, Post Regulations, Public Laws, MIL-SPECS, and so forth. Amateur proposal writers usually slide over these references with something like, "XYZ Corp. will comply with . . . ," and let it go at that without even knowing what it is they promised to comply with. *Don't do it!* I have often found these references to be enormously helpful, and that is what the customer put them in there for—to help you. In any case, let the reader know that you are familiar with the reference by applying it to your response. Otherwise, again you might be ruled nonresponsive by the evaluators.

Research the Subject Matter

Read any available material pertaining to your requirement: marketing reports, trip reports, consultant briefings, pertinent parts of old proposals. You want to absorb all the background you can in order to get a feel for this environment that you are going to be working in.

Look At the Other SOW Sections

Determine if there are other SOW sections with which you will have interface responsibility. If so, you will have to coordinate your input with that of the person writing that section.

Step 3. Preparations for Writing

Look Up the CDRLs and DIDs

You have done all the background reading, collected the pertinent references, located the SOW items you are going to address, and have read and reread that portion of the SOW. If your SOW section contains any reference to the contract data requirements list (CDRL) or the contract data list (CDL), then you must turn to this section of the RFP (usually listed in a directory of attachments). Each CDRL and CDL item identifies a report that will be rendered as a contract requirement. Each item is delineated on a standard form that states the name of the report, the frequency thereof, the contract reference, and various other data such as code numbers, but virtually nothing of what the report consists of. To find that out, you have to turn to the corresponding data item description (DID). The DID will describe the report's nature, format, desired content, purpose, and use, and give instructions for its preparation.

A really good RFP will contain all these CDRLs and the corresponding DIDs, but somehow it is the exception rather than the rule that they are all there, especially the DIDs. If the referenced CDL or DID is missing, it is up to your management to see that you get it. And you may have to pound on some more desks if they start dragging their feet, because *you need these documents before you proceed.* The reason is that in most cases, the customer will want to know how you are going to gather the data with which you prepare these reports, who will be responsible, what raw data you will use, and so on. The customer didn't list those things in the RFP just to be filling squares. The standard response I see in proposals (if any at all) is, "Dumdum Corp will provide reports as required in CDRL __." This is no response at all, and I would accordingly mark you nonresponsive if I were the evaluator.

The Detailed Outline

Now you are ready for one of the most important steps in proposal preparation. If you do this step right, the rest is easy. It's all downhill from there on.

First, locate your SOW requirement in the general outline. Let's say it is "Organization and Policies." There should be an "Organization and Policies" heading in the outline. (Generally the outline must follow the same sequence as the RFP, and it *should use the same headings* as the RFP so far as possible. This is in order to enable evaluators to find what they are looking for without playing detective.) This is the subject you have to write to, and it is your responsibility to determine the best way to respond to this subject, not anyone else's.

If you find there are additional subheadings provided in the general outline, cross them out and let the proposal manager know that he or she doesn't have to do your thinking for you—that you will take it from that point. The reason I make an issue of this is because so many times I've seen managers turn over an important job like making this outline to an English major who, instead of using any common sense or technical judgment, simply outlines the RFP. Well, any fool can do that! What is called for here is a knowledgeable person making an intelligible presentation of an often complex subject involving the application of engineering or management experience. You, the writer, are presumably in possession of some expertise in the subject matter and should be the best qualified on how to organize your presentation. Of course, you must follow the sequence of the RFP so far as practicable. But sometimes the RFP is not organized in a sensible manner.

Oftentimes the writer of the RFP will set out requirements for quality control, for example, then go to another subject and then later come back to quality control again. Well, if you slavishly follow the sequence of the SOW without using a little common sense, you will end up with an incoherent mess. Or sometimes you will have a subsection of the SOW that is there solely for information purposes. Yet I've frequently seen cases where some idiot outlines this background information as something the proposal writer must respond to also.

Now let's take a real-life example to demonstrate how you go about making your detailed outline. Figure 4.2 is an excerpt from a government RFP management section. You have been assigned to write this portion of the proposal. You are about to construct your detailed outline. A good way to analyze this SOW section is to go through it carefully, underlining all the *key nouns* together with their modifiers. You will find that these nouns taken in sequence will practically dictate your outline for you.

For example, study Figure 4.2. You will note that paragraph (2)(a) is concerned with "Organization and Policies," the general heading, but here are the key words:

- Mission contract requirements (line 2)
- Integrated management system (line 4)
- Requirements of a mission contract (line 5)

Now you have to conclude that in paragraph (2)(a) they want to see what you know about managing this *mission-type* contract. And that is all they want you to talk about in responding to this SOW paragraph. Now take paragraph (2)(b):

(2) Organization and Policies

    (a) The proposer shall describe his organization and management policies to accomplish the <u>mission contract requirements.</u> A thorough treatment of these items shall be provided to enable an understanding of the proposer's rationale for an <u>integrated management system</u> specifically tailored to the requirements of <u>a mission contract.</u>

    (b) The proposer shall provide <u>organization charts</u> which show the entire proposed organizational structure, including relationship to the <u>corporate and/or division organization.</u> Complete rationale for the structure can be provided. A description of the proposer's <u>internal lines of responsibility and authority,</u> and the <u>interface relationships</u> with the Government and any subcontractors shall be shown. The <u>interrelationship</u> of the planning, operational, and management responsibilities of the various <u>organizational elements,</u> including element size, shall be provided. <u>Organizational features</u> which contribute to maintaining flexibility and efficiency throughout the performance of the contract requirements shall be described. If work is performed by the contractor for commercial organizations or other Government agencies, the extent to which this proposed effort will be <u>organizationally integrated</u> with that work, and supporting rationale, shall be provided.

    (c) The proposer shall provide <u>functional policies, techniques, and procedures</u> applicable to the management of the mission contract effort. Such policies as <u>delegation of authority and/or responsibility,</u> <u>degree of management autonomy,</u> and subcontract management, which the proposer would require to adequately direct the overall contract effort, shall be included. The proposer is encouraged to show evidence of <u>proven management policies and procedures</u> that are effectively operating within his parent organization or on other contract effort that can be applied to the particular demand of this contract.

Figure 4.2 An excerpt from a government RFP management section.

- Organization charts (line 1)
- Organizational structure (line 2)
- Corporate and/or division organization (line 3)
- Internal lines of responsibility and authority (line 5)
- Interface relationships (line 5)
- Interrelationship (line 7)

- Organizational elements (line 8)
- Organizationally integrated (line 14)

Obviously, you had better talk about *organization and interfaces* in this paragraph and *nothing else*. Furthermore, you must address each of these items, insofar as logically possible, in the same order that they appear. In other words, don't talk about interfaces before you talk about organizational structure.

Now take paragraph (2)(c):

- Functional policies, techniques, procedures (line 1)
- Delegation of authority and/or responsibility (line 3)
- Degree of management autonomy (line 4)
- Subcontract management (line 4)
- Proven management policies and procedures (line 7)

As you can readily see, they want you to talk about management *policies, techniques, and procedures* here, not as pertains to mission contracts (you covered that in the first paragraph), not as regards organization (you covered that in the second paragraph).

So the main subheadings under paragraph (2) would be:

(2) Organization and Policies
(a) Mission Contract Management
(b) Organizational Structure
(c) Management Policies and Procedures

Now you will want to insert the subheadings too, but you can see how they will be dictated by the listings as I have shown. But it is up to you as to how to organize the sequence of these subheadings so that your presentation will flow in a sensible and logical manner. For example, it might make more sense to you in paragraph (2)(a) to talk about integrated management systems before addressing mission contract requirements. That's your prerogative.

So this is what you do in preparing your detailed outline for each major section of the SOW. If you are the radar expert on the proposal team, the proposal manager will probably assign you the job of responding to every SOW item that concerns radar. So you will make a detailed outline for each of those items set out in the general outline just as we have done here.

The Thematic Outline

This is a kind of fancy title for a rather mundane item but for want of a better one, it will have to suffice. What you need to do here is simply expand your detailed outline with notations of what you will want to include in your write-up under each of your subheadings. For example, under the subheading, "Subcontract Management" under Sect. 2 (c) in the previous example, you would list all the things you will want to include under this heading: The names of your subcontractors, the degree of autonomy, their reporting procedures, the pertinent CDRL reference, other references or regulations governing subcontracting, the rationale for subcontracting this particular item, and so forth. Include anything that occurs to you as pertinent to this subject. Don't worry about the sequence for now; you can rearrange these items later. What you are striving for now is to make sure you have included *everything* that has a significant bearing on this subject. Now go back over your detailed outline, searching for items that can be illuminated or clarified by use of graphics. Sometimes a graph or chart or picture can save you a thousand words or make clear what you have been trying to describe without any further explanation. So rough out what you want the graphic to look like and indicate where it is to be inserted. When you are finished, check your work for completeness against the SOW and all related references.

Of course, one of the graphics that will be required in most cases for any input is the detailed organization chart showing your particular function, broken down to the last man. This graphic should be near the beginning of your input and should show the exact breakdown of your organization and how it fits into the parent (next higher) organizational element.

Now you are just about ready to start writing your input. But first there is one other item that most proposal writers must address in almost any proposal. That is the job of staffing for your area of responsibility. Whether it is an R&D, an O&M, or even a study-type contract, you—as the expert in this particular segment of the contract—must come up with your recommendations as to what it will take to perform the contract requirement. In order to keep costs down, you must be very careful in establishing both the number of personnel the job will require and also the proper skill mix. You must remember to staff only for actual programmed requirements within the scope of work. Do not staff for things you think would be nice to have, or for surge requirements (i.e., peak load requirements that occur only intermittently). You must staff only for work which in your best judgment will require the expenditure of 2,080 hours per year. And only in specialized cases will you staff for coverage of sick leave, vacations, and other absences (attrition, etc.). We all know that if you staff up to fill such contingencies, some other hungry bidder is going to eat your lunch by underbidding you. And in this game, there are no rewards for second place. As for those specialized cases, it's up to your team leader or proposal manager to advise you or make special adjustments accordingly, based on legal interpretations of the language of the RFP.

Congratulations! You are just about finished with your preliminary preparations prior to writing your contribution to the proposal. Now there is just one more step before you start to write.

How to Evaluate Your Thematic Outline

Here is a checklist for evaluating your thematic outline.

1. Have you checked the sequence of your outline? Have you presented each major item strictly in the same sequence as it is presented in the RFP? The sequence is determined by (a) the proposal instructions and (b) the SOW.
2. Have you faithfully complied with the other details of the proposal instructions (Sect L of the RFP) as literally interpreted—thoroughly and to the letter?
3. Have you addressed each and every requirement, express and implied in the SOW requirement. Including CDRL/DID items, government regulations, MIL-STDs, other references, and so forth?
4. Have you addressed any other pertinent items that you may have noted in your perusal of the RFP as pertinent to your area of responsibility, including interfaces?
5. Did you examine the evaluation criteria (Section M) of the RFP? This section may be very detailed or very sketchy, depending on the vagaries of the contracting office in charge of this procurement. But, like the instructions in Section L, it is to be taken very seriously and very literally. Check your proposal input against these criteria point by point as rigorously as you can. If you don't feel completely comfortable with your response to each of the delineated criteria, then fall back and regroup. You have more work to do, because if you have the slightest discomfort, you can be assured that the evaluator will, and you will either be marked down or get a deficiency that will come back to haunt and embarrass you later.

When you have completed this exercise, by all means find some knowledgeable colleagues and go over the whole thing with them. They may have some suggestions. In any case, the old adage, two heads are better than one applies. Discuss the approaches you are taking and the technical decisions you proposed in your write-up. Discuss with them any alternative approaches you may have considered and rejected. If doubts or disagreements arise at this point, then it's best to consider falling back and regrouping again. Perhaps more research is indicated; maybe you should consult with outside sources; maybe you need to research the literature some more. Don't be in too much of a hurry to get on with writing the proposal, because what you are doing here is the very foundation of your whole effort. If you get this part right, the rest is easy. So don't rush it. And remember this: It is immeasurably easier to take your time and do it right the first time than it is to do it over again.

There is a popular misconception that you can just throw out a pile of garbage for a first draft and then turn it into a gourmet meal later. Don't believe it. No matter what you've heard, you only compound the problem that way. Trust me.

After you have resolved all problems, gone over your check lists, discussed your outline with knowledgeable colleagues, and otherwise assured yourself that your outline is perfect—the very best you can do—then and only then turn it in to your team leader or proposal manager, as the case may be, for approval. Then and only then are you ready to start writing.

How to Get Started Writing

Now at last we are ready to start writing the input. So here are a few tips on how to get started and how you should go about presenting your input. Some of what follows may sound familiar, but it is worth reviewing again here, because this is where many proposal writers come up against a blank (mental) wall. But believe it or not, if you have done everything right up to this point, the rest is a piece of cake.

Generally, for each major segment, you should start out with telling the customer who in the organization is going to perform this requirement, what this section is supposed to do (the mission), and the most salient feature or critical area or the biggest problem you see in achieving success. (There may be none; if so, move on to next step.)

Technical Approach

Tell them how you are going to organize your resources to perform the mission. Who is going to manage it and who this person reports to. If interfacing is an important part of the function, explain how you interface and with whom. Now give them your organization chart, complete with manning by skill level, if possible. (Some organizations will be too large to do this without hopelessly messing up your organization chart. In that case, you will have to show your manning elsewhere.)

Describe the duties and responsibilities of the manager and any other key personnel. Explain your rationale for manning and how the organization will function to perform the SOW requirements.

Weave in the CDRL/DID requirements in your proposal—not just that you will comply, but *how*. Use the MIL-STDS, ARs, AFRs, and the like to help you respond to the RFP; again, not just referencing them but *using* them in responding. They can be a big help to you in telling how you will perform the function. Let the customer know you've read, understand, and know *how* to comply with them.

You must tell the evaluator how you are going to perform this function. But you must do it in few words. So you must keep it at the management/supervisor level—how you direct, guide, prioritize, supervise, monitor, plan, coordinate, and organize the successful performance of this task. *Do not* get bogged down in writing procedural details—like telling how you operate a pH meter. You do not have enough pages for that. You are not writing an operations manual or an SOP. You are just trying to prove to a group of strangers that you have enough expertise to see this job is done right.

By way of illustrating how you should approach a proposal contribution assignment, let's use an analogy. Let's suppose you are the supervisor of the beacon repair shop, which is a small part of a very large contract located on a major military installation. The commanding general is scheduled to visit your shop in the morning and he wants you to brief him on your operation. Well, first you would tell him who you are, what your responsibility is, where your shop fits into the overall organization, and who you interface with in this government contract. Then you would state briefly how you *control* the operation.

The defective beacons are logged in, inspected, defects noted, repair work assigned, quality control procedures fulfilled, finally inspected, tested, logged out, and returned to the user. You might explain that your testing devices are calibrated periodically (which you specify) and by whom and according to what standards. You might explain what your biggest problem area is and how you cope with it. And you might conclude by telling him you have been doing this for *x* number of years and that all your technicians are certified and given special training in beacon repair. You have thus told the general all he wants to know without wasting his valuable time on trivial details or irrelevant information.

So the general walks away knowing all he needs to know to give him a warm feeling of confidence that you and your subordinates know what you are doing and have a good handle on the situation. He is relieved to know that, at least in this area, he has nothing to worry about. Now this is essentially the same thing a good proposal should accomplish, and you do it in the same way. But *not necessarily* in the same sequence. You and you alone must decide the most logical and clear way to present your write-up within the framework of the RFP mandated format.

To summarize, a good proposal input should proceed in a *logical sequence* to present the following (but not necessarily in this order):

- Who (what unit) is responsible for this function.
- Where this function fits in the organization.
- The mission and extent of responsibility.
- Interfaces: customer counterparts, your company's supporting elements, other supporting contractors or government agencies.
- Management/supervision: How the operation is controlled; working concept, work flow, priorities, and so forth; compliance with CDRLs, MIL-STDs, ARs, and the like; training; QC procedure.
- Critical areas (if any) and how you cope with them.
- Innovative ideas for improvement of operation.

Writing Style

Just a few words here on writing style. (There will be much more on this subject later in the book.) In very general terms for now: Your style should be informative without being pedantic; factual without being boring; logically organized without being rigid; thorough to the extent of showing the readers everything they want to see; and no more. Thought processes should flow—generally, from the generic to the specific; from the known to the unknown; from the simple to the complex; and from the past to the present to the future. The whole purpose of the proposal is to convince the reader that you know and understand the problem and know what to do about it.

You would be amazed at how many people in this business do not understand this. Some people think you can overwhelm the reader with eloquence, or recitation of past accomplishments, or other irrelevancies. First and foremost, you are *responding* to an RFP, and you must do so with an economy of words. Many technical people have a tendency to assume that the reader knows all about the subject, so they don't want to bore him with the details. They forget the purpose of the proposal is to *let the reader know that you know* these details—not to educate him or her.

And then you have the other extreme: those perfectionists with a penchant for too much thoroughness. These people want to tell you everything they know about any subject. You ask them for the time and they tell you about Naval Observatory time and its relationship to time code generators. And all you wanted to know was what time it was.

In conclusion, insofar as writing style is concerned, there is no substitute for expertise in the subject matter. When you really know your subject, you know what is important enough to talk about and what isn't; you can easily empathize with the reader; and your writing will have the flavor of authority. When you don't know your subject, you will have a tendency to ramble, to throw in irrelevant or unimportant details, and try to snow the reader. You are winging it, and they will know it.

Or you will try to get away with the cut-and-paste routine. I can spot this fraud instantaneously, and so can the evaluator. So the bottom line is, "Do your homework before you start to write." Research your subject thoroughly, organize it carefully, and the rest will take care of itself.

Let me quote from a critique I made of a proposal a few years ago to illustrate some of the points I've made.

> **Conclusion:** Your proposal still needs much work. Some good material but too generic. Need more *who, what, where, when, and why.* Specific people doing specific things to make specific things happen. Need graphics to illustrate and bolster your text.
>
> I'm sorry to say if I were the evaluator, I just would not have a warm feeling of confidence that you know how to manage this project

from what I've seen here. It's too much a statement of objectives without specifics of how you propose to achieve those objectives. There is virtually no indication of a dynamic manager taking charge or of a manaagement team assisting him to make decisions, set priorities, track costs, allocate responsibilities, track work progress and performance, and do all the other things that an aggressive, dynamic management team is supposed to do. There is too much of "We want to do the work and we know how, *trust us.*"

I have to tell you about an experience I had once, because it illustrates some of the points I've been making here. I was managing a very complex proposal that involved a multiplicity of sensor systems integrated into a missile range support system. One of these was a telemetry (TM) station. We had dragooned a super tech (that's an engineer without a degree) to write this portion, because he had many years experience, he was an acknowledged expert in this field, and he was available—unlike the few degreed engineers we had with TM experience. I should say we dragged him kicking and screaming into this proposal. Nobody likes to write proposals, especially engineers and, more especially, super techs. He came to my office sullen, querulous—the typical "Why me?" attitude. I gently explained what we needed. (I say gently, because he was all we had, and besides, he did come highly recommended.) He grudgingly took his extract of the SOW, the proposal plan, and the proposal instructions and grumbled his way out the door.

A few days later I got the usual mishmash one gets from someone who had had no training or experience in proposal writing: some cut-and-paste stuff obviously out of another proposal, some regurgitation of the RFP, and a description of a TM station we once operated in Idaho or somewhere. I read it over and asked him in a nice way to come back and let's talk.

I didn't say anything about his unsuitable input, but instead got him talking about the way this proposed TM station was equipped. It was obvious that he had much enthusiasm for telemetry operations and was really expert and knowledgeable. At this point I put on a dumb act (which, for me was easy) and asked, "I've always wondered just what they mean by 'stripping the data.' Could you explain that to me?" His eyes lit up and he went to the chalkboard and gave me a 20-minute dissertation on how TM stations operated and how he would organize and manage this TM station if he were running it. When he finished, I said, "Now that is exactly what I want to see in your input for this proposal."

"But they already know all that," he said.

"Maybe so," I said, "but the idea is, the customer wants us to prove to him that *we know that!*"

"Okay, no problem," and he was out the door. The next day I got one of the best inputs of the whole proposal.

This is because his input was informative, factual, and to the point. He wrote with authority, because he was an expert in his field. He didn't waste words rambling or beating around the bush, or trying to snow the customer, because he knew exactly what he wanted to say in order to tell the customer how this telemetry facility was supposed to work and how to operate and maintain it.

And that is the essence of what distinguishes a good proposal from the usual garbage one sees: a mishmash of cut-and-paste irrelevancies, strident sales pitches, boring accounts of past accomplishments, and endless, turgid prose.

So now, dear readers, I've said all I can say to help you get started and, I hope, get started on the right foot. And if you faithfully follow the procedure I've outlined here, there is every reason to believe you will have an outstanding proposal input, and you will forever after bask in the adoration of your team leader and your proposal manager. And (gasp!) maybe the company president will even invite you out to lunch sometime.

Chapter 5

Writing Techniques:
The Good, The Bad, and The Ugly

"Of all those arts in which the wise excel,
Nature's chief masterpiece is writing well."
—John Sheffield

Lest any of you be intimidated by the quote above, let me hasten to assure you that you do not have to be a gifted writer to be a good proposal writer. Here for example, is an excerpt from *Ulysses* by James Joyce, one of the giants of the literary world, right up there with George Bernard Shaw:

> Onward to the dead sea they tramp to drink, unslaked and with horrible gulpings, the salt somnolent inexhaustible flood. And the equine portent grows again, magnified in the deserted heaven's own magnitude till it looms, vast, over the house of Virgo.

And so on. See, you wouldn't want this guy writing proposals for you, would you?

What is important is that you write with sincerity, honesty, and enthusiasm for your subject. You do not have to impress the reader with your erudition or cleverness or creativity. What you do need to do is present simple, straightforward truths in an organized manner with the objective of responding to the requirements set out in the RFP and with as few words as possible. Of course this is easier said than done, so the purpose of this chapter is to provide you with a few dos and don'ts and show you how to master some of the techniques of the proposal writer.

First let us review some basics. A proposal is a response to an RFP. It is a document that tells the customer how you propose to fulfill a list of requirements that the customer has set out in the RFP. As such, it is an offer by you to perform certain acts for a specified consideration, and upon acceptance by the customer it becomes a binding contract between you and him. Now, in order for the customer to evaluate your proposal, he wants to see a response to each and every one of the requirements he has set out. And he doesn't want to search all over the document to find these responses. And he doesn't want to sift through a plethora of irrelevant hogwash to find it. And he doesn't want to see answers to questions he didn't ask.

The Golden Rule

Let me put this in the form of a rule. You might call it the golden rule of proposal writing, because almost all other rules flow therefrom:

Golden Rule: "You must forthrightly and honestly respond to each and every one of the requirements set out in the RFP in a manner that makes it as easy as possible for the reader to understand and evaluate your proposal."

Sounds simple enough, doesn't it? And yet in my work as a consultant, I find over and over and over again some yahoo who has worked on two or three proposals and therefore thinks he is an expert and even knows more than the customer about what he (the customer) wants.

To give you an example, I reviewed a proposal a while back, and because time was of the essence, the marketing director called a meeting of his proposal team to hear my comments via a teleconference call. So, after citing several errors of omission, my next comment was to the effect that they didn't address paragraph *xx* of the proposal instructions at all. I could hear the marketing director asking the proposal manager why this hadn't been done. The proposal manager says, "Well, we considered that but felt it wasn't as important as some of the other requirements, so we just skipped it; we just used our own judgment." I could almost hear the marketing director grinding his teeth as he told him, "Well that was your first mistake." And I had the impression that was probably his last mistake too, at least for that company.

Now a good proposal manager will make it almost impossible for you to make a mistake like that, because his outline for the proposal will address each and every one of the proposal instructions and incorporate each and every one of the items in the SOW and the evaluation criteria. But alas! All proposal managers are not necessarily good proposal managers.

The Cardinal Rules

What follows are what you might call the cardinal rules of proposal writing. These general rules may not be all inclusive, but, if conscientiously applied, they will probably eliminate at least 90% of the *macro* problems I constantly see in proposals I review.

Rule 1: Conform to the Format of the RFP

Not just in the sequence of your presentation, but also in the terminology, spelling, titles, and usage. If they capitalize "government," then you capitalize Government; if they call a helicopter a rotary wing airplane, then you call it a rotary wing airplane; if they say you report to the technical director, then you report to the technical director, even though you know he is really the project manager. If they want your program manager to stand on his or her head for five minutes at the beginning of each work day, then promise them accordingly. After all, they are the customer and the customer is always right.

Rule 2: Make Your Narrative Flow

From the past to the present to the future; from the simple to the complex; from the known to the unknown; from the problem to the solution. Each subject must be addressed in an orderly, logical manner. This is the reason why it is imperative that you develop a detailed outline of what you intend to say before you start to write. That way you have a roadmap to follow as you write; you avoid rambling, and you will develop a crispness in your presentation that will make the evaluator love you for your brevity.

Rule 3: Put Yourself in the Evaluators' Shoes

Empathize. Project yourself into their environment and imagine what they would like to see as your response to this requirement. You know they want a straightforward answer to the problem without wading through a lot of blah, blah, blah about your past experience and other irrelevancies to get there. This is because they are looking for specific responses to their requirements as defined in the RFP, and anything else just gets in the way.

Rule 4: Tell Them What They Want to Know and No More

If you ask someone how to get to Atlanta, you don't want him to tell you about his last trip there and that he visited his Aunt Agatha who lives there. You just want to know how to get to Atlanta. So spare them the tutorial lectures. Just answer the question raised by the RFP item.

Rule 5: Use Positive Statements

Don't ever criticize the competition or find fault with other third parties. Evaluators don't want to read that. For example, if you know of deficiencies of an incumbent contractor on a service contract, emphasize the measures you will take to overcome these kinds of problems rather than pointing out these problems to the customer. When reviewing your input, try to rephrase any negative statements by turning them into positive statements.

Rule 6: Make the Format Pleasing to the Eye

Nobody wants to read pages and pages of monotonous type. Spice it up with graphics, illustrations, "cherry boxes[1]," or whatever it takes to make your proposal easy to read. But with a purpose. I once worked for a company that wanted some kind of graphic on every page, so we had pictures of electronic banks that looked just like a row of footlockers, and so forth. Every illustration or graphic should illuminate the text and enhance the understanding of what the printed word conveys. Another suggestion: publish your proposal in double columns. Believe it or not, you can get more words per page in a double-column format than you can in single column.

Rule 7: Do Not Propose Anything Bigger, Better, Faster, or More Sophisticated Than What They Asked for in the RFP if It is Going to Cost More Money

To do so will simply price you out of the competition.[2] If you really think the customer has the money and would be interested in the more expensive item, then propose it in an alternate proposal. (I have a suspicion that nobody ever reads alternate proposals, but if you have the time and inclination, go ahead.)

Rule 8: Back Up Every Statement With Proof

This is the most pervasive (and unforgivable) error I see in the proposals I've reviewed. You can't expect the reader to be impressed with such statements as, "We fully understand the complexities involved in development of the XYZ system." And so much for conveying your understanding of their problem. Or, "Our many years of experience in software development have given us a keen insight into the type of problems encountered in this project." Those sentences are fine as premises, but they need to be followed by proof or they are just mere throwaway lines worth absolutely nothing. You must explain in sufficient detail and specificity just *why* and *how* you understand those complexities. You must describe specifically what experience you have had in dealing with similar software problems and just how this experience relates to this proposal and how it has given you this keen insight into this specific problem.

---

1. A "cherry box" is a shaded rectangular box that usually appears in the upper right-hand corner of the first page of a section. It contains a list or summary of the salient features presented in that section.

2. For a description of a major exception for negotiated contascts, see "The 'Best Value' Concept" in Chapter 6.

Rule 9: Be Specific

The reader wants to know who does what to whom as well as how, why, when, and where. This is another area where I commonly see the most appallingly sloppy writing. Some proposal writers think they have responded to the RFP requirement by simply *stating goals*, without describing how these goals are achieved. You must have an organization chart in front of you and clearly understand who is going to perform the task and by whose direction, by what means, and in coordination with whom, and then convey this understanding to the evaluator.

The use of vague, glittering generalities is one of my pet peeves, and I can just imagine how it must drive the evaluator bananas trying to find some meat where there is nothing but fluff.

Rule 10: Set the Stage

Suppose you are watching a movie. While the titles and credits are still appearing on the screen, superimposed on the opening scenes you see a street scene, heavy traffic, sidewalks crowded with mostly well-dressed pedestrians walking briskly past and in and out of adjoining buildings. A man carrying a briefcase emerges from the pedestrians and enters one of the high-rise buildings. The next scene shows him getting into the elevator. We then see him him emerging from the elevator and entering an office with a name on the door and "Attorney-at-Law" printed underneath the name. He waves casually at the secretary as he enters the suite of inner offices. Without a word being spoken, you know his name and that he is an attorney in an apparently prestigious law firm. The director has set the scene.

Now suppose that instead of the above, the movie starts out with this attorney sitting in an office, talking to someone about a murder case. Pretty soon you would be asking yourself, "*Who* on earth are these people, and *what* are they talking about, and *where are we*? And *how* did we get here? And if you don't get some answers pretty soon, you are going to say to yourself, "*What* am I doing here?" and get up and go home.

The director in the first example had the good sense to "set the stage." The director in the second case didn't, so he probably will end up directing Grade C movies somewhere in lower Slobovia.

And the same sort of thing can happen to you as a proposal writer if you plunge into the middle of a subject without first setting the stage. Otherwise, the poor befuddled evaluator never can tell who and what you are talking about. You do not want evaluators to be asking himself, "*Who? What? Where?*", or they may end up saying to themselves, "*What* am I doing here?" as they toss your proposal in the waste basket so *they* can go home.

Having thus set the stage for you with these ten cardinal rules, it is time to move on to some of the nitty-gritty details of the techniques of writing, especially the bad techniques to be avoided. Readers of my previous book on this subject will recognize some of what follows, because I am repeating some of its words of wisdom. Bad proposal writing techniques don't change much (they seem to be passed down from generation to generation), so there is no way I can cover this subject without repeating some of the most common and egregious examples of bad proposal writing.

Some Ants in Your Picnic Lunch

There are some words and expressions that just make me gag; I can go through almost any proposal and pick them out like ants in a picnic lunch or pebbles in my shoe. Here are a few (but not necessarily all) of the expressions I despise. The phrase in the previous sentence in parentheses is one of them. This is typical bureaucratese cover-your-behind talk. Leave the bureaucratese to the bureaucrats. Using such expressions tells the reader you are not sure of what you are saying or whether you have said it all, so you think it would be a good idea to leave yourself an escape hatch. Here are some other (ugh) expressions:

1. "Cognizant." As in "The cognizant engineer will ensure that all safety precautions are taken . . ." Well, who in blazes is the *cognizant* engineer? That is just the point. Obviously, the writer didn't know. Maybe it should be the radar supervisor, maybe it's the QC manager, maybe it's the operations manager, or . . . hmmm. So he takes the easy way out and says, "the cognizant engineer," which tells the reader he doesn't know and isn't going to trouble himself to figure it out.
2. "Philosophy." As in "Our management philosophy is blah, blah, blah, zzzz . . ." Leave philosophy to the philosophers. Stick to the facts, man; you are dealing with realities not abstractions; you are dealing with numbers, reasons, proof, decisions, and the like, not philosophy.
3. "Adherence." As in "Supervisors will ensure adherence to quality control procedures." This is just a throwaway sentence. Any damn fool can say this (and they do), but it doesn't mean a thing. How do you "adhere" anyhow? "Adhere" means to stick to something. Just another example of sloppy writing. What you must do is *comply with specific, designated procedures or directives by performing specific, designated acts.*
4. "Facets." As in "Our experience covers all facets of the contract . . ." This seems to be one of those overused cliches so dear to the hearts of some writers. "Facet," according to the dictionary, means "polished, plane surfaces of a cut gem," and that's about all you ever get when you see that word. You never really get the gem, just the surfaces.
5. "Established procedures," "existing procedures," "standard practice," and "generally accepted practice." All these glittering generalities will buy you nothing, because they are too vague and imprecise to form the basis of a

contract obligation, and because the evaluator has no standard upon which to compare what you are promising versus any other competitor. In nearly all cases, the use of these expressions by a proposal writer is just a cop-out to avoid doing the necessary research and analysis to be more specific.

6. "Optimum." As in, "We will provide *optimum* on-the-job cross-training for all personnel." Another glittering generality. What is "optimum"? To me, it means that whenever you feel like it, you will try to see that some people get a little cross-training. What are the criteria? What are the objectives? Are they to get cross-training in one job only? Are any records to be kept, or any standards by which to measure the effectiveness of the cross-training? Who will be responsible for the cross-training and how will it be supervised? Does the writer think that by just saying "optimum" all these questions are answered? No. He is too lazy and sloppy to have figured out that there are such questions.

Along with these unfortunate expressions, I have two other bones to pick with many proposal writers: the imprecise use of words and the use of the passive voice.

One sees so much imprecise writing these days, because we now have two generations raised on television, on images instead of the written word. So they say, "I am sending you this treatise for your *pursual*, and tell me what you think."

They mean "perusal," of course, but the two words sound alike, so what the heck. And then the secretary mindlessly types it pursual whether it makes any sense or not.

But there are two pairs of words which drive me up the wall: The verbs *affect/effect* and *imply/infer*. "Affect" means to influence. "Tobacco affects health adversely." "Effect" means to bring about or accomplish. "Abstinence effects an improvement in one's health." (Abstinence of tobacco, that is!) And another thing; *affect* is never, never used as a noun. Every day I can pick up a newspaper and see such inanities as, "The antitrust suit will have no *affect* on local business . . .," which is what I saw in the paper just today. Another example of how the media are corrupting our youth. Whatever happened to proofreaders?

And another: Imply is to *throw* as infer is to *catch*. Correct: "I implied that he was correct, and he inferred that I had approved." Wrong: "I inferred that I had approved. . ."

The use of the passive voice should be avoided. The passive voice is used when the doer of the act is vague. Example: "It was decided to replace the travel arrangements group in the White House." The writer either did not know who made the decision, or he or she doesn't want you to know who made the decision. As such, the passive voice is the favorite artifice of bureaucrats. Because that way, it is almost impossible to fix the blame where it belongs when something goes wrong. But the proposal writer is only showing his ignorance as well as making the evaluator very frustrated and angry with such evasiveness.

And it seems most writers today were looking out the window when their teacher was teaching grammar. "Managers must back up their subordinates." Not

"Managers must back-up their subordinates." What kind of logic is there in putting a hyphen between a verb and its adverb? You use the hyphen when the words involved are used as an adjective. Correct: "We specialize in state-of-the-art systems for improving the state of the art."

More examples of sloppy writing: This in a statement from a Congressperson. "We must stop the perpetration of crime and terror which is stalking our streets." Perpetration is stalking our streets? Terror may be stalking our streets, but the subject of the clause is "which," which is in apposition to the noun, "perpetration." "Terror" cannot be the subject of the verb "is stalking" because it is part of the prepositional phrase that is a modifier of the word "perpetration." "Perpetration" is the subject and "is stalking" is the predicate. The trouble is, we stopped teaching kids how to diagram sentences about 40 years ago (too challenging), so educators decreed that it was more important to keep them entertained and to bolster their self esteem by "dumbing" everything down.

One more example: This from an executive summary. "In the management plan, we will present a brief history of our company, our facility, our cost control methods, . . . etc." They will present a history of their facility, their cost-accounting methods? Who wants to read a history of their facility—or a history of their cost-accounting methods? Everything that follows "history" is a compound prepositional phrase that modifies the word, "history." This is just plain sloppy writing, and if you do not understand the logic of these past two paragraphs, then it is advisable that you hire an English major to edit all your stuff before it gets out of your office.

The Six Deadly Sins of Proposal Writers

So much for the merely irritating "crackers-in-your-bed" kinds of bad proposal writing. Now for the really ugly stuff that can seriously impact the quality of your proposal. I call them the six deadly sins of proposal writers.

1. Regurgitating the RFP

Early in my proposal writing career (that is to say, I had worked on only about a dozen proposals), the proposal manager and I went to the bidders conference leaving our newly formed proposal team behind to start work on the proposal. They were all good, competent engineers, dependable and respected, but with little or no proposal writing experience. What we expected them to do was to study and analyze the RFP, research the problem, brainstorm the problem areas, and start to organize their tentative approaches during the time we were gone. When we returned the next day, I had that sinking feeling as soon as we walked in the door, because they were all writing furiously. My suspicions were confirmed as soon as I took a look at what they were writing.

If the RFP requested, "A progress report will be submitted weekly, in accordance with CDRL #3," they would write, "Progress reports will be submitted weekly in accordance with CDRL #3." Where the RFP requested ". . . . compliance with the safety requirements contained in the safety documents referenced in DR #4," the writer would put down, "XYZ Company will comply with safety requirements referenced in DR #4," and so on and on. And this is just about what you will get every time with neophyte proposal writers unless the proposal manager sets everyone down in the very beginning and gives the proposal team a little pep talk on how to prepare to write proposals. What these writers should have done was research CDRL #3 and DR #4 and tell the evaluator specifically what we proposed to put in those weekly reports, where and how we would gather the information that went into the reports, who would be responsible for compiling the report, what approvals and reviews would be required before it is submitted to the customer, and so on. They should have looked up the DR #4 references and any other pertinent references, for that matter, and told just how we were going to comply, who would be responsible for ensuring compliance, what reports would be required, what feedback systems would be set up in order to keep the program manager informed of compliance, and so on.

Simply regurgitating the RFP buys you absolutely nothing; it will earn the evaluator's disgust with your ineptness, or worse yet, his everlasting hatred for your insult to his intelligence.

2. The Cutting and Pasting Syndrome

This is perhaps the secondmost (behind regurgitation) evil and reprehensible addiction to be found in the proposal writing field. The last two multibillion dollar companies I have worked for were among the most egregious practitioners of this fakery. (Why is it so much harder to get through to employees of *big* companies than small companies?) In both of these frustrating experiences, there was always some pompous middle management idiot somewhere who would take anything I wrote and interlace it with paragraphs, sentences, even phrases from some of the company's old proposals.

In this way they managed to take almost everything I wrote and turn it into jerky, disjointed, irrelevant gibberish. When I remonstrated, they would say, "Well, this came out of one of our winning proposals, so it must be good." Sure, it might have been good for *that other* proposal, but this is a different proposal. Each proposal is unique. Each requires specific, original responses to unique situations. How many times do I have to say this: There is no substitute for the research, study, and analysis that enables you to provide intelligent, well-reasoned, straightforward, specific responses to specific RFP requirements.

True, there is a place for the use of old proposals (whether they were winning ones or not is irrelevant). But these old proposals should serve one of two objectives: (a) To refresh your memory or alert you to points you might have missed, or to provide you with ideas to help you get started; and (b) to use for the boilerplate items of your proposal. By boilerplate, I mean those items that will be pretty much the same in any proposal, to wit: your company's personnel procedures, including the EEO, promotion policies, compensation policies; company experience, industrial safety, security procedures; and—well, you get the idea. But you must be very careful in your cutting and pasting to make sure *every word* conforms to the letter of the proposal instructions (Section L in Government RFPs).

3. Rambling—Going Around in Circles

This is the product of a disorganized mind, and it is usually incurable. If you are a proposal manager and you have ramblers on your proposal team, get rid of them early on. How can you tell? By the kind of detailed outline they submit during the outline phase. If they can't organize the subject material in a coherent and logical outline, they will never be able to write a coherent input. A ramblers can drive a proposal evaluator crazy, because the evaluator will read something and say to himself, "This must be where he is going to address hardware interfaces." Then he sees something a few pages farther on and he says, "No, I guess *this* is where he is going to address hardware interfaces." And so on and so on. Pretty soon the evaluator is going to become enraged and frustrated and start telling everyone else on the SSEB what he thinks of your proposal and also what he thinks of your company. (More on SSEBs in the next chapter.)

4. Bare, Unsupported Statements

"Our 14 years experience in laser devices provides us with unsurpassed expertise in solving the problems encountered in laser ranging systems."

"Our quality assurance procedures will eliminate any chance of malfunctions in the anastigmat."

"XYZ's proven configuration management system will ensure that any design errors are immediately identified."

None of the above statements proves anything at all. And yet you can read almost any proposal and pick out statements like this on every few pages. Oh, you may often find such statements followed by several sentences of a general nature. Such as, "We were congratulated by Gen Dingbat on our QA system." Or, "XYZ's configuration management system is considered the best in the Western Hemisphere." You still haven't proved anything. Two *un*supported statements do not make a supported statement. Evaluators will just slide right over this kind of thing, slightly irritated at this sort of puffery they always see in proposals written by amateurs.

You must start with the premise that the reader doesn't believe a thing you say without proof. I got a sardonic laugh out of a proposal I worked on recently where the writer bragged about an existing company procedure that they would implement to solve all the customer's missile-range safety problems. I warned them without success that they should take this out, because the referenced procedure would be wholly unworkable and irrelevant without a substantial outlay for software changes. Well would you believe the customer in the Q & A session demanded to see the procedure? So after much hemming and hawing and stuttering and stammering, the proposal manager shamefacedly declared they had made a mistake, and there was no such procedure. You might say this was an extreme case of a bare, unsupported statement coming back to haunt them.

5. Obfuscating the Problem

This is a common trick used by lawyers who know they have a weak case. The idea is to throw up a smokescreen so as to confuse the jury as to what the real issues are. The idea in proposal writing is to throw out a cloud of verbiage disguised as intelligent thought but which evades the issue, because your knowledge of the subject matter is too limited for you to address the subject matter head on. The writer hopes in this way to confuse the evaluator into thinking he knows what he is talking about.

Obfuscation sometimes works in court, because juries are made up of average, ordinary people, often not too smart. Evaluation teams are (usually) made up of professional people, expert and experienced in the subject matter, somewhat suspicious and adversarial by nature, and therefore not likely to be fooled by such Machiavellian tactics. You're blowing smoke, and they know it.

So the remedy for you, the proposal writer, is to get out the reference books and study and analyze the subject matter until you can write with authority on the subject. If you don't feel you are smart enough to do it this way or don't have the time to acquire this much expertise, then hire a consultant who has a proven record and background in this field and ask him to help you out. (Caveat: Before hiring a consultant, see what I have to say about consultants in Chapter 9.)

6. Chinese Crossword Puzzles

Last, but by no means least important, is the problem of the busy graphic. Engineers especially, with their penchant for thoroughness, have an uncontrollable tendency to stuff everything they know about a subject into each graphic. This makes for diagrams that are about as unintelligible as Chinese crossword puzzles. The overriding, inflexible rule for graphics should be, "Keep it simple." If readers have to spend more than two minutes figuring out *the purpose* of your graphic, they are simply going to cast it aside and go on to something else. If they have to spend more than five minutes[3] (at the very most, ten) studying your graphic, they will likely do the same. A graphic should have no more than one central idea to present. A flowchart,

---

3. An exception, of course, would be the organization/function charts, which must be as complete and detailed as the RFP directs.

for instance, should not try to incorporate command and control functions when its main purpose is to show the work flow of a widget moving through the widget repair shop. If there are certain exceptions or anomalies in a process that would affect the flowchart under certain exceptional circumstances, don't try to present this in the flowchart. Describe the effect of these anomalies in your text. Never present a graphic without text to explain it and its significance.

Well-designed graphics should illuminate and enhance the accompanying text. The judicious use of graphics can eliminate an excess of boring, sleep-inducing text. They can enable you to present an enormous amount of detailed information in a comparatively small space. Let's take, for instance, the case where you have one of those RFPs that spells out in excruciating detail all the nit-picking jobs you have to perform on a contract. (You often find this sort of thing on O & M or "housekeeping" jobs.) Here is an example of what I mean, taken from an actual RFP:

> **The SOW (Statement of Work) requires:**
> C.12.3.17.4.1   Review justification of work and approve or disapprove.
> C.6.12.3.17.4.2   Assign Job Order Numbers and prioritize work.
> C.6.12.3.17.4.3   Determine means by which work will be accomplished.
> C.6.12.3.17.4.4   Establish and maintain an Official Project File.

And so on, *ad infinitum,* or so it seems. Okay, you want to respond to all this, but how can you do that without "regurgitating" the RFP? The best way to do this and with a minimum of space is to use a graphic. You go through these long lists in the SOW and correlate them in a sensible fashion, like lumping all the items according to who is the responsible person for accomplishing them, or listing them in sequence in a flowchart, or whatever fits the situation.

Figure 5.1 shows an example of how you can accomplish this even in a very complex engineering development effort. This graphic gives the reader an overview of this project in little more than half a page. It would take many pages to describe this, and the effect would still be inadequate. This flowchart may seem a little too busy at first glance, but it provides the reader a roadmap for the many pages of text that will follow. The numbers above the blocks designate the corresponding SOW paragraph that applies to that block. Evaluators can see what your purpose is in two minutes. They can follow the chart through easily in five minutes. They also have a reference now to refer back to whenever they wish to check it against other things.

Figure 5.2 shows a graphic that I think is too busy and almost guaranteed to make evaluators throw up their hands in despair and go on by. You must remember that the evaluators themselves do not enjoy reviewing a number of proposals any

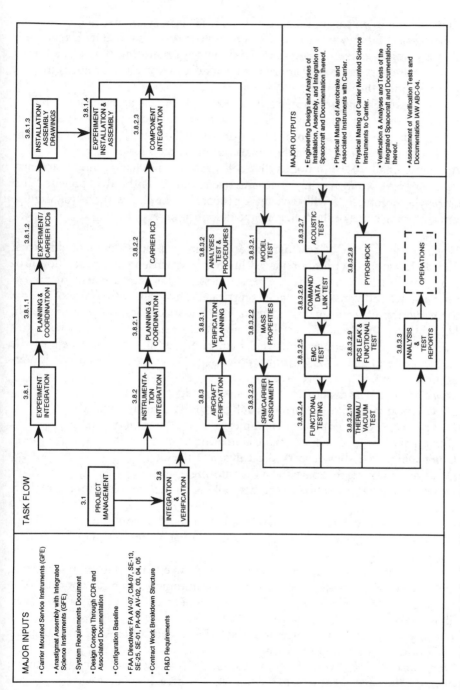

Figure 5.1 A well-defined graphic for an R&D proposal.

more than you enjoy preparing them. It is a tedious and demanding job, evaluating several proposals, and they want to get it over with as soon as possible. If they see a chart that is going to take up more than ten minutes of their time, chances are they will perceive the chart as nothing more than a road block in their progress toward getting to the end of the job.

Figure 5.2 might be appropriate in a textbook or a master's thesis. But in those cases, the reader is more highly motivated to try to understand every detail of the graphic. Not true of the proposal evaluator, so my last bit of advice on this subject is: Better to use two simple graphics than one busy, busy intimidating one.

And now, finally, a list of don'ts that will wrap up this chapter and, I fervently hope, will improve your writing style and technique if faithfully applied. Who knows? Maybe eventually I will pick up a proposal some day without (ugh, gulp, gasp, cringe) seeing some of the follies I have described here.

- *Don't* make a habit of starting sentences with a prepositional or adverbial phrase. Example: "With the renewed interest in environmental protection programs and plans to upgrade the sensor systems for measurement of atmospheric state, and considering the sophisticated advances in the state of the art for gathering of such quantified data, the XYZ Corporation proposes blah, blah, blah . . ." (Wrong.) People like me with ordinary-size brains just can't carry all that long-winded baggage in memory until the writer gets to the point. Rather: "The XYZ Corp. proposes . . . . We feel that the renewed interest in environmental . . ." (Correct.)
- *Don't* harp on past experience. It turns people off.
- *Don't* repeat yourself or return to a subject you've already covered.
- *Don't* use excessive verbiage. Lengthiness is not a criterion of quality.
- *Don't* make unsupported, dogmatic statements.
- *Don't* submit busy-busy charts, diagrams, and the like.
- *Don't* preach or teach. Spare them the tutoring.
- *Don't* use vague generalities. You are talking to real people about a real-life specific, problem.
- *Don't* try to snow the reader. He or she is smarter than you think.
- *Don't* use the imperative,"shall." You are writing a proposal, not a specification or an RFP.
- *Don't* string a dozen adjectives together. Example. "The data obtained from the servo-driven, low-light level, recording, automatic, digital, optical, laser-ranging and tracking device . . ." Same comment as for the adverbial clause above. Better to break it up into two sentences.
- *Don't* present important decisions, solutions, conclusions, or declarations without rationale to support them.
- *Don't* just tell *what* you are going to do. This is essentially merely stating a goal. Readers also want to know who, when, where, how, and why.

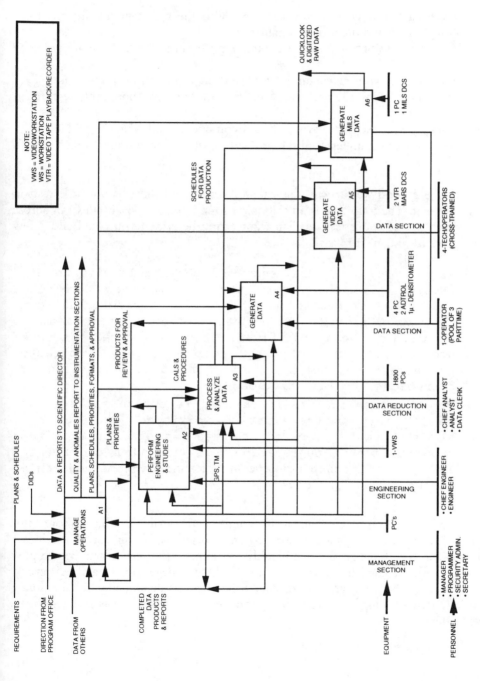

Figure 5.2   A chart that is a little too busy for most proposals.

- *Don't* start writing until you have reviewed the pertinent instructions from both the RFP and the proposal manager.
- *Don't* start writing until you have made an outline of what you are going to say.
- *Don't* pick up your pencil until you have thought the problem through.
- *Don't* try to think the problem through until you have thoroughly researched the problem.
- *Don't* try to research the problem until you understand what the problem is.
- *Don't* think you understand the problem until you have brainstormed it with other competent people.

Maybe a good way to end this chapter would be to give you a little test on sloppy writing. The following is an example I found in a proposal that I ran across a few years ago. I count no less than eight errors here, and you could add a few more errors of judgment to that.

```
We recognize the challenges of phasing-in with no dis-
ruption of test support and infusing new technology
into the system development process. Hopefully our com-
pany will provide the experienced management team to
accomplish these objectives. They have excellent back-
grounds with us and our partner on related contracts,
and access to the electronics and data processing re-
sources of two industry leaders.
We have assured ourself through retention surveys that
we can rely on the existing workforce. Therefore, we
are thoroughly prepared to phase-in and continue test
support without degradation. We will then provide the
infusion of technology and new management methodologies
in support of the government.
```

Sigh . . . and oh, dear! One has to wonder if the writer is talking about infusion or *con*fusion there. Okay, my parting shot to you is: If you can't find at least five errors in the above quote, then I highly recommend that henceforth you employ a person with an English major from an accredited college to read and edit everything you write before it gets out of your office (as this person should have done), especially if it is going into a proposal, and more especially if it is going into the cover letter.

Chapter 6

How the Customer Evaluates Your Proposal

"In the land of the blind, the one-eyed man is—ostracized."
—Helgeson

For most of us on the contractor side of the house, the mechanics of how the customer analyzes and evaluates our proposals is wrapped in mystery. In the case of proposals for government contracts, some of the mystery is necessitated by the Federal Acquisition Regulations (FAR)—some of it by the desire to ensure fairness in the conduct of the evaluation, and some of it to cover up the chicanery practiced by bureaucracies when they have the opportunity to operate in secrecy. But the bottom line is: The FAR has been ingeniously and painstakingly designed to ensure fairness in the procurement process.

Our objective here is to describe the system as it was meant to function according to the FAR and the applicable law of contracts. And, I might say, this is the way it does function in the vast majority of cases. I might also add that, in my opinion, if more contractors would exercise their right of protest when they see blatant violations of the FAR, we would eventually have a much fairer and consistently honest selection process for the award of government contracts.

So let us begin by analyzing how the government's selection process works. "Why," you may be asking, "do I need to know anything about the customer's proposal evaluation process?" The reason is you must know what readers will be looking for, what their thought processes are, and how they expect your proposal to be organized, so that you will know how to evaluate your own proposal before submitting it. You must know this in order for you to respond most effectively in your proposal. Also, knowing this will enable you to empathize with the evaluators and thus make their lives easier. Bear in mind that the sole purpose of writing a proposal is to convince these evaluators that your company is the most capable of performing this particular contract.

This chapter will present a general overview of the proposal evaluation system that has been set up by the FAR and other laws and regulations in order to ensure fairness in the award of government contracts. The terminology and the details may vary somewhat between the various government agencies, but the principles are essentially the same throughout the government. Underlying the procurement process, of course are the rules of contract law as codified in Federal statutes and regulations and the interpretation thereof by the Federal courts, which constitutes the case law applying to the entire procurement system.

Proposal Evaluation Boards—
the Source Selection Authority, the Source Selection Advisory Committee, and the Source Selection Evaluation Board

Figure 6.1 shows the functional organization of a typical government procurement structure. The Source Selection Authority (SSA) for large procurements is usually the senior government official having an interest in the subject matter of the procurement. In the military, this would be the commanding general of the activity or command that would have primary responsibility for the use or control of the procured item. The SSA makes the final decision for contract award. This person may overrule any recommendations of the Source Selection Advisory Committee (SSAC) or the Source Selection Evaluation Board (SSEB), or may even refuse to accept recommendations. That is, he may request that their reports contain only the facts and findings.However, his decision *should* be supported by the documentation—that is, the evaluation submitted by the SSEB and the findings submitted by the SSAC. This is because he may have to justify his decision to higher authority, and (the more ominous possibilities) a formal protest, a General Accounting Office (GAO) investigation, a contractor's resort to the Court of Appeals, or (horrors) a Congressional investigation!

While these remedies seldom provide any finite relief to the victimized contractor who spent several hundred thousand dollars preparing a good proposal, they probably have some penumbra type of effect in restraining otherwise unscrupulous government officials from blithely awarding contracts to their friends or their relatives, or perhaps providing some "divine guidance" on costing or other matters to a favored bidder.

The SSEB performs 90% of the work of evaluating the proposal. The people on the SSEB are those who compare, in detail, your proposal versus the requirements stated in the RFP. The chairman of the SSEB may or may not be the program manager for the program, that is, the user of the particular goods or services being procured. In my opinion, he or she should be, because who else would be in a better position to judge the acceptability of what is being proposed? But alas, that is not the way it usually works in the real world. More often than not, the chairman of the SSEB will be a senior official who has no interest in the outcome of the procure-

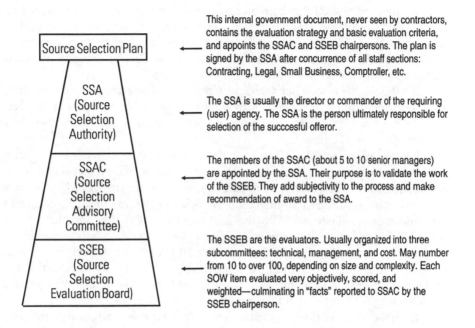

Figure 6.1 The functional organization of a typical government procurement structure.

ment. The logic being that the intended user might be biased in favor of certain contractors with whom he or she is most familiar. There is something to be said for both theories, of course.

In any case, the chairman of the SSEB is the most important person in the entire evaluation process. He or she is responsible for implementing the source selection plan, which includes all instructions to the SSEB, including the evaluation criteria and rating techniques to be applied. The source selection plan and the RFP are generally prepared by a team of specialists located within the command of the SSA. These are procurement specialists who also have no stake in the outcome of the procurement. Here again, there is a problem, not so much in the system as in the way it is implemented. The success of the system depends on meticulous coordination between (a) the procurement specialists who prepare the RFP and the source selection plan and (b) the field personnel who will be the users. And again, you must have thorough coordination between the procurement specialists and the SSEB. Ideally, there should be a complete meeting of the minds on the interpretation of the RFP and the source selection plan among all three parties: the procurement specialists, the SSEB, and the users.

The trouble is, such coordination is seldom realized. What often happens is that the procurement people go their own way, thinking they know better than the users what they really need. (Sound familiar?) The people on the SSEB put their own interpretation on the RFP requirements, in effect adding or modifying the requirements, which results in standards that were neither intended nor desired by either the users in the field or the procurement specialists. So the SSEB ends up declaring a deficiency on the bidder, based on something that was never actually intended to be a requirement in the RFP.

It all goes back to what I said in Chapter 2: Coordination (or anything else) doesn't happen unless a certain individual is responsible to make it happen. And here we have a case where the chain of command lines are fuzzy and the consequences for error ill defined.

I know of a case that illustrates the problem. A lens system was being procured for missile-tracking purposes. The procurement people stipulated a lens surface distortion of one-quarter wave length, a much more stringent requirement than necessary. This resulted in an unacceptable delay in the procurement coupled with a horrendous price. When asked by the field personnel why they set such an impractical specification, the procurement people replied, "Because it is possible and any good vendor should be able to meet this spec." I guess it never occurred to them that the people in the field ought to have something to say about it. And there was no mechanism to ensure that they did. (I might add that this foolish requirement doubled the cost, both in time and dollars.)

It might make you feel better to know that no one really wants the job of being on the SSEB. It is a tedious, exacting, and often boring job, and they probably don't enjoy reading the proposal any more than you do writing it. Furthermore, they are usually brought in from the field (partly to avoid contractor bias and often because the special expertise may not be available locally) and then given a deadline to perform this onerous task in which they have no particular interest or stake in the outcome.

Source Selection Process

For an overview of the government evaluation process, see Figure 6.2, which depicts the various steps that every proposal is subjected to before an award decision is made.

The Source Selection Plan

Proposals, these days, are almost always required to be submitted in loose-leaf binders. There is a good reason for this. Upon receipt, the chairman of the SSEB breaks down the proposal into sections and parcels them out to the various members of the board. Each section is assigned to a member of the board who (presumably) has special expertise in that section of the proposal. The chairman then explains the ground rules for the evaluation procedures and issues a set of standards upon which the evaluators are to base their evaluations. These standards are supposed to have

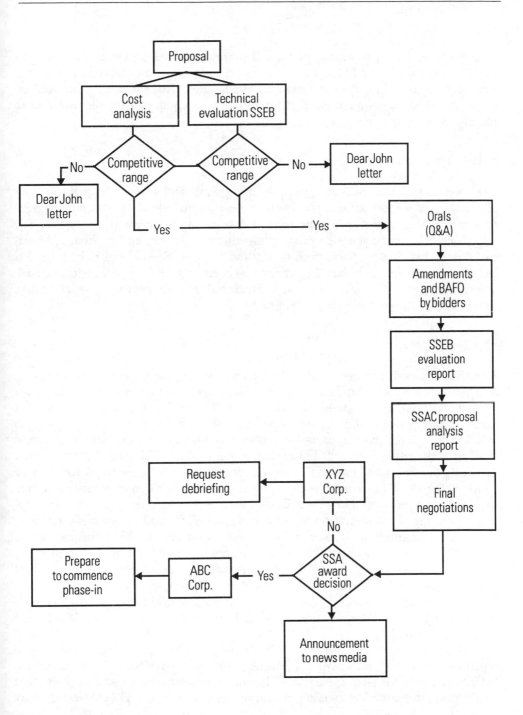

Figure 6.2 The various steps that every proposal is subjected to before an award decision is made.

been prepared by the technical people and submitted to the procurement specialists before issuance of the RFP, and are the only criteria that the evaluators are to take into account in making their evaluations. The SSEB is also required (before RFP release) to make a determination of the minimum score required for the proposal to remain in the zone of consideration.

SSEB Procedures

The members of the SSEB are given a scoring sheet and sent off to perform their evaluation. When evaluation is complete, the scores are added up for each competitor, and those failing to reach the zone of consideration are eliminated. Note: The government is reluctant to eliminate competition, however, and so final approval for elimination of a proposal must be secured from the SSA. If he or she feels that the deficiencies are such that they cannot be corrected, the proposal is eliminated. The government is anxious to avoid elimination of a competitor, especially when there are a small number of bids submitted.

Q and A Phase

The SSEB has now narrowed down the bids to those whose technical, management, and cost submittals are sufficiently acceptable to warrant further consideration. But don't think your work is finished when you have turned in the proposal. The next phase is the question and answer phase, sometimes called the "orals" or "Q and A's." However, the practice of having just one meeting in which questions are asked orally and the answers provided immediately seems to be a thing of the past. Instead of asking questions and having the contractor respond orally, the trend seems to be to have everything in writing, or else to have a series of written questions for which both a written response and an oral discussion is expected.

First, the SSEB wants you to correct minor errors, inadvertent misstatements, typos, and misunderstandings or ambiguities in the proposal. This is the last chance you will have to clarify or amplify any statements you made and the last chance you will have to clean up any sloppy inept writing that may have slipped by the proposal manager and the Red Team.[1] (I had the misfortune recently to work on a proposal that had an inept proposal manager, a screwed-up proposal team, and an incompetent Red Team, resulting in a greater effort being put in to this phase than on the original proposal.)

The purpose of the Q and A phase is to give each qualifying contractor an equal opportunity to make minor corrections that may have been the result of misinterpretation of the language in the RFP, simple inadvertence, or whatever else that might prevent a complete meeting of the minds. However the Q & A session may

---

1. The coordination of Red Team function is the responsibility of the proposal manager. This is described in detail in Chapter 9.

not involve the bidder's essential qualifications, or basic technical approaches, or unrealistic cost for performing the contract. (They already eliminated those bidders.)

The BAFO

The next and final step for the bidder is the best and final offer (BAFO), which gives the government a final chance to squeeze the last drop of blood (if any) from the contractor before making the award. If you have slaved away on the proposal for weeks and weeks or months and months, you may take heart at this point, or more likely, *resign yourself* to the fact that the fate of your proposal is now in the hands of the bean counters!

Oftentimes a bidder will hold out a little up to this point; then the government thinks they have made a helluva deal when he shaves off a little more at this time (which he always intended to do). I would strongly recommend you not follow this practice. For one thing, the boilerplate in every proposal now warns you that there may not necessarily be a BAFO. So you may end up holding the bag, because some other bidder underbid you by the amount you were going to shave off. I know of exactly such an instance actually happening.

SSAC Actions

Having obtained the BAFO from all the qualified bidders, and having completed the technical evaluation of all the bids, the SSEB chairman will now prepare the SSEB report and submit it to the SSAC. The SSAC in turn prepares the proposal analysis report (a somewhat condensed form of the SSEB report) and forwards it to the SSA for an award decision. The members of the SSAC are appointed by the SSA. You might say they do about 8% of the source evaluation work (compared to 90% by the SSEB and 2% by the SSA).[2] It is also worthy of note that, whereas the SSEB performs a digital function, the SSAC performs an analog function. In other words, the SSEB comes up with a numerical rating that the SSAC converts to an adjectival rating. The SSEB must use digital ratings as a matter of necessity, because it is impossible to add adjectives in computing an overall rating.

SSA Award Decision

When the SSA makes his decision, he may simply announce the award, and the contractor prepares to take over his new responsibilities. However, for large, multimillion dollar contracts, it is not quite that simple. First, the announcement will be that the government is commencing negotiations exclusively with the selected contractor.

---

2. Bear in mind that the SSAC and SSEB are supported by the staff elements of the command or agency, such as legal, cost accounting, the Small Business Administration (SBA), the Defense Contract Audit Agency (DCAA), and so on.

These final negotiations may involve a multitude of details that in the aggregate may amount to a significant amount of money. Such negotiations, however, cannot involve any issues that go to the heart of the contract—the essence thereof—otherwise there would be grounds for protest, with resultant heartburn for all concerned. When the negotiations are concluded, the government is ready to make the announcement of contract award.

But wait! There is still one more important detail. The government must find a Congressperson who is not off on a junket somewhere like Paris, Rome, or the Riviera (on important government business) so that they can have this Congressperson make the announcement. This is mandatory, so that the Congressperson can take credit for this herculean effort he or she has made to bring this lucrative government contract to his or her district. This way, his or her incumbency is assured for a few more years, and the grateful Congressperson will assuredly support that government agency in future budget requests.

I had that experience once. We had won the contract, and the government was ready to make the announcement Christmas week. (Our takeover date was supposed to be January 1.) Well, they just couldn't find the Congressperson from our district. They tried Acapulco, the Bahamas, Waikiki, Aspen, and all the other places where Congresspersons might be expected to have important government business going on at that time of year, but in vain. So the announcement was not made until January 5, four days after we were to assume responsibility for the contract!

The Evaluation Process

So much for the overview of the evaluation process. Let's get down to some details. Let's take a closer look at the work of the SSEB in the evaluation process.

Three Basic Criteria

Remember that the standards are statements of the government's criteria upon which the members of the SSEB evaluate your proposal. These are the detailed criteria that the evaluators will have propped up in front of them as they grade each segment of your proposal.

You might say there are three kinds of criteria:

1. The evaluation criteria that you see in the RFP (Section M).
2. The evaluation criteria seen only by the government (i.e., the standards).
3. The criteria that nobody ever sees (i.e., the biases, preferences, prejudices, emotional attachments, and so on that affect the judgment of the evaluator.

The first kind, those that appear in the RFP, are the ones that you, the proposal writer, are most concerned with, because you must use these criteria to critique your own proposal. If you haven't responded to these criteria in all respects, you still have more work to do before turning in your proposal.

The second kind, the standards, you will never see, but you should try to envision what they might be as you prepare your proposal. This is not as impossible as it may seem, because they *must* track with the evaluation criteria in the RFP and with the proposal instructions. The standards can not contain anything which is not required and directed by the RFP.

The third kind, your company image, you the proposal writer can do something about by providing a well-organized, easy-to-follow proposal that faithfully complies with the proposal instructions (Sect. L of the RFP) and responds implicitly to all requirements of the RFP as spelled out in the SOW. That will most assuredly give your company a good image as far as the evaluator is concerned. And that is all *you* can do. The up-front marketing people have to do the rest by creating a favorable image of your company long before the RFP hits the streets.

I suppose this is as good a place as any to unload on another of my pet peeves. Over and over again I run into some nitwit who wants to ignore the proposal instructions and base the proposal outline on the *evaluation criteria*, or even outline the SOW! The general outline of any proposal *has got to follow the proposal instructions (Sect. L) to the letter*. No ifs, ands, or buts, no matter what anybody tells you. (The instructions to all bidders for preparation of the proposal are contained in Sect. L—always.)

The following is a short extract of an actual evaluation criteria section (for a government procurement of technical services), and following that is an extract of a *standards* section. You will note that the *standards* track with the evaluation criteria. You may find the following analysis somewhat boring and have a tendency to skip over it, but I implore you to take the time to understand what follows, because you can't write good, responsive proposals until you do.

Excerpt of Evaluation Criteria from an RFP

M.2 Evaluation Criteria

A. **Go/No Go Evaluation.** Key personnel must be rated a "Go" *in order for the offeror to be further considered for award.* [Italics mine.] The contractor must have in its employ or have commitments for employment, individuals which meet the education and experience requirements specified in the SOW for all positions classified as key personnel.

B. **Evaluation Factors For Award.** The evaluation criteria are delineated in this section by areas and elements within an area and factors within an element. The four *areas* of evaluation include technical, management, cost, and past performance. The technical area is slightly more important than the management area. The management area is approximately one and one-half times as important as cost.

1. The technical *areas* consist of three *elements*: (a) approach for processing and control of work, (b) adequacy of personnel, and (c) contractor furnished equipment...

   (a) Element 1: Approach for processing and control of work includes the following *factors*:

      (i) Procedure for planning and estimating work;

      (ii) Procedure for receiving, scheduling, processing and statusing work;

      (iii)Procedure for technical reporting

[Other factors omitted]

   (b) Element 2: The offeror's understanding of the SOW as shown by the adequacy of personnel includes the *factors* listed below:

      (i) Appropriate number of employees

      (ii) Qualifications, skill levels, and skill mix

      (iii)Accomplishment of cyclic requirements and workload fluctuations.

   (c) *[Other factors omitted]*

Before we move on to the *corresponding excerpt of a government standard,* let me point out some features of the previous evaluation criteria. Note that there are explicit go/no go criteria here. That means you must propose key personnel who meet the qualifications and experience stipulated in the RFP or you are dead. And don't think you can get away with a little "poetic license" on this. They will verify the information in the resumes you provide through their own investigation.

Note that in this RFP the hierarchy of evaluation factors is: *Areas, Elements, Factors,* and *Subfactors.* We have included above only some of the factors of *two of the elements* of the technical area. The proposal instructions for this RFP direct that these evaluation criteria be applied for each of the *functions* specified in the RFP. In other words, *all* these evaluation criteria are to be applied in turn to *each* of the *functions*—that is, "Boiler and Heating Plants," "Transportation," "Electrical Services," and so on.

Now for a look at the corresponding government rating sheets and then the standards by which the evaluators measure your proposal response. The following is an excerpt from the government's evaluation standards. Remember, you will never see these documents in the course of your proposal writing career, but you will note that they track with the evaluation criteria.

Excerpt 1 from the Government's Evaluation Standards

FUNCTION
BOILER AND HEATING PLANTS

GO/NO GO FACTOR
Personnel:
  (a) Boiler plants shall be attended by operators as speci-
     fied in AR 420-49, Table 2-1, Operating Personnel Re-
     quirements for Automatically Fired Steam and Hot Water
     Plants.
  (b) Plant operators shall be properly trained and certified
     IAW AR 420-15 and DARCOM supplements thereto.

ELEMENT 1: Processing and Control of Work
FACTORS

	Score	Weight	Total Score
a. Procedures for planning and estimating work	____	____	____
b. Procedure for receiving, scheduling, processing and statusing work	____	____	____
c. Procedure for technical reporting	____	____	____
d. Procedure for accomplishment of cyclic requirements and workload fluctuation	____	____	____

ELEMENT 2: Organization and Policies
FACTORS
  a. Appropriate number of employees
  b. Qualifications, skill level and skill mix
  c. Accomplishment of cyclic requirements

Note that the Go/No Go factors reference an AR and other references. This means you had better get out these references, study them, and respond to the letter of the regulation. Can't you just imagine what the evaluator will do with your proposal if you put down, as so many are wont to do: "XYZ will provide operators as specified in AR 420-49 . . . blah, blah" without even looking up this AR? You will be dead, kaput, finito.

Note also that the rating sheet here *tracks exactly with the evaluation criteria published in the RFP*: the Go/No Go criteria; the elements and the factors. Now for a look at the standards, the written criteria upon which the evaluators base their ratings of your proposal. Note: For sake of brevity, we are providing the standard for Element 2 only, Organization and Policies.

Excerpt 2 from the Government's Evaluation Standards

STANDARDS FOR SCORING ORGANIZATION AND POLICIES

Adjectival Rating	Score	Description
Exceptional	100	Proposer has a clear understanding and proposes an exceptional organization to accomplish the task set forth in Section C (the SOW) of the RFP.
Acceptable	75	Proposer demonstrates a firm grasp of the Army's requirements and proposes a good proven organization. Those deficiencies not considered minor can be easily corrected with the offeror's expenditure of time and funds.
Marginal	50	Proposer indicates a shallow understanding of the requirements and the proposed organization barely meets the technical requirements.
Unacceptable	0	Proposer's interpretation of the requirements, as reflected in the proposer's approach, is so incomplete, vague, incompatible, incomprehensible or incorrect that it is unsatisfactory.

Let's return to the definition of standards. Standards are written statements of conditions necessary to achieve minimum acceptable performance. Standards are the measurement guides—the detailed instructions provided to the evaluators to help measure the adequacy of the proposal in meeting the requirements set out in the RFP. Standards must measure acceptability of the proposed solution. That is to say, that any criterion that measures anything *other than acceptability* (that is, to achieve minimum acceptable performance) cannot be considered a standard.

Conversely, a proposed approach that exceeds minimum acceptable performance cannot receive a higher grade than one that just meets acceptability. Presumably, if the customer wanted the higher performance, they would have so stated. The message here is simply: "Don't think you will get a higher grade by proposing something nice to have and thus beat the competition." It may not do you any harm, as long as it does not cost any more. Likewise, it will not do you any good either. (But see the "Best Value Concept" section at the end of this chapter for a major exception.)

Standards should be prepared by the users and/or procurement specialists *prior* to the issuance of the RFP. In any case, they *must* be prepared prior to the receipt of the proposals. Otherwise, there could be charges of fraud and collusion in the procurement.

Failure to address a standard in the proposal will result in a deficiency, so I repeat: it is important to try to deduce the standards from a judicious analysis of the RFP. You should be able to do this by taking each of the evaluation criteria in turn and apply them to each of the SOW items that you are responding to and determine what you must write to fulfill the criteria.

A standard is set out in four parts: area, item, factor, and subfactor. (Air Force terminology.) The terminology may differ in different agencies (as in the example above, the Army uses the term, "element" instead of "item"), but the result is the same. Evaluation is made at the factor and subfactor level, the area and item elements being merely titles or headings for management purposes. As in the example following, there may be several factors and subfactors within an item. The factor/subfactor descriptions will contain detailed descriptions or instructions for evaluating these criteria.

Example of a Standard from Air Force Procurement

```
Item: Design and develop communication subsystem.
Factor: Technical control element. Evaluated IAW factor
description.
Factor: Voice communication element
Subfactor: Automatic audio switch. Evaluated IAW subfactor
description.
Subfactor:  Emergency manual service
```

Rating Techniques

Now a word about the rating techniques. All instructions to the members of the SSEB are included in the source selection plan, including the rating instructions. For very large procurements, the SSEB is organized into various hierarchies to facilitate evaluation and surveillance of the evaluators. *Areas* may be in overall control of managers (selected by the SSEB Chairman). *Items* (or "elements") are assigned to "item captains;" *factors* and *subfactors* to "evaluators." If both narrative and numerical scoring is used, the evaluator usually provides the numerical rating and the item captain writes the narrative. Color coding (in lieu of numerical rating) is sometimes used, especially in the Air Force. This facilitates quick-look review by the SSAC or SSA where many proposals are evaluated for one procurement.

Once a proposal has been scored, no changes in scoring are permitted *except* to evaluate changes to the proposal, made as a request by the SSEB chairman to a bidder in the Q and A phase. In that case, a narrative justification should accompany any change in the numerical score.

Costs are never scored in Air Force or Army procurements, but in some agencies (for example, the Navy and the Department of Commerce) they may be scored according to a prearranged formula, which may or may not be published in the RFP.

Figure 6.3 is another example of a rating sheet for numerical scoring of proposals. There is no standard form for all proposals, the format usually being left up to the chairman of the SSEB. Note that each factor is given a percent weighting and that each subfactor is given a rating within the factor.

Contract Considerations

Some RFPs include a model contract. If so, this must be considered in writing your proposal. The purchasing and contract officer (PCO) will compare your proposal with the model to verify that there are no conflicts. If your proposal is inconsistent with the model contract or fails to acknowledge substantive obligations therein (for example compliance with the contract data requirements list (CDRL), you are, in effect, taking exception to a portion of what the customer said he wants. If these discrepancies are minor in nature, you will be so advised during the Q and A phase and be given a chance to amend your proposal accordingly. You may take exceptions to any portion of the model contract (or to the RFP), of course, but my advice in general is don't do it if you want the contract.

The PCO will also take a look at the price quoted to determine if the price is realistic in relation to the contract. If not realistic, your proposal will probably be peremptorily dropped from the zone of consideration, whether it be unrealistically high or unrealistically low. (Remember, I'm telling it the way it is supposed to be, not necessarily the way it is. I know of a contract awarded out of Nellis AFB some years back where all of the proposers conscientiously bid realistic costs and thus fell neatly into a realistic bracket except one. That one was awarded the contract. That one was the low bid, of course. One has to wonder why they didn't just auction off the contract to the low bidder and save everybody all the trouble of writing proposals and then evaluating them.)

Date:

Item: _____

Spec

Bidder: _____

Evaluator: _____

RATING

.0 Unacceptable
.1 Poor
.2 Below average/marginal
.3 Average
.4 Above average
.5 Excellent

FACTOR #3–MANAGEMENT	MAXUMUM	ACCEPTABLE	RATING	WEIGHTING	SCORE
A. PROJECT MANAGEMENT = 30%					
1. Degree of managerial support					
2. Number and specialization of personnel					
3. Qualification of key personnel					
B. MANAGEMENT APPROACH = 30%					
1. Project schedule controls					
2. Coordination of activities					
3. Vendor control and liaison					
C. MANAGEMENT CAPABILITY = 40%					
1. Previous related experience					
2. In-house capability					

Figure 6.3 Rating sheet for the numerical scoring of proposals.

Deficiencies

A deficiency is defined as any part of an offer or proposal that fails to meet the customer's minimum requirements established in the solicitation.

Any one of the four conditions below may constitute a deficiency. If deficiencies found in a proposal are such as to constitute a fundamental flaw in concept, or otherwise are of such a magnitude as to be incapable of being corrected without major revision, the proposal will not fall within the zone of consideration (competitive range) and will therefore be eliminated from further consideration.

A deficiency is any part of a contractor's proposal that:

- Fails to meet the minimum requirements represented by the standard; or
- Proposes an approach that poses unacceptable risk; or
- Represents an omission of fact that makes it impossible to assess compliance with the standard for that requirement; or
- Describes an approach taken by the offerer in the design of its system that yields undesirable performance.

Minor deficiencies may be corrected in the Q and A phase. The greater the number of proposals submitted, however, the greater the chance of your proposal being eliminated for deficiencies.

Many RFPs will list major critical areas and stipulate that a failing score in *any one* of these major areas will disqualify your proposal from the zone of consideration, regardless of how how well you score in other areas. You saw an example of that previously where the evaluation criteria stipulated certain Go/No Go criteria.

Don't feel bad when the contracting officer starts talking to you about "deficiencies" in your proposal. Even if a proposal were perfect, they would probably find at least one somehow. Moreover, the term is used only in the strict sense of the definitions above. And many deficiencies are merely inadvertent omissions or errors that your Red Team or your proposal manager should have caught. Also, a careless SSEB chairman may have a tendency to blur the distinction between a deficiency and a clarification. A clarification should involve no penalty in the scoring whatever. It simply means the evaluator is not sure he or she understands what you meant to say.

Let us examine in more detail each of the conditions that constitute a deficiency.

1. *Failure to meet minimum requirements represented by the standard.* Suppose you have proposed an engineer who doesn't have a degree, and the RFP requires that all engineers have a degree in engineering. If he is one of the key personnel as defined in the RFP, and if the evaluation criteria read

like the example I used above (the Go/No Go criteria[3]), then you have a serious deficiency. In fact, you're dead if you don't replace him pronto.

But suppose he is not key personnel. Then you probably have only a minor deficiency. You will be downgraded a bit in the evaluation for this item, but it will not be fatal. You know the nondegreed engineer you proposed can do the job. My advice is: find another resume; the idea is to win the contract first. Then you can worry about such minor details of running it.

2. *Proposes an approach that poses unacceptable risk.* This is not an attempt by the customer to discourage innovative approaches. What it does mean is that you have to do a thoroughly meticulous job of convincing the customer that your approach is feasible, that there are no uncertainties and (for hardware systems) that your design is feasible, that you have tested it, and that you have the documentation to prove it. If you cannot positively eliminate the uncertainties, then you had better propose a different, safer approach. You can't expect the customer to buy a "pig in a poke."

3. *Has an omission of fact that makes it impossible to assess compliance with the standard for that requirement.* This is the most pervasive of all deficiencies, and paradoxically the most easily avoided. It simply means that you have to address *all* requirements set out in the RFP including all facts and data to enable the customer to fully evaluate your proposal.

If you fail to address any particular of the RFP requirements, express or implied, you can be certain of getting yourself tagged with a deficiency. That is why I have been harping on preparing the proposal in a systematic, orderly manner, starting with the preliminary preparations, research, analysis of the RFP, making a detailed outline, reviewing, critiquing, and rewriting. There are no shortcuts.

4. *Describes an approach taken by the offeror in the design of its system that yields undesirable performance.* This is like item (2) above except that in that case the customer has *uncertainties.* In this case he (or she) *knows* it won't work, either because he has seen it tried before, or (to him, at least) concludes that it is patently unworkable. If you really think your approach is feasible, you have simply failed to prove your case. As a general rule, don't try out any unorthodox, way-out solutions or approaches in a proposal. The people who evaluate proposals are generally engineering or science-oriented or business-type people. Such people are usually conservative minded and careful to avoid high-risk decisions. If they weren't, they would not last long in their business. Again, you must win the contract first. Then you might have the time and the resources to convince the customer of the feasibility of your approach. Or, alternatively, look into the

---

3. Para. M2, A, p.114.

possibility of getting a grant, if you are convinced you have something there. It is much easier to get a grant for high-risk ventures. (See Chapter 8.)

Since you, the proposal writer or manager, will never get a chance to see the standards prepared by the procuring agency, I am including some more real-world samples of standards to close out this presentation. This should give you some valuable insight into the careful analysis that a good procurement agency will give your proposal through the in-depth questions the SSEB will pose for the evaluators. The agency that prepared the standards that you are about to see did its homework—conscientiously and with admirable thoroughness. A pity that all procurement agencies are not as dedicated as this one. A pity that such dedication is sometimes wasted by the chicanery of decision makers higher up the chain of command.

Examples of Standards and Weighting from a NASA Procurement

A. **Technical and Management Understanding** Total 450 points.
  1. Operating Plan— 300 points
     a. Supervisory authority and responsibility
        (1) Does offeror set forth supervisory responsibility for each succeeding layer of organization?
        (2) Does each functional manager have the necessary authority to carry out his or her proposed assignments?
        (3) Are supervisory positions consistent with functions requiring monitoring?
        (4) Are supervisory positions described in the text consistent with organization charts?
     b. Managerial control devices
        (1) What techniques are proposed for each level of supervision to monitor succeeding levels of supervision?
        (2) How will parallel functional supervisors communicate with each other on matters of joint concern?
     c. Work flow and assignments
        (1) What procedures are set forth for how assignments will be made?
        (2) How are work priorities established?
        (3) Who establishes priorities?
        (4) What provisions are made for assuring a closed loop?

(5) What techniques are proposed to determine assignment status?

(6) How is status reported to NASA Director on a timely basis?

d. Cost Controls

(1) What are proposed techniques for controlling expenditures made on equipment maintenance and supplies?

(2) What does offeror propose as a method of assuring utilization of existing equipment?

e. Training

(1) What is proposed for initial training for new employees in each functional area?

(2) What provisions are made for inservice training?

(3) Is cross-training to be accomplished? How?

(4) What is proposed for (2) and (3) above for supervisory personnel?

(5) Does proposed depth of training meet government needs?

f. Does proposer cite any pivotal or crucial factors for a successful operation?

g. Overtime

(1) What are the proposed controls concerning overtime utilization?

(2) At what levels of authority may overtime be approved?

(3) At what levels of supervision will overtime not be allowed?

(4) What is the proposed policy concerning the supervision of those assigned to unique or one-of-a-kind tasks?

h. Emergency Planning

(1) Does proposer present a plan for major fire or disaster?

(2) Does plan provide for cross-utilization of manpower?

(3) Does plan provide a means of call for assistance beyond company capabilities?

i. Phase-in

      (1) Does proposer describe a phase-in plan that will provide for optimum operations during transition period?

      (2) What other manpower resources will be made available from within the company?

      (3) Is a plan provided for recruitment of new personnel? Is it adequate?

      (4) Is sufficient time provided for relocation of personnel to accomplish transition?

      (5) What percentage of existing work force is proposer planning to recruit?

  j. Utilization of Personnel

      (1) What plans are offered concerning interface between off-site and on-site personnel?

      (2) What plans are offered to permit flexibility to meet shifting or peak work loads?

2. Organization and Management— 150 points

  a. Organization

      (1) Are the functions assigned to each level of organization clearly identified?

      (2) Are the functions logically grouped? Is there any unnecessary duplication of functions?

      (3) Will the proposed groupings create problems in accomplishing the work?

      (4) Are the proposed lines of communications within the project organization simple and direct?

      (5) What is the relationship of the project organization to company or home office organization?

      (6) Is the plan for subcontract management effective?

  b. Management

      (1) Does the project manager have the necessary authority to do the job?

      (2) Do the supervisors of major functions have the requisite authority?

      (3) What support is contemplated from the front office? Too much? Too little?

      (4) What management techniques will be used at the project manager level to ensure success of this effort?

(5) Are the interface relationships between the government and contractor organizations on site adequately covered? Are these relationships workable?

Please bear in mind that these standards were devised for a specific RFP involving a specific contract and cannot be applied blindly to any other procurement situation. They are included here to show you the kind of in-depth questions a good SSEB team will come up with in analyzing your proposal. The hope is that they will give you an insight into the kind of questions your proposal is supposed to answer.

These are the kinds of questions a good, competent Red Team manager will devise for his Red Team when they start reviewing your proposal. But Red Teams are seldom that well prepared. So you, the proposal writer must try to anticipate the kind of questions the SSEB is going to be asking. Then make sure your proposal input answers them.

Frequently, the failure of proposal writers to respond fully and precisely to the RFP requirements is attributable to confusion in interpreting the language in the RFP accurately. Generally speaking, RFPs are not written by talented or professional writers and certainly not with the precision of most legal documents. The language is often obscure, sloppy, poorly organized, and ineptly phrased. I have seen some RFPs that were about as indecipherable as that quote from *Ulysses* at the beginning of Chapter 5!

I am not saying this by way of commiseration, but once again, to emphasize that you must analyze, dissect, reread, and brainstorm the various sections of the RFP until you are sure you understand exactly what the customer wants. If you have any doubts, check with your proposal manager and other team members to see if they have the same interpretation you do. Too many times I have seen even experienced proposal managers starting off about 90 degrees off course, because they *thought* they understood the proposal instructions.

It has crossed my mind that possibly some of this obscure ambiguous language in RFPs is intentional. Could it be that there are some crafty procurement offices around the country who deliberately and with malice aforethought design the RFP in such a manner that only the most intelligent and perceptive contractors will make the zone of consideration? In other words, "If you are too dumb to understand what we mean, you are too dumb to be able to perform this contract competently."

What is Wrong with the Government's Evaluation Process? And What is Being Done to Correct It?

Back in the beginning of this chapter, I said that the procurement process was ingeniously designed to ensure fairness in the award of government contracts. And in the vast majority of cases, the system functions as it was intended.

The very fact that the news media can make such a big deal out of a $200 hammer or an exorbitantly priced ash tray is itself proof that a system that administers the expenditure of such sums as $300 billion a year by DOD alone must be working pretty well. In fact I doubt anyone could find a system elsewhere that works better.[4] And further, consider what DOD got for its money: a sophisticated array of weaponry such as the world has never seen; and such as the rest of the world will never in the foreseeable future ever match. A military capability that inflicted some 300,000 casualties on the fourth largest army in the world at a cost of less than 200 of our own troops. An "arms race" that bankrupted and destroyed the mighty Soviet Union and ended the cold war and the threat of nuclear holocaust. And a military establishment by far the most powerful in the world, which can bring its power to bear in days' or even hours' notice to any spot on earth where America's vital interests are threatened.

But any system subject to the intervention of the human element will occasionally be flawed. And in the field of government contracting, such flaws have led to scandal, reaction, and overreaction such as we have seen in recent times with Ill Wind. Suffice it to say that Ill Wind will not be the end of unscrupulous procurement practices, nor have we seen the last of punitive actions taken against individuals and corporations as a result of fraudulently awarded contracts made in violation of the law of the land.

The Three Flaws in the System

There are three basic flaws in the procurement system:

(a) The power of the SSA to make an award for reasons known only to himself and without regard to the recommendations of the SSEB (whose *raison d'etre* is to ensure fairness).
(b) The difficulty of proving government malfeasance when the government itself controls access to the facts through classification of documents.
(c) The failure of the SSEBs to ensure cost realism through feasibility analyses of the proposals. SSEBs are supposed to be made up of technical experts who can break down a contract into its component segments and make a rational analysis of what it should cost in staffing and material to perform each segment.

From my observations, the problems arising from government malfeasance occur mostly in the award of services contracts—for example, the O & M portion of

---

4. A friend of mine, working as a consultant to the Japanese government, after a meeting with the contractor that the Japanese government had selected to perform the contract (to build a missile tracking range), asked his Japanese counterpart why they had selected a contractor who was clearly unprepared and unqualified to do the job. The Japanese government official, astonished at the question, replied, "Why, because it was their turn!"

the DOD budget that in cold war days ran into the neighborhood of $90 billion per year. One of the reasons for this is the difficulty of quantifying costs for services with the same precision as for hardware contracts. Another is the greater scrutiny given to hardware as compared to services contracts. Another is the idiotic, politically inspired mandates tacked on by Congress, in its infinite wisdom, to anything involving labor.

But let us take a look at each of the three major flaws in the system as outlined above. Actually, two of them are not flaws in the system but are really flaws in the *application* of a generally good system.

First, the *authority of the SSA to disregard the recommendations of the SSEB without having to justify his decision.* This authority enables the SSA in effect, to vitiate the very expensive and detailed work of the SSEB in securing an honest evaluation, not to mention opening up the whole system to fraud and collusion. I talked to one government engineer who told me he hated to work on SSEBs simply because the SSA always made up his mind who he was going to award the contract to beforehand, and they were just performing a tedious but useless exercise.

Of course, you will never find an SSA who will disregard the recommendation of the SSAC, because he can and does appoint individuals to that committee who will make the recommendation he wants. And if by some weird accident they don't, he can send the recommendation back until they do. So in the event of a protest or a GAO inquiry, the SSA is always clean. He just acted upon the recommendation of that amorphous bureaucratic invention that can obfuscate any issue with a smokescreen of bureaucratic weasel words to the point that even the FBI would throw up their hands in despair. So much for Flaw (a).

Onward to the second flaw, (b): *the difficulty of proving government malfeasance when the government itself controls all the documentation through classification of documents.*

The trouble is that the bidder is under a major handicap in bringing legal action against the government, because the government is in possession of most of the documentation that could support the bidder's case, most of which may be inaccessible even to a Freedom of Information (FOIA) request.

And furthermore, notwithstanding the fact that the government is in a position to cover their tracks through classification of documents, the bidder has the burden of showing that the government violated the provisions of the FAR or the proper application of contract law. Well, in any case, we will have to leave that to the legal eagles whose arcane sorcery dominates so much of our lives for better or worse.

In the field of tort law, there is a rule called *res ipsa loquitor* that says that where circumstances causing injury are in the defendant's (the government's) exclusive control, he is *presumed* negligent where plaintiff's injury (due to the illegal application of the FAR) does not ordinarily happen in the absence of negligence. Too bad this rule is not applied in these cases.

So why am I belaboring this subject in a book on how to write proposals? Because I think it is high time contractors started demanding fairness in government contracting. Some procurement agencies award contracts like dealing a deck of cards. Thousands of manhours of government employee time are wasted in simply going through the motions of complying with the regulations when everybody knows (eventually) that the SSA had already made up his mind whom he or she was going to award the contract to before the whole process had even started.

Too many times I have seen companies waste hundreds of thousands of dollars responding honestly to an RFP and bidding a realistic cost, only to be defeated by an unscrupulous competitor (probably in collusion with one or more of the government procurement people). He buys into the contract and after a decent interval of time (that is, after the time has expired for a protest), he gets his big fat mod (modification to the contract) and laughs all the way to the bank.

And then there is the other extreme, where the customer has developed a nice, comfortable incestuous relationship with the incumbent contractor over the years and he is going to award the contract to this incumbent come hell or high water, no matter what. I managed a proposal once where the customer (the Department of Commerce, this time), blatantly evaluated all the proposals according to how close they came to the proposal submitted by the incumbent. In other words, if you proposed less staffing or a different organization chart than the incumbent, you were penalized accordingly, presumably for not understanding the situation.

I think the last straw in my experience was a case in point, a procurement where the Air Force awarded the contract to the *highest* bidder (the incumbent, of course) even though the two losing bidders were at least as qualified as the winner. I have ample reason to know our proposal was technically superior to that of the winner (although there is no way of ever proving this, because the government is authorized to keep the findings of the SSEB forever secret from the public). Furthermore, our proposal contained a no-strike agreement with the labor union involved; the winner's proposal did not. So, as predictable as night follows day, within months after the contract was awarded, (to the *highest* bidder, remember) the union began strike preparations—preparing for the picket lines, printing placards for the strikers to carry, and so forth. Then magically out of the subterranean bowels of the Air Force bureaucracy came a miraculous solution which made everyone happy. Guess what it was.

No protests were filed, a few half-hearted inquiries dismissed with the usual vague, meaningless cliches. "The selection was based on *technical risks* involved in the various proposals." Our company had virtually invented the technology which was the subject of the "risk." The "risks" were never defined, much less substantiated. And if there were ostensible risks, they were never raised in the orals. And so the decision stood, and no one can ever prove the real reason why. End of story.

Yes, this is a book about how to write proposals, and my advice on this subject is: when you smell something like this in the making, walk away from it. If you are a victim of this sort of a scam, exercise your right of protest. In my previous book on this subject, I advised against going the protest route, because protests were almost never successful. That was then; this is now. I know of several protests in the multi-hundred-million-dollar range that were upheld in recent times, one at Redstone Arsenal (Army), ordered by the GAO and another at Kennedy Space Center (NASA) to name two. There have been several in the billion-dollar range in recent years involving hardware systems contracts. One government official was heard to remark, "When you put out a contract for a billion dollars, you can almost expect an automatic protest."

Before we go on to Flaw (c), I should also remind you of the dire consequences you as a contractor are exposed to when you win a contract by misrepresentation. Here is an excerpt from a current newspaper item: "The EPA blocked the XYZ Corporation from receiving any new federal contracts until an investigation and possible *debarment* proceedings are complete . . . . There has been a pattern of XYZ's including false and misleading statements in proposals,' the EPA memo said." In other words, this company was facing the possibility of being prohibited from bidding on any government contracts during the period of debarment, which could be months or even years.

Flaw (c): *The failure of the SSEBs to ensure cost realism through feasibility analyses of the proposals.* This flaw is most assuredly a flaw in the way the system is allowed to work—that is, the failure of the SSEBs to ensure cost realism in evaluation of proposals. Every RFP has boilerplate that pays lip service to the government's determination to evaluate the proposals based on cost realism and the best interests of the government, blah, blah, blah . . . just words. And every government procurement package includes an independent government cost estimate (IGCE) that is supposed to determine the realistic cost to the government.

This is a classic illustration of how the government mutilates a good system by carelessness or, more likely, by the malfeasance of bureaucrats with an axe to grind in favor of one contractor over the others. How? The Q and A phase is seldom characterized by questions that go to the *feasibility* of the bidder's proposed course of action. And awareness of this fact is exactly why bidders commonly buy into a contract, knowing full well they can not adequately perform under the bid price. In far too many cases, the government awards the contract to the low bidder when they know full well (or should know full well) that the contractor can not perform at his bid price. So what happens? Why, the government, even though they know the contract was obtained by fraud and deceit (which is what deliberate underbidding is), nevertheless generously modifies the contract after a few months to bail out the winning contractor. This practice usually costs the taxpayer more in the end than if they had selected the highest bidder in the first place.

Of course, none of the other bidders complain or file a protest. How can they argue that the government shouldn't make the award to the low bidder? Economy and frugality are right up there with motherhood. And besides for many government contractors, the government is the only customer they have. And bureaucrats have long memories where protests are concerned.

The obvious remedy to this sort of thing (which has become rampant in the service contracting field), is for the panel of experts (presumably) on the SSEB to ask the right questions of the various bidders and weigh their answers carefully on the scale of reasonableness.

To illustrate, suppose Foxy Corp. bids five people to perform mess kit repair. Joe Blow on the SSEB, who is the panel's expert on mess kit repair, knows (or *should know*) that this job absolutely, positively cannot be done with less than ten people, unless Foxy Corp. has found some new revolutionary way to repair mess kits with 100% more efficiency. So he asks the Foxy Corp. delegate at the Q & A session, "What makes you think you can repair all these mess kits with just five people?" If Foxy Corp. can't explain in detail exactly what each person assigned this task does and how they can do it twice as fast as what Joe Blow thinks it should take, then their credibility is severely damaged, and they are in a heap of trouble. After a few more lies like this are uncovered, then Foxy's proposal should be rejected for failing the test of cost realism and also because Foxy Corp. fails to understand the problem.

That is the way the system is supposed to work, but more often than not, in my observation, the government blindly awards the contract to the low bidder. Everybody knows that six months later there will be a mod to the contract and both the contractor and the government will get well again at the taxpayer's expense.

How does the government get away with this? Well, believe it or not, they often plead incompetence. That is, they will say in effect, "It is impossible for poor little ol' us to make an accurate estimate of the probable cost of performing such a complicated contract. We have to rely on the contractor's estimates." This is how many multibillion dollar weapons system contracts—for example, the B-1 and B-2 bombers, the A-12, the C-5A and the C-17—end up in horrendous cost overruns.

The government is responsible for making an IGCE on all such contracts. (Another one of those things that is forever kept secret from the public.) Are we to believe that, notwithstanding all the resources at the disposal of the United States government, it is incapable of performing this cost accounting function? Cost accounting has been developed into a science such that the cost of any project can be forecasted with reasonable accuracy, even the cost of putting a man on the moon. There were no scandalous overruns on that project. And furthermore, how can the government pretend it knows how to manage a program if it cannot make a reasonable estimate of the actual cost of the program? C'mon, gimme a break!

One might concede that for certain contracts, cost estimating is somewhat more difficult. Software development, engineering development, and R & D contracts come to mind. But there are well-established ways of controlling even these contracts so that they can be awarded on realistic bids in a manner that is fair to all competitors. And that is what brings me to the last and most important part of this chapter for those who bid on high-technology contracts. Why? Because now the government is making a difficult transition in trying to correct some of the evils I have been discussing.

The Best Value Concept

For years and years we have had boilerplate in every major RFP to the effect that "award will be made to the offeror whose offer is the most advantageous to the Government, price and other factors considered." Until recent years, we all read this statement and said to ourselves, "Yeah, sure." And then we went about writing a proposal knowing full well the customer would award the contract to the lowest technically qualified bid.

So we aimed to provide the very minimum the RFP required while still meeting the technical requirements in order to keep the cost at a minimum. Why? Because regardless of what the boilerplate said, most government contracts were awarded in a two-step process. First the evaluators eliminated all but the most technically qualified proposals and then awarded the contract to the proposal that was in this zone of consideration which had the lowest cost.

In recent years, there has been a new wrinkle in the government's application of this boilerplate. That is to say, the government is now applying a literal interpretation to their boilerplate!

So now we have a whole new ball game whenever the following two areas of contracting are involved: Professional and technical services and contracts where innovative solutions are paramount. Predictably, this has caused confusion and consternation in the business community, ensuing in a number of protests and litigation in this area that we will get to later in this chapter.

First, let us define exactly what we are talking about here. I have gone about asking various people I know, "What is this so-called 'best value concept'?," and I have received mostly expletives and unprintable comments about the ancestry of bureaucrats, but that hasn't been much help. So obviously we need some explication of this subject for starters.

Let's start out with the invitation for bid (IFB). In an IFB, the contract award goes to the lowest responsible bidder. The customer issues IFBs to a list of bidders he has compiled, having first made a reasonable effort to ascertain that they are responsible bidders. Then the bids are opened publicly and the lowest bidder declared the winner. That's all there is to it. Obviously such procedures must be limited to common, mundane items that are normally obtainable off the shelf and usable without any modification or processing. Potatoes, for example, or shoes, blankets, or widgets, all of which must meet specific standardized specifications. Same thing for nonprofessional services, say janitorial services.

Now when you get into more complicated items, such as a radar antenna or O&M of an established facility, the customer needs to know much more about the bidder's capabilities other than simply knowing he is responsible. There are many different approaches to building a radar antenna or providing O&M of a facility—say, a power plant. So you put out an RFP instead of an IFB, and demand that the bidder tell you just how and what he proposes to provide you with to meet your requirements. The RFP will state exactly what the radar antenna must be capable of doing or just what the facility consists of and what standards of O&M you expect. In other words, the RFP sets out minimum performance requirements, and it is up to the bidder to tell the customer how he proposes to meet them. The correct boilerplate would have language to the effect that ". . . award will be made to the bidder who proposes the lowest cost, in the technically acceptable range." The evaluation criteria in Section M of the RFP will be based on the *minimum* requirements that will enable the customer to perform his or her mission. If bidders propose some other things that are nice to have or that exceed the RFP minimum requirements, it will avail them nothing unless they have met all the minimum requirements *and* they have the lowest price.

This has been pretty much the way most procurements have been conducted for anything but the most mundane products or services until the past few years. The trouble is that this method encouraged "buying in" to a contract. Bidders deliberately bid unrealistically low costs in order to win the contract. Then, when it was too late to turn back and start over again, the winning bidder would present the customer with a humongous cost overrun. So then the Government would have to "modify" the contract to prevent a disastrous work stoppage or an unacceptable delay in fulfilling its mission. And the procurement authorities, aware of this possibility but fearful of criticism for not being frugal enough with the taxpayers' money, awarded the contract to the low bidder anyhow. This, in spite of the fact that they already had the statutory authority to award the contract to the proposal which was the "most advantageous to the Government," a clause that, as I stated in the beginning, was often included in the boilerplate, but ignored in evaluating the proposals.

This is the situation as it still exists today with the procurement of equipment that, while complex, is not pushing the state of the art or is not inherently adapted to innovative solutions or does not require uniquely professional services. One might say that this is a gray area intermediate between the IFB where award clearly is made to the lowest bidder, period, and the other type of procurement (which we will address next), where it is clear that the "best value" concept is virtually mandated.

And this would be the class of negotiated procurements that involve highly professional services or where such services are required in the production of hardware or software where innovation is a key requirement. The evaluation of proposals in such cases involves a balancing of the bidder's proposed cost with other criteria *beyond technical acceptability which would enhance the value to the government of the item being procured.* Examples of such criteria would be: quality of the product or services, reliability of ontime delivery (where time is of the essence to the user), bidder's past performance, and risk of technology obsolescence, to list a few. A perfect illustration would be the case I described previously in the Air Force proposal where we had a binding no-strike agreement with the labor union involved and the competition did not.

While the general application of best value is relatively recent, it has nevertheless become entrenched in the government's evaluation procedures through the application of both statutory and regulatory authority. Its statutory basis is established in the Competition in Contracting Act of 1984 and has been impleented by the FAR and other regulatory directives.

On April 15, 1991, the Office of Federal Procurement Policy, in a policy letter, stated, "Agencies shall use competitive negotiations for acquisitions where the quality of performance over and above the minimum acceptable level *will enhance mission accomplishment and be worth the corresponding increase in cost.*" *(OFPP Letter 91-2, emphasis mine.)*

And from FAR 15.605 (c): "In certain acquisitions, the Government may select the source whose proposal offers the greatest value to the Government in terms of performance and other factors. This may be the case, for example, in the acquisition of research and development or professional services or when cost reimbursement contracting is anticipated." (This is the regulatory authority to which I referred earlier but which has been used sparingly until recent times.)

GSA Guidelines further direct that: "a) Hidden criteria or standards must enable the agency to perform its mission more effectively and, b) The agency must be able to show what value the government is getting to justify the additional cost." (GSA Guidelines at 5-1, 5-2.)

This regulatory authority has been bolstered by some landmark legal cases. Perhaps the leading case in this field is *Lockheed Missiles and Space versus Department of Treasury*, GSBCA Nos. 11776-P, 11777-P, 93-1 BCA 25,401, a case brought before the General Services Board of Contract Appeals (GSBCA). This case resulted from several protests arising from the award of a conract to AT&T at a price of more than $500 million *higher* than one bidder and $700 million higher than another!

The salient features of this decision which are crucial to an understanding of the best value concept are as follows:

- The decision was based on a cost/technical trade-off. Productivity analysis, risk analysis, and the other factors considered were inherent in any cost/technical trade-off.
- Subjective standards applied in the award decision and *not announced* in the RFP (Sect M of the evaluation criteria) were: the degree of expandability and flexibility of the proposed system, an assessment of past performance on timely availability of equipment, and the impact of the bidder's organizational structure on performance. (Refer back to Chapter II for a horrible example of an organizational structure that would lose a contract under best value.)
- All of the best value standards were *developed after the receipt of the proposals, and all were based on assessments of the proposals, balanced against user needs.*

Needless to say, this decision gives the government a much wider latitude in making an evaluation and justifying an award than previously thought possible by most of us. The GSBCA defined the extent of government's permissible discretion as follows (paraphrased): "The RFP's provisions need contain no real limitation on the *methods* that might be used in conducting a cost/technical trade-off analysis, so long as the price trade-off is reasonably commensurate with the technical advantage to be gained."

So what should we as proposal writers learn from all this?

- First, when you see words like "most advantageous to the government," "greatest value, cost and other factors considered," and "cost/technical trade-off," you might as well conclude that best value technique will be applied in evaluating your proposal.
- Second, when you see these phrases, you must analyze the proposal instructions and evaluation criteria with great care. If the criteria appear too vague or general, challenge them at the bidders conference. Perhaps you can smoke out a little more detail or at least get some clues as to what these hidden criteria are. Some cases have implied that the government's award decision might have been overruled if the bidder had challenged the RFP on these grounds.
- Third, put your marketing people to work, redoubling their efforts to find out these hidden criteria. They should review everything they ever heard about the government's needs, hot buttons, perceived risks, crucial mission requirements, or, if you are lucky, maybe what the government included in the source selection plan.
- Fourth, reassess your company's capabilities to provide a significantly improved product or service which (a) enhances the government's ability to fulfill its mission in a practical and identifiable way, *and* (b) can be provided at a relatively small increase in cost.
- Fifth, review your preliminary proposal approaches with a critical eye to eliminate any perception by the customer of:

    (a) Any technical risks inherent in your approach such as: technology obsolescence, restrictions on flexibility, expandability, technology advances in the state of the art.
    (b) Potential financial risks impacting the program.
    (c) Production risks (strikes, interruptions of supplies, competence of subcontractors, reliability of equipment, etc.).
    (d) Schedule risks involving technical approach or logistics.
    (e) Any problematic past performance in similar efforts
    (f) A lack of cost realism of your proposal. (If there are doubts as to your cost realism, there will certainly be doubts as to the realism of your best value approach.)

- Sixth, rewrite your themes to reflect any changes in your approach.

Application of the Best Value Concept in Proposal Evaluation

While the government indeed has wide discretion in applying the best value concept, GSBCA and the GAO decisions as a result of the many protests that have arisen therefrom indicate some firm restrictions. And it would behoove corporate executives to study the case law on this subject, both for the purpose of tailoring their proposals accordingly and to enable them to make the right decision whether or not to protest an award decision.

Certain rules have emerged. For one thing, the higher technical cost must justify the higher price. A recent GAO decision ruled that an award "should be supported by a specific, documented determination that the technical superiority of the higher priced offer *warrants the additional cost involved*, even where...cost is stated to be the least important factor." Sturm, Ruger & Co., Inc., January 14,1993,93–1 CPD Sect. 42 at 2. and Dewberry & Davis, B-247115, May 5, 1992, 92–1 CPD Sect 452.

Second, the government cannot announce one basis for evaluation and then make the award on a different basis. Nor can unannounced criteria (standards) be used unless there is a rational relationship between the standards and the announced evaluation criteria set out in the RFP. Greenhorne & O'Mara, B-247116.3, B-247116.4, October 7, 1992, 92–2 CPD para. 229.

Third, the source selection decision must be consistent with the documentation prepared by the SSEB unless the SSA can offer a rational basis justifying the award on another basis. A higher cost must result in greater benefit to the government. The decision of the SSA must document this position.

Generally, it is easier to support a protest based on a services contract than it is for a hardware contract. And it is easier to prevail where the government has established rigid and detailed criteria (and failed to apply them consistently) than where they have left themselves more discretion.

While it is true that statistically, relatively few protests are successful, one must take into account that many protests are filed frivolously in the heat of anger at being rejected. (Of 3,000 protests per year filed with GAO, about half are dropped within a week. But 700 go to a full decision. Of 400 filed with GSA, about 100 went to a decision.) Others are filed in frustration at the often high-handed methods employed by the government in evaluating and awarding contracts. (Such as the Air Force contract I mentioned previously.) However, a recent compilation by the GAO concluded that in *protests with merit*, over 35% of them had some success. About 100 protests per year end up in the Federal courts.

Most successful protests are attributable to three types of errors by the government:

1. Award based on best value was not based on actual government needs. Do not propose things just because they are nice to have if it is going to cost any more. You will be pricing yourself out of the competition, and the extra

feature will avail you nothing. That of course is the way it is supposed to work in a "lowest cost in the technically acceptable range" type of procurement. On the other hand, in a best-value type of procurement, the government is authorized to pay the additional cost for the extra benefit *if it can be proved that the extra feature serves an actual need to the user.* And it would appear from the documented rulings that the burden of proof is on the government to show this need in responding to a protest. "Nice to have" won't cut it. In fact, it has been held that the government must place a value to the technically superior feature and to trade off that value against a lower rated, lower priced offer. (*Grumman Data Systems Corp. versus Department of Air Force*, GSBCA 11635–P, 92–2 BCA Sect 24,999.)

2. Award was made without regard to amendments made to the original RFP. Oftentimes, the response to the many questions asked at the bidders' conference in themselves constitute a material amendment to the original terms of the solicitation. Then the government makes an evaluation and award based on the original criteria without regard to the amendments. (Probably a case of the right hand not knowing what the left hand was doing.)

3. Evaluation is made based on standards that do not relate to the evaluation criteria published in the solicitation. The standards, while not revealed to the public, nevertheless must track with the evaluation criteria (Section M) of the solicitation? Even in a best-value-type procurement, the standards, whether quantifiable or not, must bear a positive relationship to the evaluation criteria. The cost/technical trade-off must be made in the context of the criteria in the solicitation, or there are grounds for protest.

In summary, the best value concept is not new by any means. It has been with us for many years, but only in recent years has there been some attempt to implement it through the Office of Federal Procurement Policy, the GSA, and the various agencies through implementation memoranda. A significant body of case law has accumulated over the past two years that clarifies the application of the concept better than any policy letter could ever do.

The best value concept is limited to negotiated procurements which involve professional and technical services or the use of such services in producing products which are highly dependent on innovative approaches or solutions.

- The best-value approach authorizes the government to use wide discretion in the selection of a bidder who proposes a higher cost, if it can be proved that this higher cost actually meets a government need that falls within the general criteria published in the solicitation.
- The solicitation must stipulate that a contract will be awarded for the proposal that is "most advantageous to the government, price and other factors considered," or words to that effect.
- There must be a rational basis for cost/technical trade-offs taking into account the actual need for the technically superior feature, the application of the hid-

den criteria (standards) in relation to the evaluation criteria of the RFP; and the relative benefit to be gained as compared with an evaluated lower cost bid.

So there you have it. I hope I haven't discouraged anyone by pointing out the pitfalls, the aberrations, and the monkey business. But the prudent company would be wise to take into account these things before spending several hundred thousand dollars only to find out later that it was a lost cause from the beginning and the government was just leading you down the primrose path. I cannot emphasize enough the importance of having a marketing section that is capable of smelling out these things before you spend your money. Or in the alternative, having some of these factors working in your favor instead of against you. The competition is getting keener, and in direct proportion, the sophistication of both proposal writing techniques and the methods of evaluating them will grow. You can depend on it.

Chapter 7

Why Some Proposals Don't Make the Grade

"He who works with turkeys will never soar with eagles."
—Anonymous

Just about everything you find in this chapter, I've alluded to elsewhere in this book, but this is not a review. Now we are going to get into the nitty-gritty details of why proposals fail and how to avoid these failures. Let me tell you, when you don't make it to the BAFO, you have failed. And that can be a most embarrassing, humiliating experience. It happened to me just once, early in my career. However, that turned out to be a great learning experience. We went to the debriefing, which was presented in a commendably thorough and professional manner. Actually, it was a kind of turning point for me, because for the first time I got a faint inkling of what the proposal writing business is all about. (There were virtually no books on this subject at that time.) I honestly believe that if you absorb the contents of this book and apply what you have learned here conscientiously, you will never have to go through such an embarrassing experience.

The Six Reasons Why Proposals Fail to Make the Grade

I firmly believe that there are six fundamental reasons why proposals fail to reach the BAFO stage. Six and *only* six. I mentioned them in the Introduction of this book. Now we will examine them in detail.

1. Failure to *Organize* A *Disciplined* Proposal *Team*

I have italicized the operating words in the above heading, because they are all important: *organize, disciplined, team*.

Proposal writing is not what you would call a recreational activity. (One might think so, to observe the way some of them are conducted.) It requires a concerted effort, involving the integration of a multitude of disciplines, performed by people working in a compressed time frame, usually on an *ad hoc* basis, who often have little in common, and (sadly) have little stake in the outcome. We will get into that aspect of the problem in Chapter 9, but for now, we need only to look pragmatically at the means required to avoid failure.

The place to start, as always, in building an organized, disciplined team is with the organizational structure. The concept that underlies the success of any organizational structure is based on two factors: (a) the necessity of fixing responsibility for the achievement of well-defined goals in a specific, discrete, identifiable individual, and (b) a finite, recognizable incentive for the team to achieve that goal or else to expose themselves to potentially unpleasant consequences for negligence in not achieving it.

Remember back in Chapter 1 where we had a marketing organizational structure with a built-in chain of command with responsibility fixed from a designated individual in corporate management right on down through the corporate division that would be responsible for the performance of the contract when it was won? Well, now we are concerned with the extension of that organization down into the proposal team. And the concept and the principles are exactly the same here as there.

See Figure 7.1 for a model proposal organization. The proposal manager, remember, reports to the head of the sponsoring organization (the corporate entity that will be responsible for performance of the contract after it is awarded). The proposal manager reports to the individual who has ultimate responsibility for winning the contract. Why this individual? Because he or she is the only person who has control of all the resources (or the authority to obtain them) necessary to prepare the proposal and to perform the contract after it is won.

It is patently unfair to expect proposal managers to have this responsibility when they do not control the required resources—that is, the personnel, funding, facilities, and access to corporate management. The division president does have these resources. And when corporate management makes it clear to him that he (the division chief) will be held responsible for the outcome of the proposal, then like magic, his resources will become available to support the proposal manager. Why? Because the division chief has just as much stake in the outcome as the proposal manager.

You will note that I have a deputy proposal manager here. Of course you are going to say, "Ahah! He is contradicting what he said in Chapter 2 about the redundancy of deputies." Correct. But this is a special case. I have also stated that the proposal manager must be the person who will manage the contract after it is won. If the proposal manager has a demonstrated ability to manage proposals and knows how to write and critique others' writing, then fine, you don't need a deputy. But more often than not, the person who is best capable of managing the new contract

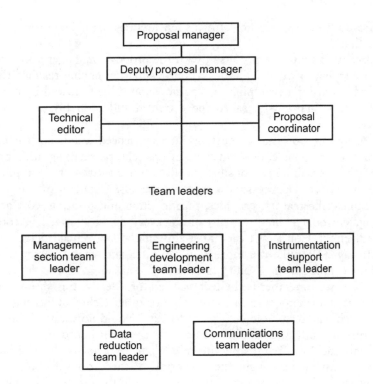

Figure 7.1 Organization of proposal team.

does not know beans about writing or managing proposals. Proposal preparation is a specialty requiring both a special talent and substantial experience to do it well.

So the solution is to appoint a deputy proposal manager who has these special qualifications to handle the day-to-day technical details of managing the proposal under the general supervision of the proposal manager. What? You can't afford the "luxury" of bringing in a deputy proposal manager? Go back to square one; revisit the Bid/No Bid decision. Either you should not bid this job, or there is not enough profit in this job to justify the expense of a deputy for two or three months. If you can't afford to do the proposal right, don't do the proposal.

Where do you find this individual? Either from the staff of the division chief or from corporate staff. Any corporation or corporate division that does not have such a person on its staff should set about obtaining one, or else start grooming one to be this person.

Moving down the organization chart, we find a "proposal coordinator" on the proposal management staff. The function of this individual is to relieve the proposal manager of the myriad of minor administrative details involved in the proposal, so that proposal managers can focus on what they are there for—to manage.

I remember when I first proposed this to my boss in one of the screwed-up companies I used to work for. He bestowed upon me his benevolent, condescending smile and said, "Don, we can not afford such luxuries here. The proposal manager can handle that."

So three weeks into the proposal, with the proposal manager about to become a basket case trying to work 18-hour days, the situation having reached the state of compounded confusion developing into panic, soon to be followed by paralysis, we finally got a coordinator who saved the proposal and probably just about everyone's sanity.

The proposal coordinator must be an experienced administrator capable of handling all types of people, devoted to detail, patient, persevering, unflappable, but decisive. He or she will be responsible for all administrative details: typing, acquiring the necessary word processors, security procedures, control of the paper flow, editing, technical illustrators, graphics, reproduction and printing, cost accounting, timekeeping, personnel—in short, just about every detail involved in coordinating the proposal effort. Control of the paper flow alone is a crucial detail. For a proposal worth say, $50 million or more, you can't imagine what a horrendous job just this one thing can be if you haven't been there.

The other staff member is the technical editor. Ideally, this should be an English major with some exposure to engineering or other technical writing, enough to understand technical terminology. This individual would normally come from division or corporate staff and would not have to come on board until after the first draft has had the Red Team and the management review. The technical editor should be the last person—with the exception of the proposal manager—who is allowed to even look at the proposal before it goes to the printer. This person is the professional who has the proper training to pick up the dangling participles; repair the split infinitives; rehabilitate the fractured syntax; find the missing commas, colons, and apostrophes; corral the rambling discourse so common to amateur writers, and in general make the whole proposal look like it had been exposed to some English-speaking person who has been educated beyond the 8th grade. If anyone messes with it after the technical editor has finished with it, it is guaranteed to get screwed up.

Next we come to the very heart and soul of the proposal organization, the team leaders. I regret to say that I've had a little trouble getting this concept across to the management people I've worked with around the country. It is unfathomable to me why anyone would prefer that the proposal manager should try to wade through reams of half-baked, raw proposal inputs to the point of exhaustion, when the process can be so easily remedied by a little decentralized supervision.

The team leaders should be chosen on the basis of who is going to run the organization after the contract is won, just as the proposal manager is chosen as the person who will manage the contract. The reason for this is obvious. If the key personnel who are going to perform the contract know they will be the ones who are going to live with it, then they have the incentive to ensure that the proposal (which will become the contract) is done right. Show me a proposal that is put together by people who have no stake in the outcome, and I'll show you a loser.

The individual who is going to be the business manager or administrator of the new contract, then, will be the team leader for all the administrative portions of the proposal—that is, personnel, payroll and accounting, industrial security, and so forth. Then logically, since the business manager or administrator is going to manage these functions on the contract, he or she should be the one who manages these functions in the proposal. He or she would be the person best qualified to review and critique the section on cost accounting or personnel and administration. The business manager or adminstrator would also be the person who would review the input from the industrial safety specialist, and, if it was not adequate or went off in the wrong direction, would set the specialist straight and return the input for another rewrite. When the business manager or administrator is satisfied that the safety input fulfills the requirements of the RFP and his or her concept of what the safety section should do and complies with the directions of the proposal manager, then and only then is it submitted to the proposal manager.

In this same manner each key management person proposed on the contract is personally responsible for supervising his or her corresponding segment of the proposal. Key management people thus have a personal stake in correcting this part of the proposal to the best of their ability. Furthermore, they become intimately familiar with the details of that entire section so that they will be fully prepared to answer questions at the orals.

Likewise, proposal managers, freed from the time-consuming ordeal of nitpicking their way through piles of garbage that careless or inexperienced contributors cut and pasted from irrelevant proposals and the like, will now have time to focus on the crucial thing they were selected to do—manage the proposal.

The duties of the team leaders then, will include giving guidance to the various contributors, reviewing their inputs, disseminating the information pertaining to the proposal effort, and ensuring that deadlines are met and that all required interaction with proposal management is accomplished.

The team leader concept decentralizes the burden of supervision so as to enable proposal managers to devote their time to the macro responsibilities of management. But it has the further and no less important virtue of establishing an operating chain of command without which no organization can function in a disciplined and orderly manner. Furthermore, the team leader concept facilitates the cohesion and teamwork that makes the whole proposal effort work. No one likes to work in an atmosphere where he or she is not sure whom he reports to or whether anyone will recognize him for doing a good job. No one wants to be part of a huge amorphous mass of people lost in the confusion and bureaucratic bumbling of a large, unstructured proposal effort. The typical proposal contributor, as is the case with any worker, anywhere, wants to feel that he or she is part of an identifiable, recognizable *team* whose final product is an achievement that will be acknowledged as such.

And, finally, the organization presented here, by fixing responsibility for specific segments of the proposal in specific ways, forces the key people to do their homework early on or else expose their lack of preparedness for all the world to see. No one wants to find himself in this position, so he will be impelled to buckle down and apply himself to the job, start the research, make his own preparations, study and analyze the available documents, and eschew the bull sessions.

2. Failure to Compose an Adequate Proposal Plan

No one can launch any kind of major endeavor successfully without first preparing a detailed plan of action. The purpose of a proposal plan is to document a complete, well-thought-out course of action to serve as a roadmap for the proposal team; a means of documenting the proposal manager's decisions, requirements, and intended use thereof; and, finally, a standard means of disseminating all pertinent proposal information to all members of the proposal team. Without a proposal plan, everyone drifts around in the dark, groping for the answer to the question, "What am I doing here?"

To be informed is to be involved, and the sooner the proposal team is fully informed of all background and other pertinent details, the sooner the proposal team will start looking like a team with a stated goal and the motivation to achieve that goal.

The proposal plan should be a manning document, a logistical document, and a coordinating document. It should also be an open-ended document, so that all information acquired or directives issued after the initial publication will be published as addenda to the original document.

The following is abbreviated example of a typical proposal plan.

Example of Proposal Plan

```
1.0   Basic Assumptions
      Expected RFP release date: o/a_____.
      Proposal due date o/a_____.
      Type of contract:  CPAF  (CPFF, FFP, or ?)
      Location of proposal preparation_____.
      Place of performance (POP) of contract_____.
      Expected competitors_____.
      Value of the contract: About_____ covering the full
      five five years of a 3 + 2 contract.
      Pre-RFP Bidders conference scheduled for_____at_____
      Technical proposal will be page limited to _____ pages.
      Management proposal will be limited to _____pages.
      Contract will be managed as a separate cost center.
      We will bid as prime. Five percent set-aside for small
      business subcontracts.
```

Phase-in period _____ days.

2.0   Organization of Proposal Team

Proposal Manager is John Doe.

Deputy Proposal Manager is Jane Doe.

Proposal Coordinator is Mary Lou Smith.

All other key personnel will be announced NLT end of month.

See Encl.1 for organization chart of proposal team *(Fig 7-1)*.

3.0   Duties of Key Personnel

Team Leaders will be responsible for all proposal inputs within their respective assigned areas. For example, the Instrumentation Support Team Leader will be responsible for everything listed in Section 3.0 of the SOW IAW Sect. L of the RFP and in fulfillment of criteria of Sect M. of the RFP. This will include guidance to the various contributors to this section, review of their inputs, dissemination of information pertaining to the proposal effort, ensuring that deadlines are met, and that all required interface with proposal management is accomplished.

The proposal coordinator (Mary Lou Smith) will be responsible for all administrative and logistic support to enable the proposal team to function. This will include arrangements for equipment and supplies, graphic arts and typing support, security of proposal material, work flow control, assembling of final draft, printing, binding, and distribution. She will be responsible for maintenance of the master volume of both the first draft and the final draft.

4.0   Proposal Procedures

The Proposal Manager will issue a general outline to the proposal team within five days after RFP release. Each team leader will ensure that detailed outlines be prepared in conformance to the general outline and submitted on time in accordance with the milestone chart (Encl 2). *(Fig. 7-2.)*

In general, follow the same sequence in proposal contributions as appears in the SOW.

Each major section will be separated by a tab divider. This divider will be imprinted with the overall organization chart for the contract, with the organizational units *responsible for performance of that section* highlighted to help the reader identify which organizational elements are responsible for performance of that particular function of the contract.

Use the following hierarchy for job titles:

Program Manager

(Department) Managers

(Section) Supervisors

Unit Leadman

Senior Technicians

Technician A, Technician B, Technician C

The contract organization chart and the work breakdown structure will be posted on the wall of the conference room NLT five days after RFP release.

Resumes. Team Leaders will be responsible for providing resumes of key personnel within their area of responsibility. Resumes will be limited to two pages and will be formatted in strict compliance with RFP instructions.

There will be only two official drafts of this proposal, both to be maintained by the Proposal Coordinator. The first draft will be delivered to the Proposal Manager only after Team Leaders have reviewed, critiqued, sent back to writers for rewrite and finally approved as fulfilling all RFP requirements.

After review by the Proposal Manager, these drafts will be turned over to the Proposal Coordinator for inclusion in the First Draft Volume. When the Proposal Manager has determined that this volume is ready for Red Team and management review, he will release it to the Red Team with instructions for their review. He will turn over an identical copy for management review to be conducted concurrently.

After Red Team and management reviews are completed, the Proposal Manager will direct the necessary rewrite, correction, make a final review and release it to the Editor for final edit.

```
5.0 Reference Material
```
Each proposal contributor will be provided a proposal package containing pertinent portions of the RFP, special instructions, and anything else deemed necessary to prepare the respective portions of the proposal. A library of additional information will be maintained at the proposal management office. All proposal contributors are *required* to familiarize themselves with the contents thereof.

```
6.0 Addenda
```
This is to be considered an open-ended plan. As changes occur and new information is acquired, addenda to this plan will be published. All members of the proposal team will keep a file of this plan plus the addenda, so that all instructions throughout the entire proposal cycle will be integrated into this one document.

Now here you have an example of an organization that knows how to prepare for a proposal effort. This company has the forethought to appoint the three most important key people to the task well in advance of the release of the RFP. The proposal manager has already done his homework by getting together with the marketing people and gathering an abundance of preliminary information on this endeavor, which he has compiled for this first iteration of the proposal plan. Some of the information must necessarily be speculative, but it is accurate enough for planning purposes. Remember, these are *assumptions*, and as further information is developed, it will be published in the form of addenda.

Obviously the proposal manager has been coordinating with the sponsoring organization manager and his staff, because he has already obtained their concurrence on the assignment of the two other key personnel to the proposal team. Note also that the propsal manager has worked out the broad outlines of the proposal strategy with management by announcing the decision to bid it as prime (no teaming arrangements or major subcontractor). Furthermore, he has worked out an agreement on administrative and logistical support, because he knows exactly where the proposal will be prepared. The remainder of the proposal team, the team leaders, are in the process of being selected. (It takes more time to extract these people from their current assignments because of the normal resistance of the field managers to relinquishing their "indispensable" subordinates for a month or two to work on a proposal.)

And, lastly, observe that the proposal manager has stated his *modus operandi* right up front, so that all will know what is expected of them from the very start. He has clearly set out the duties of the proposal coordinator and the team leaders. And he has shown the good sense to let them know what they can expect from him. He will publish a general outline and a contract organization chart within a specified time frame, so that the proposal team can proceed with their work without the usual dithering while the proposal manager spends his time enjoying the problem.

3. Failure to Establish A Timely Proposal General Outline

Why did the proposal manager commit himself to issuing the general outline within five days after release of the RFP? Because he knew from working on proposals himself that it is nearly impossible to start composing your portion of the proposal without knowing where it is going to fit in, knowing the general format, knowing how other pieces of the proposal fit together, and having some assurance that everyone is singing off the same sheet of music.

Let's take a look at the reasons why you have to have a general outline. The general outline:

- Constitutes the proposal manager's *interpretation* of the proposal instructions in the RFP.
- Incorporates into one document the roadmap for complying with the proposal instructions, the proposal evaluation criteria, and the method of addressing the SOW.
- Establishes the format of the proposal.
- Provides the starting point for the preparation of the detailed outlines that must be submitted by each contributor and approved by their respective team leaders.
- Facilitates the *assignment* of responsibility for the various segments of the proposal. "Paragraph 3.5 and paragraph 4.5.6 are assigned to Mr. Able."
- Is indispensable for the *coordination* of all elements of the proposal effort.

As the basic document of the entire proposal effort, the general outline is not a matter for the tinkering of amateurs or neophytes. This is a prime example of a case where the proposal manager, no matter how *technically qualified in his or her field*, should seek the active assistance of an experienced proposal specialist (the deputy proposal manager, if available).

I am appalled at some of the ineptness I've seen in the preparation of general outlines. I have seen cases where the whole RFP was outlined, even the general information provided as background for the bidders! How could the writer be expected to respond to that? In other cases, the *evaluation criteria* (Section M) was outlined—as a general outline! In others, the SOW was outlined, contrary to the proposal instructions. These are examples I've encountered in large companies, even with consultants, people who, one would think, had enough proposal experience to know better. I had to argue with management for four hours about this recently. I finally told them this is like arguing for four hours with the Flat Earth Society. In another case, I never was able to convince management how to best prepare an outline until a retired civil servant showed up at the meeting with a copy of the standards they had used on the SSEB the last time that contract was competed. It was the exact mirror image of the outline I had provided them. That convinced them.

I'll say it one more time. The general outline must incorporate (a) the proposal instructions, (b) the evaluation criteria, and (c) the SOW. The proposal instructions are the basis. It is mandatory that the outline comply with this, literally. All the rest has to fit into these instructions. The evaluation criteria must be the criteria upon which you judge the responsiveness of your outline. The SOW constitutes the meat that must be addressed in the proposal, and the outline should indicate the method of addressing the SOW, but *you do not outline the SOW or the evaluation criteria!*

4. Failure to Establish An Organization Chart

The proposed organization chart for the contract is the third pillar in the structure that the proposal manager prepares as the basis of all ensuing proposal activity. These three pillars—the proposal plan, the general outline, and the organization chart—must be prepared and issued by the proposal manager as soon as possible after RFP release, because the proposal team cannot proceed until they are. Any proposal manager worth his or her salt should be able to come up with a working organization chart down to the supervisor level within five working days after he or she gets his hands on the RFP.[1]

This five-day period is about right for the proposal team to settle in and analyze the RFP, do some preliminary research, locate the references it will need, and start to develop its concept of how it will address its respective portions of the RFP. Not until the members of the proposal team have the general outline and the organization chart in their hot little hands can they prepare their detailed outlines, their staffing requirements, and the organization of the operating elements (that is, below the supervisor level).

A word of caution here. Do not confuse the organizational structure with the work breakdown structure or contract work breakdown structure (CWBS), which is sometimes an RFP requirement (especially for large contracts and especially it seems, for Air Force and NASA procurements). The work breakdown structure is based on work packages; the contract organization is based on other criteria as fully described in Chapter 2.

Here again, I have seen the most inconceivable ineptness by some proposal managers leading to indescribable chaos in the proposal effort. I was brought in on one proposal where the proposal team was in the *last week* of the schedule and still did not have an organization chart to write to! Here was a proposal manager putting in 18-hour days trying to rewrite everyone's sloppy inputs, but he hadn't had time to come up with an organization chart. Of course the inputs were sloppy. No one knew who his or her supervisor was to report to in the contract organization,

---

1. Of equal importance in hardware contracts, especially those involving engineering development, system integration, and the like, are the block diagrams that define the system. This topic will be discussed in Chapter 8.

with whom or where he or she were to interface, or what staff elements—or line elements, for that matter—there would be. So all the inputs were weasel-worded generalities, mostly cut-and-pasted stuff from other proposals. Truly a disaster.

Even the smallest contributor to a proposal effort needs the perspective that only a well-drawn organization chart can provide. As to the technique of drawing up an organization chart that makes sense, I refer you back to Chapter 2. If you are to be a key person on any proposal, and if you have not fully absorbed the concepts propounded there, I advise you to go back and reread that chapter.

5. Failure to Establish A Hard-Nosed Schedule

This is another area where, I am sure, every proposal manager who ever lived has suffered grievous frustration. This is the area where discipline or lack thereof really manifests itself. There is absolutely no need for those 18-hour days that characterize so many proposal efforts. There is ample time provided by any RFP to complete any proposal without that sort of thing *if the proposal effort is done right*.

The problem often arises because the proposal manager is too circumspect about his own commitment to the schedule. He will be late in devising it, then post it without fanfare in an inconspicuous place, then let a few of the early deadlines go by without raising any fuss. So pretty soon, nobody takes the schedule seriously, and the next thing the proposal manager knows, it's panic time.

But more often this problem arises because there is no way of enforcing any discipline on the proposal team. And that is why I strongly advocate that the proposal team should to the greatest extent possible reflect the organization that will be performing the contract. That way there is a chain of command in place that will extend into the new contract, and there is an incentive for everyone to do his or her best, because winning the new contract means promotions and/or pay raises for all concerned.

As for the technique of preparing hard-nosed schedules that everyone can live with, see Figure 7.2 for a typical example. Note that about one-half of the allotted time is provided for the preparation of the first draft. Given the foibles of human nature, you can almost be sure that this deadline will slip a little, because, for one thing, it is most important that this first draft be done right. You can slip a little into the second half of the schedule, say as much as 10%, without serious consequences. (But don't tell that to anybody.) But what is most important is that proposal managers impress upon the team early on that slippages will be taken seriously and could have dire consequences for the members who miss deadlines. They accomplish this by setting some intermediate deadlines, such as the submission of detailed outlines and/or the operating element staffing tables. Then they scream like banshees when someone misses these deadlines (and someone will, as surely as night follows day). That way, everyone should get the idea that the schedule is to be taken seriously, and, if you are lucky, you might at least get the first draft submitted within a reasonable time.

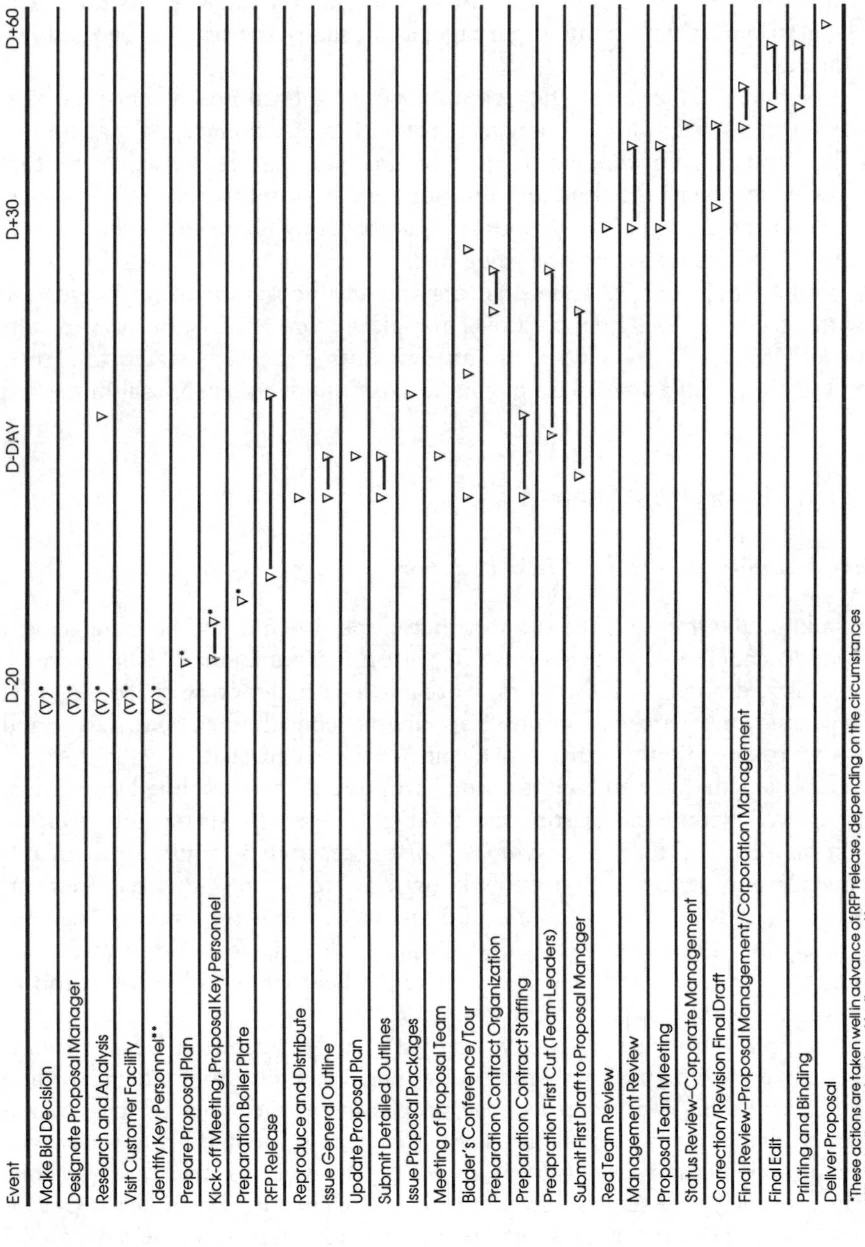

Event	D-20	D-DAY	D+30	D+60
Make Bid Decision	(∇)*			
Designate Proposal Manager	(∇)*			
Research and Analysis	(∇)*	∇		
Visit Customer Facility	(∇)*			
Identify Key Personnel**	(∇)*			
Prepare Proposal Plan	∇*			
Kick-off Meeting, Proposal Key Personnel	∇—∇*			
Preparation Boiler Plate	∇*			
RFP Release	∇——∇			
Reproduce and Distribute		∇		
Issue General Outline		∇—∇		
Update Proposal Plan		∇		
Submit Detailed Outlines		∇—∇		
Issue Proposal Packages		∇		
Meeting of Proposal Team		∇		
Bidder's Conference/Tour		∇	∇	
Preparation Contract Organization			∇—∇	
Preparation Contract Staffing		∇—∇		
Preparation First Cut (Team Leaders)		∇—∇		
Submit First Draft to Proposal Manager		∇		
Red Team Review			∇	
Management Review			∇—∇	
Proposal Team Meeting			∇—∇	
Status Review–Corporate Management				∇
Correction/Revision Final Draft			∇—∇	
Final Review–Proposal Management/Corporation Management				∇
Final Edit				∇—∇
Printing and Binding				∇—∇
Deliver Proposal				∇

*These actions are taken well in advance of RFP release, depending on the circumstances
**Both for the contract and for the proposal team.
(D-Day is the RFP Release Day.)

Figure 7.2 Milestone chart.

The biggest mistake I've seen in regard to schedules is that some over-eager (and under-equipped) proposal manager (or more often, middle-management type) will insist on "something he can look at" about a week after the RFP hits the street. So what he gets in that time frame is garbage, and usually the proposal goes down hill from there.

So, in summary, the successful proposal needs a hard-nosed schedule, prepared early on and posted in a prominent place with much fanfare, so that no one can miss the importance of abiding by it or be unaware of dire consequences that might follow in the event the deadlines are not met. It would be advisable to post alongside the schedule a list of the proposal assignments by name and a chart showing whether the deadline for each was being met.

The ultimate objective, of course, is to avoid at all costs the usual Wagnerian climax (with people dropping dead all over the place from exhaustion) that results when proposal teams take too cavalier an attitude during the early stages with their endless bull sessions and now end up having to write the whole proposal in the last ten days.

6. Failures in Management Support

Insufficient Administrative and Logistical Support

What I'm talking about here is the support that corporate and middle management must provide to enable the proposal team to perform its function. This support includes the typists, draftsmen, illustrators, word processors, working space, security, professional assistance (editors, proposal specialists, consultants), and, lastly and especially, the support of other corporate elements when requested.

For example, you have an RFP that your proposal team is qualified to address. Everything is well within the existing capabilities of the sponsoring organization from which the proposal team is drawn *with one exception*: a requirement for underwater metric photography. You don't know how to address this requirement, but you know there is a corporate unit 3,000 miles away that specializes in just exactly this discipline. My experience is that tapping into this corporate expertise is like pulling teeth. In fact, I've found it harder to get help from within the corporation in cases like this than to get it from strangers.

This example epitomizes what is wrong with the leadership in large corporations. No one in corporate has been specifically assigned responsibility for providing this support, so nothing ever happens. The proposal manager goes to the division chief (the sponsoring organization), and says, "We need some help from the corporate Oceanography Division on this SOW item." So the division chief calls someone in corporate and relays the request. So some guy in the corporate office calls Oceanography and says, "Hey, those guys out there in Nevada want some help on a proposal." And he forwards an extract of the SOW requirement that he received from the proposal manager to the Oceanography division. Well, the last thing this guy in

Oceanography wants is to send someone (especially any of his *capable* people) 3,000 miles to help someone he doesn't even know to work on a proposal. So he calls on the telephone and gives them some lip service. And if that doesn't satisfy them, he will give them some lip. "Well, the first thing you guys gotta do is hire some scuba divers."

"How many?"

"Oh, maybe four or five or maybe eight or ten."

"Well gosh, that is not much to go on. Can't you write up this part of the proposal for us and fax it?"

"Hey, whatta you think this is; we got our own work to do here. I gotta go now."

"The nerve of those guys," Mr. Oceanography mutters to himself before hanging up the phone and hurrying off to join his colleagues for a three-martini, two-hour lunch. And so it goes, while the poor beleaguered proposal manager starts getting ulcers on top of his ulcers.

The remedy, of course, as I have said over and over again in this book, is for the corporate CEO or equivalent to appoint a specific individual to be responsible for corporate support of each proposal—*not only the proposal*, but also for corporate support of the contract after it is awarded. This way, there is a specific named individual in corporate management who has a personal stake in the success of the proposal and a continuing responsibility after the contract is awarded. This way, any malfeasance, misfeasance, or nonfeasance by corporate management in its responsibility to support the proposal properly will inevitably come back to haunt that individual.

That is the most common administrative problem concerning the lack of *corporate* support. The most common problem concerning the lack of administrative and logistical support to be provided by the *sponsoring organization* is simply a general failure of prior preparation. Management consistently underestimates the magnitude and cost of a proposal effort. So you start out with one word processor, a proposal manager, and a couple of zombies to write it. Suddenly, after wasting much precious time going around in circles, it dawns on everyone that you are way behind the power curve, and you end up with a cast of thousands trying to avert disaster, which compounds the disaster.

The next most common problem is the habit of some organizations to put the whole proposal team in a conference room with telephones ringing, smokers smoking, talkers talking, and people running in and out. Total confusion! These "work places" are commonly called "boiler rooms" or "bull pens"—the latter, I would say, being the more appropriate term. How on earth can anyone do any analytical thinking or serious researching of problems under these conditions? No wonder so many proposals end up as nothing but a mishmash of cut-and-paste platitudes.

The conference room should be used for conferences. Each proposal writers should have a quiet space where he or she can think, meditate, reflect, research, create, write—with a minimum of interruptions. But, you know something? I have a hard time getting this concept across too sometimes. Why? Because it seems like there are a lot of windbags in the proposal business, and windbags need someone to listen to them.

Lack of Prior Preparation by Marketing

Some companies have aggressive, effective, "cracker jack" marketing organizations. Some have a collection of duds who do a barely passable job of impersonating a marketing organization. That is to say, they attend all the bidders' conferences, study the CBD, shuffle papers around to create the illusion of activity, and generally make a nuisance of themselves while using up their expense accounts, but never come up with a winner. If you work for the second type of company, and they want you to manage a proposal, it's best if you plead terminal illness and start updating your resume. Chances are, no matter how good a proposal you write, you will never overcome the company image that your inept marketing section has already created.

That is the first duty of a good marketing group—creating a favorable image of your company. The second is gathering intelligence. Not just on future bidding opportunities, but also on your competition—their weaknesses, their strengths, their intentions, and their political connections. The company thus armed will seldom make a foolish Bid/No Bid decision, because it will have all the necessary information on the procurement and on the competitive environment at its fingertips.

But all that information is virtually worthless unless it is disseminated in timely fashion to the people who need it. And that is the weak link I have observed even in outfits that have a great marketing organization. There is generally not enough—or not any—coordination between marketeers and that proposal team down in the foxholes.

Most marketeers work hard on the company image thing. They wine and dine and entertain the customer; they shake a multitude of hands and slap a lot of backs, and talk, talk, talk. But when it comes to taking notes, writing reports, conferring with proposal teams, coordinating their intelligence activities with the people who are going to write the proposal . . . well, they have more important things to do. And when it comes time to write the proposal, they are long gone.

I could count on one hand the times I have commenced work on a proposal in full coordination with the marketing people. And each time was an exhilarating experience. I was presented with a folder several inches thick describing almost everything I needed to know about the procurement as well as the expected competition, the weaknesses and strengths from which I could devise our themes, even accurate information on staffing and costs. This is what a really good marketing group can do.

Proposal Team Organization and Training

Many companies have the idea that all you have to do is gather together a proposal manager and several bodies and presto, you have a proposal team. As I have said before, proposal preparation is a specialty that must be learned. There is never sufficient time after the RFP comes out for a completely green team to learn what it needs to know through on-the-job training. That is why you need experienced proposal managers (or deputy proposal managers) and proposal coordinators. On-the-job training should be limited to some of the contributors (or writers) under the supervision of experienced team leaders. The wise company manager would be advised to hold company in-house seminars on proposal writing, especially for engineers and senior technicians who thus can someday be effective team leaders.

But a word of caution on whom you select for these seminars. Some people can write and some can't. It doesn't really correlate with intelligence or good job performance. Some people can talk, some can write, some have big feet, some have big ears. The ability to write well is a talent. And paradoxically, good talkers are seldom good writers. So you need to find the people who have the ability to express themselves well *on paper* before you send them to a seminar and plan to make team leaders out of them. The reason, of course, is that team leaders must know how to guide and correct proposal contributors in preparing responsive and articulate inputs. They must be able to recognize the difference between a well-thought-out input and the hot air of someone who is winging it. They must be able to tell a writer how to sort out an incoherent mess and turn it into an RFP-responsive input.

Lack of Management Coordination

The occasional detached, casual attitude of management as illustrated above in regard to the selection and training of proposal teams is manifested in another way: the lack of coordination of the work of the proposal team with that of the field units that are called upon to support the proposal. I mentioned in the Introduction the experience I had where all the key people I had in mind for the proposal team were allowed to schedule their vacations at about the time the RFP came out. (Believe it or not, the last proposal I worked on, they let the *proposal manager* go on a cruise midway through the proposal effort!

Other examples abound. The marketing people are off doing their own thing instead of being available to brief the proposal team on everything they know about the procurement and the competition. Reference material called out in the RFP is unavailable, because no one thought to stock such obvious documents as MIL-STDs, DOD regulations, and the like. Marketing knew there was a Tempest requirement in the proposal but neglected to tell anyone. Management knew there would be a cost/schedule control system criteria (C/SCSC) requirement, but neglected to train anyone in this technique. The RFP requires a top-secret facility clearance. No one thought to initiate action to obtain such a clearance. Once, when I was working for a billion-dollar company, I was sent 1,000 miles away on a bidders' tour only to find out halfway through the tour, that it was a small business set aside. Too many marketing directors and division vice presidents spend too much time playing "I'm the boss" and not enough time on the mundane activity of coordinating the details of what makes things work.

Another crucial area is the dire necessity for coordination of the bean counters with the technical personnel. It is natural that bean counters are interested only in the profit margin and safeguarding the company's capital. If they ignored these factors, they would not be bean counters for long. The engineer who manages the proposal, on the other hand, is mainly interested in adequately staffing the contract with well-qualified personnel, so that they can get the job done. (Especially if they are going to manage the contract.) So you have two diametrically opposite motivational factors meeting head on.

Enter the wise, experienced, commonsensical corporate management person. He knows from years of experience how to referee this argument. First he verifies that the proposal manager isn't trying to gold plate the proposal. He wisely knows that you don't bid things that are nice to have, but instead try to respond to the letter and the spirit of what the RFP requests. That is what the customer expects you to do. If he wanted gold plating, he would have specified gold plating. Applying the rules set out in Chapter 2, he streamlines the contract management staff and consolidates supervisory responsibilities in the line elements. He makes some changes in the skill distribution. "What makes you think you need all Tech A's instead of Tech B's and Tech C's in this unit?" And so on.

Then he looks at the cost proposal. "What makes you think we can win this contract with this G&A when there is virtually no risk capital involved? Take out the base fee. The competition will not bid a base fee on this type of contract. I am confident we can win at least 80% of the award fee. So what does that leave us? Not much, but that's good enough, considering there is virtually no capital investment and the fact that this contract has a great potential for growth."

Now that's the way good management wins proposals. By getting involved in the things that management should get involved in—namely the sound business judgments, the mature business decisions that come with years of experience and good common sense. Not the nit-picking and second-guessing of the mechanics of putting the proposal together (which is the proposal manager's job), or the opposite extreme—a detached, bemused indifference to the whole thing on the part of management, who knows they can just blame it on the proposal manager if it is lost, no matter their own incompetence in the process.

We had a good illustration of this in one of the companies I used to work for. The marketing director was competent enough and took an active hand in preparing the proposals, at which he was also competent. But the costing was done at corporate headquarters thousands of miles away. We would prepare the proposal and send it off to corporate for costing. We did our thing, they did theirs, and never the twain would meet. Well, given the conflicting objectives I described above and the fact that the costing was done at a higher level, it is not surprising that we were always out of the ballpark on cost and, therefore, always lost out. It might have been a big help if we could have gotten the president of the corporation to come in off the golf course once in a while to mediate the situation. So did management relieve the comptroller at corporate level? Of course not; they relieved the marketing director at the division level (the old story: search for the guilty, punishment of the innocent, and *noblesse oblige*).

Well, as it turned out, the new marketing director was shrewd enough to figure out what had been happening. And he had enough clout to demand—and get—an experienced costing specialist who reported to him right there in his own facility. Guess what. We started winning contracts one after another, a magical transformation! The only difference was, we were now able to cost our proposals realistically. And *everyone* was happy ever after, because now the comptroller could spend all his time out on the golf course with the president.

In concluding this chapter, I think it would be fitting to present to you good readers the Seven Steps to Stagnation.

1. "We've never done it that way."
2. "We're not ready for that yet."
3. "We're doing all right without it."
4. "We tried it once and it didn't work out."
5. "It costs too much."
6. "That's not our responsibility."
7. "It won't work."

The fact of the matter is, in my opinion, we have no shortage of anything in this country except good leadership. Corporate presidents with sound judgment, dedicated courageous leaders with a consuming desire for excellence and a clear vision of the future. Instead, too often what I've seen (with some notable exceptions) is a fraternity of good ol' boys, ever protective of their perks: their company cars, their golf club memberships, their expense accounts, their exalted status symbols the corner office, the ever-present yes men. This last is especially prevalent among retired military officers who have made the transition to corporate management. Whether a retired colonel or admiral, they always seem to have their private enterprise version of a valet (sycophant) whose function is still the same—namely to be the servile, flattering, fawning, obsequious flunky always there to aid and comfort them.

However, the end is near as America girds itself for the realities of the modern global economy. Even now we are going through a massive shakeout in all our industries in order to compete in a world where competition is global. We no longer can afford these anachronisms, and we no longer have any monopoly on anything. Thousands of these middle-management dinosaurs will soon become extinct, streamlined out of existence, replaced by computers, overtaken by technology and the real world out there.

Chapter 8
Special Applications

The road to engineering disasters is paved with false assumptions.
—Helgeson

So far in this book, I have tried to address the techniques of proposal writing in a generic sense. That is, what I've said up to this point will apply to about 90% of what anyone will confront as a proposal writer or manager. This chapter will attempt to address some of the remaining 10%.

Engineering Development Contracts

Engineering development is the process by which a variety of engineering disciplines is integrated through systems engineering techniques to transform a technological requirement into an operating system.

The Province of Professionals

Engineering development contracts are the province of professionals. If you don't have a staff with experience in engineering development contracts, stay away. It is no job for amateurs, no job for Joe's Garage–type operations.

I had some friends who worked for an outfit that, because of some early success in O&M contracts in the aerospace business, began to think they could walk on water. So they bid on a complex, interactive computer hardware project involving some wind tunnels. A substantial amount of software development was involved, and, would you believe, a firm fixed price contract? Well, unfortunately for them, they won the contract. Probably because every other possible bidder avoided it as one would avoid the plague.

Within months, this project was in deep trouble. Panic followed by sheer chaos followed by despair. Black boxes that nobody could tell what went into or out of, software in hopeless confusion and no end in sight. Ordinarily, the government would have canceled the contract and debarred the company. But it seems the government itself was having budget problems, so it became a low-priority project. The government thereupon craftily chose to hold the poor beleaguered contractor's feet to the fire, demanding specific performance of the contract.

My friends had to hire the services of a platoon of high-powered consultants at even higher powered salaries to pick up the pieces and sort things out. The system was finally delivered over a year late. They told me they lost $300,000 dollars on the contract. I'd believe $1,000,000. Result: End of company. End of story.

I hope that little anecdote will convince you that:

- Engineering development contracts are for the pros.
- One must be very wary of the contract terms, especially such things as fixed-price contracts and also what is in the fine print. I once did some work for a large aerospace corporation on a $100,000,000 contract, which we won. But the company walked away from it (a wise decision, in my opinion), because the fine print in the contract offered by the government imposed what amounted to strict liability for all consequences of any failure during the life cycle of the system. This could amount to several hundred million dollars.
- Finally, don't even think about bidding on an engineering development contract without some very careful planning first. And that is what I'm going to discuss next.

Mandatory Preliminary Planning Before Bid

The planning of any complex engineering development effort should begin with the preparation of a comprehensive engineering study. This study should be completed before attempting to make a preliminary Bid/No Bid decision, because an intelligent decision cannot be made without it. The engineering study must address the following:

- Definition of the problem;
- System performance requirements;
- Proposed solutions (preliminary design concepts);
- Generic cost trade-offs;
- Risk analysis;
- Feasibility assessment;
- Mathematical modeling (where appropriate);
- Logistical requirements; and
- Installation and integration requirements.

If, after such a rigorous analysis and study is made, a bid decision appears feasible, additional analysis and determinations will be made, as appropriate, *before the release of the RFP*. Normally you won't have time to perform these studies adequately in the course of the proposal period. If the customer can't or won't give you the information to make these studies before RFP release, don't bid it. You can be sure some other company somewhere has this information. You can't afford to waste your time and money with all these uncertainties facing you after the RFP comes out.

Okay, you have been provided the necessary information, you've made the engineering studies, and you've come to the conclusion that it is a viable bid opportunity. So here are some of the other things you should be doing as best you can with the information available to you *before* the RFP comes out:

- Determine an overall WBS;
- Determine system design trade-offs;
- Identify specific hardware components;
- Identify and define all GFE interfaces, especially software;
- Determine the magnitude of software development;
- Determine the nature of all external interface requirements;
- Finalize the system design concept and prepare block diagrams;
- Determine allocation of CI/CPCIs;
- Determine make-or-buy decisions;
- Commence preliminary negotiation of teaming arrangements;
- Commence preliminary negotiation of subcontracts;
- Identify vendors and get planning bids on hardware items;
- Price out software effort, if subcontracted;
- Compile estimated life cycle cost data;
- Gather all applicable reference material.

Don't be deterred by the fact that you do not have enough information to complete *all* these tasks; you rarely will. But this is what you should aim for, and in the course of your effort to acquire all this information, you will find exactly where the gaps are in your data bank and what you need to do to fill them.

Bid Strategy

Now, a few words about bid strategy. Every situation is different, of course, but here are a few rules that I think every manager should at least consider in the course of drawing up his proposal plan.

1. If follow-on production is indicated for the winner, bid low, even to the point of taking some risk. You can make it up in the production stage. The competition is keen and always will be. This is what the competition will

do, and you will never win anything without some risk. That's what free enterprise is all about.

2. Plan to subcontract anything you think can be done more economically by others. In any engineering development contract, 90 to 99% of the *components* that form the system already exist, either in the lab or off the shelf. Many otherwise intelligent managers keep trying to reinvent the wheel by in-house fabrication, running costs out of sight and ending up with an inferior product besides. Engineering development is essentially a systems engineering exercise, and don't ever forget it.

3. Corollary to #2: For components or subsystems you think you must develop in-house, first explore the R&D community. You will probably find that someone has already done a large amount of the R&D work or has already breadboarded a component similar to the one you need. Never underestimate the vast expanse and depth of expertise readily available out there. Our industrial prowess is such that anything can be built (or probably has been), so long as it does not violate the laws of physics or chemistry.

4. Make full use of all government furnished property (GFP/GFE) or customer furnished property (CFP). Sometimes there are such things available that are not listed in the RFP, and the government is happy to supply them at a fraction of the cost. I worked on a proposal once where transportation to a remote island in the Pacific was a requirement. With a little digging, we found that an amphibious seagoing craft was available, operated by the government for just such contingencies at a fraction of the cost of any commercially available vessel. And our customer in the government didn't even know it existed.

My final bit of advice, especially for those who have little experience in engineering development contracts is: Get a copy of every MIL-STD, MIL-Spec, AFR, AR, and DOD regulation and any other government publication that could possibly have a bearing on this procurement and make sure your staff is familiar with them, and, more importantly, that they apply them in every step of preparing the proposal. These documents are there to help and guide you in writing *any* proposal, but for anything involving hardware or software systems, they are your bible. Ignore them and you're dead.

Preliminary Planning Must Focus on Feasibility

The focus of your staff should be on gathering information. Don't let them get bogged down in the microdetails of the project. Engineers in general have a tendency to get too enthralled in pursuing the technical details of a problem to the bitter end without first gathering all the information required to consider alternative approaches. Keep the preliminary effort on the macro level and on the information-gathering level. If this part has been done adequately, the details will come much easier when you are ready for the system development phase.

Grants

This book is basically a book about winning contracts, and a grant is not a contract. As a matter of fact, the preparation of proposals for grants is generally a much lesser effort than the preparation of proposals for the contracts we have been studying in this book. There are, however, many similarities between these two types of effort, and because of that and the fact many proposal managers eventually get drawn into the world of grants, I'm including an abbreviated treatment of the subject here. I once started to write a book on the subject, but concluded that there were already enough good books on grants and that the world didn't really need another one. So I'm giving it a broad-brush treatment here and if you are serious about it, I'll refer you to some other references at the end of this chapter.

You may not be aware of it, but grants are big business in this country. There are currently over 30,000 private foundations, 1,500 corporate foundations, and 40,000 separate government bodies in the United States. The total of all grants in the U.S. runs to well over $100 billion annually.

History of the Grants World

First, a very brief history of grants. It was all started innocently enough by great philanthropists like Carnegie and Rockefeller, who dominated the grants world from the 1880s through the 1920s. These grants were for the purpose of improving educational advantages such as libraries and for promoting the arts, the ballet, opera, symphonies and the like. However, by 1965, we had 25,000 private foundations, 95% of which had been formed since 1945, and they will probably continue to grow in number in direct proportion to the soak-the-rich tax legislation passed by Congress. That's because, on the theory that private foundations perform a public service (not always true), they are granted tax exemption.

The doctrine of crisis intervention originated with the Roosevelt administration to meet the very serious economic emergency situation where local governments could no longer cope with the consequences of the Great Depression. And so was born the National Recovery Act (NRA), the Work Progress Administration (WPA), the Agriculture Adjustment Administration (AAA), the Civilian Conservation Corps (CCC), and so on through the alphabet. This extension of Federal constitutional powers into local government was a revolutionary step taken with the best of intentions and dictated by necessity. But, as in most revolutions, it started out with good intentions, degenerated into a prolonged period of disorganized and self-destructive excesses, and finally culminated into a somewhat more pragmatic state, which is where we are today.

Where we go from here depends on the big spenders in Congress and the patience of the long-suffering, middle-class taxpayer. For tax-free foundations do deprive the government of revenue that the middle-class taxpayer has to make up. And *government* grants, of course, are totally funded by the taxpayer. Why neither the

Congress nor the press nor other "watchdogs" of the public purse—nor the taxpaying public—has ever demanded closer scrutiny of the grants world is a mystery to me.

Of course, I'm not complaining about such respectable institutions as the National Institute of Health or the National Science Foundation or the work of the various DOD components and the many other Federal and private foundations that contribute mightily to our fund of knowledge and to scientific progress. Grants in aid to such institutions are probably largely responsible for this country's preeminence in the field of science and medicine. If you need proof of this, take a look at the list of Nobel Prize winners since the 1950s. Prior to that time, most of the winners were British or German.

But on the other hand, take a look at some of the sorry examples of profligacy and foolishness perpetrated on the working people of this country. Here is an example from Sen William Proxmire's Golden Fleece awards.

- A National Institute of Mental Health grant for $97,000 to study ethnic and class relationships among Indians and non-Indians in Peru. Title of final report: "The Peruvian Brothel, A Sexual Dispensary and Social Arena." In other words, a study of whorehouses in Peru.
- And here is a state grant of $24,000 from the California Department of Corrections for a program of transcendental meditation for convicts.

This sort of thing is still going on *ad nauseum* in spite of Proxmire and the precious few in public life who are at least trying to slow it down.

Unfortunately, this sort of thing detracts from all the positive things that can only be accomplished by grants. There is virtually no way, for example, that pure research (versus applied research) can be funded other than by grants. This is because it is difficult to frame a contract that adequately defines nebulous research projects when the outcome cannot be quantified or even predicted. So grants can and do fill this gap admirably.

So much for background. Let's get down to the nitty-gritty of preparing grant proposals. Before we go any further, however, and before you waste any time or money preparing a proposal, you must be aware of some very important limitations in acquiring a grant.

Dinstinctions Between Grants and Contracts

First, how do grants differ from contracts? Contracts are initiated by the fund*er* who advertises a need; grants are initiated by the fund*ee*, the one who wants the money. (And who identifies the need.) There is much more rigorous evaluation of performance, quality control, and budgeting in a contract than in a grant. Contract proposals are much more demanding and comprehensive than grant proposals. Generally, this is because the dimensions of a contract usually embrace a multiplicity of disciplines whereas grants are limited in extent to one topic.

Grants applications nearly always consist of standard forms to fill out. (See Figure 8.1.) The proposals, however, may sometimes run to as much as 200 or even 1,000 pages, depending on the complexity and the magnitude of the funding involved. Generally speaking, grants are funded at smaller amounts than contracts. Accordingly, grants commonly require a somewhat greater amount of proposal work per dollar of funding than contracts.

Grants are generally limited to nonprofit organizations. Grants are classified according to purpose, contracts according to method of payment (i.e., CPAF, FFP, etc.).

Elements of a Grants Proposal

Here are the key components of grant proposals:

1. *A cover letter.*
2. *An abstract* (a brief summary of the proposal).
3. *A budget.* Some foundations prescribe a budget form to fill out. In any case, you should list your personnel staffing, with a justification for the job of each person and the number of man-hours required and the cost per hour. These must be the burdened costs—that is, the basic hourly pay plus cost of all fringe benefits. Show also any donated time that is planned. Then list other direct costs (ODC) such as travel expenses, supplies, equipment, rental space, utilities, subsistence, insurance, consultants, and so forth. Then list indirect costs such as general and administrative (G&A) expense, overhead, and the cost of doing business. This is a means of recouping some of the cost of preparng your proposal.
4. *Organizational structure.* This is roughly comparable to the management plan in a contract proposal. Provide an organization and function chart showing names of key personnel and their duties. Describe how policy is made, decisions are arrived at and communicated, interfaces, and feedback systems, pretty much the same as you would for a contract organization. You need to demonstrate a capability for strict accountability of funds and time expended.

   You should provide a staffing table showing the number of dedicated personnel by type and the number of days or hours planned for each phase of the project. It is also necessary to provide resumes of all key personnel and a job description for each. Note: For many types of proposals, such as R&D or artistic performance, this could be the most important part of the proposal. Also remember to tailor the resumes so that they correlate to the project objective, leaving out the irrelevant data.

   And bear in mind that an important part of your organizational structure will involve your plan for evaluating the performance of the project. You must provide for some outside evaluation, either from the sponsor, the

Form approved
OMB No. 0925-0001

DEPARTMENT OF HEALTH AND HUMAN SERVICES PUBLIC HEALTH SERVICE	LEAVE BLANK		
	TYPE	ACTIVITY	NUMBER
GRANT APPLICATION	REVIEW GROUP		FORMERLY
FOLLOW INSTRUCTIONS CAREFULLY	COUNCIL/BOARD *(Month, year)*		DATE RECEIVED

1. TITLE OF APPLICATION *(Do not exceed 56 typewriter spaces)*

2. RESPONSE TO SPECIFIC PROGRAM ANNOUNCEMENT ☐ NO ☐ YES *(If "YES," state RFA number and/or announcement title)*

3. PRINCIPAL INVESTIGATOR/PROGRAM DIRECTOR

3a. NAME *(Last, first, middle)*	3b. SOCIAL SECURITY NUMBER
3c. POSITION TITLE	3d. MAILING ADDRESS *(Street, city, state, zip code)*
3e. DEPARTMENT, SERVICE, LABORATORY OR EQUIVALENT	
3f. MAJOR SUBDIVISION	3g. TELEPHONE *(Area code, number and extension)*

4. HUMAN SUBJECTS	5. RECOMBINANT DNA
☐ NO ☐ YES { ☐ Exemption # _____ OR ☐ Form HHS 596 enclosed	☐ NO ☐ YES

6. DATES OF ENTIRE PROPOSED PROJECT PERIOD	7. DIRECT COSTS REQUESTED FOR FIRST 12-MONTH BUD-GET PERIOD *(from page 4)*	8. DIRECT COSTS REQUESTED FOR ENTIRE PROPOSED PROJECT PERIOD *(from page 5)*
From: Through:	$	$

9. PERFORMANCE SITES *(Organizations and addresses)*	10. INVENTIONS *(Competing continuation application only)*
	☐ NO ☐ YES { ☐ Previously reported OR ☐ Not previously reported
	11. APPLICANT ORGANIZATION *(Name, address, and congressional district)*

12. TYPE OF ORGANIZATION	13. ENTITY IDENTIFICATION NUMBER
☐ Public, Specify ☐ Federal ☐ State ☐ Local ☐ Private Nonprofit ☐ For Profit *(General)* ☐ For Profit *(Small Business)*	14. ORGANIZATIONAL COMPONENT TO RECEIVE CREDIT FOR BIOMEDICAL RESEARCH SUPPORT GRANT Code ☐☐ Description

15. OFFICIAL IN BUSINESS OFFICE TO BE NOTIFIED IF AN AWARD IS MADE *(Name, title, address and telephone number.)*	16. OFFICIAL SIGNING FOR APPLICANT ORGANIZATION *(Name, title, address and telephone number)*

17. PRINCIPAL INVESTIGATOR/PROGRAM DIRECTOR ASSURANCE: I agree to accept responsibility for the scientific conduct of the project and to provide the required progress reports if a grant is awarded as a result of this application. Willful provision of false information is a criminal offense *(U.S. Code, Title 18, Section 1001)*.	SIGNATURE OF PERSON NAMED IN 3a *(In ink. "Per" signature not acceptable)*	DATE
18. CERTIFICATION AND ACCEPTANCE: I certify that the statements herein are true and complete to the best of my knowledge, and accept the obligation to comply with Public Health Service terms and conditions if a grant is awarded as the result of this application. A willfully false certification is a criminal offense *(U.S. Code, Title 18, Section 1001)*.	SIGNATURE OF PERSON NAMED IN 16 *(In ink. "Per" signature not acceptable)*	DATE

PHS 398 (Rev. 5/82)

Figure 8.1 Sample grant application.

funder, or perhaps from an auditing team where peer review is necessary as in an R&D project. So how will your organization provide the necessary interfaces, the gathering and recording of data which the evaluator needs to measure the success of the project?

5. *Related experience.* This is the place to cite your experience in achieving other similar objectives either through grants or contracts. Provide a brief history of your company, a description of your facility, your resources both in personnel and equipment, a statement of your financial status, other financial backing, a history of your cost control experience, and anything else that would persuade the funder that you are reliable, competent, and experienced in performing the kind of work that will further the aims and objectives of the funder.

6. *An introduction.* Here you outline the basic concept, the nature and scope of the problem you want to solve; the geographic area of activity, the benefits to be achieved, the importance and significance of the project, and your credentials for performing it. This is where you establish the theme, set the tone and focus of the proposal. The introduction should be a brief overview, a selling job, very much comparable to the executive summary of a contract proposal. But here the emphasis is somewhat different. Here you *must* show how your project will *further the funder's goals.* Show the relationship between your project and the avowed objectives of the funder. But be brief and concise. The proof and backup for your statements can come later.

7. *Purpose and objectives.* Start with a broad overall statement of the purpose, the mission, or goal of the project and then list the specific objectives (a breakdown of the overall objective) and the benefits to be achieved. You must convince the reader of three things here: (a) that your objective is practical (especially that it serves the purposes of the foundation), (b) that your objective is attainable, and, finally, (c) that its success is measurable in finite terms. The objective must state actions—followed by a measurable result thereof. Do not get confused with methods here. That will come later.

8. *Problem definition and need.* Here is where you demonstrate your familiarity with the problem, your recognition of its complexities and ramifications, and your credibility for understanding the problem. The problem must be described using hard, provable facts, not speculation, and by applying clear logic in setting out the parameters and significance of the problem. There are a number of ways available to help you document the need.

   a. Show evidence of a demand for action by citing news media coverage, statements of public figures, government surveys, etc.

   b. Statistical data gathered by independent studies, other foundations, "think tanks," activist groups, and lobby groups.

   c. Documentation of limitations of existing programs, prior failures, and alternative programs.

   d. Comparison of actions taken in other countries to solve the problem. (Generally, funders hate to see other countries getting ahead of us.)
   e. References to the scientific literature bearing on the problem and its relevance to subject project.
 9. *Methodology.* Start with an introductory statement that establishes that: (a) you know what has been accomplished already in this field and what has been tried and what has failed; (b) you are aware of the potential hazards, impediments, or challenges to be overcome; and (c) you are aware of the various options or alternatives available and the relative merits of each.

   Next you must present a practical, step-by-step plan for carrying out your objective. This is the place where you must really show your in-depth expertise on the subject. Present your activities in logical sequence, chronologically from beginning to end, from generic to detailed, from simple to complex. Both the what and the how and usually how many or how much. This will require the use of milestone charts, flow charts, or even pictures to illuminate your explanation or make it clear and understandable to the reader.

10. *Evaluation and reporting.* Many neophytes in this environment are shocked when they find out that a plan for objective performance data, evaluation, and reporting are also required for a grant proposal. They think it is sufficient to propose a pie-in-the-sky program and just hope that some good will come of it. Any prudently managed foundation or agency will not consider your proposal without a convincing plan for evaluation of its success or failure.

   Other than measuring how well the project succeeds in meeting its stated objectives, the evaluation process serves other purposes. It provides a feedback mechanism for monitoring the progress of the project. It provides the basis for determining whether funding should continue or be terminated. It provides, especially for government-funded programs, a comparison of the success of the project with other similar projects elsewhere, or a comparison with other baselines such as no program or a similarly funded program. Here are a few of the tasks that a good evaluation plan should address.
   a. A clear definition of the project objective in quantitative, measurable terms;
   b. Identification of the variables that affect the outcome.
   c. Data collection methods.
   d. Data analysis procedures.
   e. Reporting procedures.
   f. Responsibility for and distribution of the final report.

Why Most Grant Proposals Are Rejected

Many studies have been conducted for the purpose of analyzing the reasons for the rejection of grant proposals. These studies are in general agreement that the major causes for rejection are (a) carelessly or inadequately prepared proposals and (b) uncertainty about the competence of the applicant. You might say that these two factors are tied together. If your proposal is sloppy, chances are you are deemed incompetent too.

Other reasons why proposals fail to get funded include missing the deadline, ignoring the page limits set by the funding agency, failing to adequately justify every person assigned to the project or every proposed purchase, and, oftentimes, poor writing skills.

From what I've seen, I would say that most unfavorable impressions are due to inarticulate proposal writers. They may be brilliant in their technical field but inept at expressing themselves on paper. If this be the case, hire a consultant. Because organizing material and writing fluently is definitely even more important here than in contract proposals. The reason? You are addressing more academically oriented readers—more often than not, college professors—than is usually the case in contract proposals. And you can be sure they do not take kindly to illiteracy.

Some other suggestions: Unlike contract proposals, do not wait until the deadline to turn in your proposal. Turn it in as soon as you are satisfied with it. The earlier the better. (The rationale here is that in competitively awarded contracts that usually go on cost, there is too much chance of "leaking" the bid price of a proposal that arrives early to one of the customer's favorite bidders. This is not a factor with grants. Here it is more a case of the early bird gets the worm, or at least the most attention.)

And finally, never forget that you are trying to fill a need that is within the objectives of the funders. If you don't convince them of this, you're out of it.

Most people in the grants field would agree that the most important aspect of any grant proposal is how well the proposed idea meets the interest of the funding agency. If the idea is novel, interesting, or opens the door to new areas of research, it will get good scores. If it is something that has been done already by twenty other groups, then it does not have a chance regardless of how well it is written.

Originality of thought or process is of paramount importance. Then if you add good organization, reasonable budgeting, solid methodology, and a reliable system for measurement of results, you may have a winner.

The hit rate for most grants within the NSF and NIH (which are at the pinnacle of the grants world, professionally) is about one out of five or six. Most people do not get funded on the first attempt. However, those who have a good idea and get a modest score should keep on trying. If you respond to the comments of the reviewer in a positive fashion, your chances of being funded the next time around are excellent.

As I said in the beginning, some foundations or granting agencies will specify with varying degrees of precision what they want to see in a proposal; many will provide forms to fill out. But in the absence of specific instructions to the contrary, what I've presented here should provide the minimum you need in any grant proposal.

Bibliography

For further reading in this area, I recommend the following books:

- *The Art of Winning Foundation Grants*, Hillman & Abarbanel, Vanguard, 1975.
- *Getting a Grant*, R. Lefferts, Prentice-Hall, 1978.
- *The Money Givers*, Joseph C. Goulden. Random House, 1971.
- *Grants—How to Find and What to Do Next*, Virginia P. White, Plenum, 1975.
- *The Fleecing of America*, Senator Proxmire, Houghton Mifflin, 1980.

Research and Development Contracts

Throughout the 1970s and '80s, an enormous R&D effort, driven by the expediencies of the cold war and the very real threat to our national security from the Soviet Union, was expended in developing sophisticated military technology. And what a remarkable fallout has resulted from this effort! Incredible advances in the state of the art of computer technology, fiber optics, telecommunications, laser systems, artificial intelligence, simulation techniques, rocket propulsion systems—the list could go on and on. But most important of all, it brought on the collapse of the Soviet threat, so that we could then turn our full attention to developing the instruments of commerce and to the vision of a better world for all humanity.

The Small Business Innovative Research (SBIR) Program

So now, how to turn this vast pool of engineering and scientific talent into the production of innovative products for peaceful uses in the commercial world? Well, one way that the government is accomplishing this is through the Small Business Innovative Research (SBIR) program, which is the main subject of this section. This and similar programs will now enjoy increased emphasis as we continue the process of "turning our swords into plowshares."

The SBIR program was initiated by the Small Business Innovation Development Act of 1982 with the objectives of (a) stimulating technological innovation, (b) strengthening the role of small business in meeting R&D needs, (c) fostering and encouraging participation by minority and disadvantaged persons in technological innovation, and (d) translating the results of R&D into commercially viable products for the market place. This program is administered by the Small Business Administration (SBA) and implemented through eleven government agencies: the departments of Agriculture, Commerce (mainly through the National Oceanic and Atmospheric Administration (NOAA)), Defense (DOD), Education, Energy (DOE), Health and Human Services (HHS) (through the Public Health Service and the National Institute of Health (NIH), and Transportation, and the National Institute of Mental Health (NIMH), etc.), NASA, the National Science Foundation (NSF), the Nuclear Regulatory Commission (NRC), and the Environmental Protection Agency (EPA).

Numerous surveys have confirmed the fact that most new products and inventions emanate from the efforts of the small business community. More than half of all new product innovations are attributable to small businesses, and the SBIR program is an enlightened government's effort to encourage and perhaps accelerate this trend. Currently, the government has budgeted $1.6 billion to support this program.

The advantage to be gained by small business is that it provides an opportunity for firms with limited capital to initiate R&D programs without incurring unacceptable financial risks. The SBIR program provides funding for the early stages of R&D efforts and even some profit in certain cases.

The *quid pro quo* for the government is eminently fair. It may receive a royalty-free license in copyright material and appropriate acknowledgment in publications. It may receive a royalty-free license for the use of products that result. But copyrights and patent rights are retained by the small business. Rights in technical data, including software, remain with the contractor, with the government reserving a limited right to use such data for government purposes.

Teaming arrangements and limited partnerships are permitted so long as the eligibility requirements of a small business are met. A minimum of two-thirds of each Phase I project must be carried out by the proposing firm. For Phase II projects, a minimum of one-half. And for both Phase I and Phase II, the principal investigator must be in the employ of the proposer. (The various "phases" are described in detail in following pages.)

Ample information is available to anyone who is interested in participating in the SBIR program. The place to start is with the SBA office nearest you. Check the telephone directory. All 11 agencies issue schedules through the SBA of topics within their respective jurisdiction for which they will entertain proposals.

For in-depth information on any particular topic, contact the agency directly. The program managers within the agency are completely open and free with all information at their disposal. That's what they are there for. The only exception would be the disclosure of any information which would give an unfair advantage to one offeror over others.

There are many other sources of information available to the prospective bidder. And you should avail yourself of every one of them before you proceed with the decision to bid on one of these projects. The DOD, for example, has the Defense Technical Information Center (DTIC), which is the central source of scientific and technical information resulting from other projects and describing R&D projects that are funded by the DOD. The DTIC prepares a technical information package on each SBIR project. I cannot emphasize strongly enough the necessity of doing a prodigious amount of homework before you start.

So much for the background information. How does the program work, and how do you get started? All R&D projects under the SBIR program are conducted in three phases.

Phase I will be concerned solely with the determination of the scientific and technical merit and feasibility of ideas submitted. It will typically be just one-half person-year effort over a six-month period. The government is authorized to award up to $100,000 to the winner of an award for this Phase I effort. The object of the six-month effort will be to prove the scientific and technical feasibility and technical or scientific merit of the proposed effort. Only those who are successful in winning the Phase I award will be eligible to submit proposals for the Phase II effort. The Phase I proposal is strictly limited to 25 pages, including the cover sheet. The measure of Phase I success will include an evaluation of the extent to which Phase II results would have the potential to yield a product or process of importance to the agency *and* the private sector.

Phase II awards will be made to contractors on the basis of results from the Phase I effort and the scientific and technical merit of the Phase II proposal. Phase II awards will typically cover two to five person-years of effort over a period generaly not to exceed 24 months. Phase II is the principal R&D effort and is expected to produce a well-defined deliverable product or process. The deliverable will typically be a prototype, a breadboarded circuit, a chemical process, a diagnostic procedure, a working system in the laboratory stage, a detailed test procedure, or the like, together with a final report. Awards up to $750,000 are authorized for Phase II contracts.

Phase III of the SBIR program contemplates funding by the private sector, applying the proof of feasibility and production of prototypes envisioned by Phases I and II. Since the goal of the SBIR program is to convert government-supported R&D into commercial products, proposals that demonstrate a potential for follow-on funding by the private sector will be more favorably considered in Phases I and II. It is therefore imperative that you, the proposer, commence to secure a commitment from private industry to fund Phase III efforts and to include this commitment in your Phase I and II proposals. Also, under Phase III, federal agencies may award non-SBIR-funded follow-on contracts for products or processes that meet the mission needs of those agencies.

So that, very briefly, is how the program works. For the innovative small business entrepreneur, it provides a marvelous opportunity to fund an in-depth feasibility analysis of your idea and development of a prototype to test it, all without incurring debt. This federally funded R&D can serve as both a technical and pre-venture capital base for ideas that may have commercial potential.

Traditionally, the Department of Defense has been by far the largest participant in this program. Currently it is estimated that the DOD will fund about 1,000 Phase I proposals at about $70,000 each. A recent program solicitation that I happen to have lists 330 topics by the Army alone. Generally speaking, the larger the agency, the better the chances of winning a contract. For the Air Force, the win ratio (the ratio of proposals submitted to awards made) may be as good as five to one. All of DOD's proposal reviews are done in-house. On the other hand, the NIH, the second largest funder, subjects all their proposals to peer review from outside sources. Their win ratio is also in the neighborhood of five or six to one. These and other agencies, such as NASA, the DOE, and the NSF, account for the bulk of SBIR funding. The other agencies have a poor win ratio; the Department of Agriculture, for example, has only about a 20-to-1 win ratio.

Do Your Homework When Making a Bid/No Bid Decision

The place to start, obviously, if you are interested in proposing one of your devil-ishly clever ideas to one of the SBIR agencies, is to make a carefully considered Bid/No Bid decision. But here, even more so than with other contract bids, you have an abundance of homework to do before you arrive at that decision. First, you have a marketing job to do. For small businesses, this will usually be performed by one of your more versatile technical people. And that is just as well, because here more than ordinarily you need a depth of expertise in the field of effort just to understand what it is you are looking for.

This technical expert must make contact with his or her counterparts in the appropriate government agency and maintain this contact on a continuing basis in order to find out everything he or she can about the *modus operandi* of this agency, its funding priorities, the personalities involved, the agency's prior topics, the specifics of the technical area in which you contemplate proposing, and their past history of contract awards. Find out what the agency is really interested in and discuss the general outline of your concept with their technical staff. Such open contact is permissible up until the solicitation comes out. After that, in order to ensure fairness, they are not allowed to talk to you.

At the same time, you must make an objective appraisal of the potential of your idea for future commercial application and funding. Also its application to other agencies, because these factors are very important to the government in evaluating your proposal.

Then you must make a search of the literature and poll the scientific community, if possible, to determine the current state of the art. Possibly, someone has already thought of the idea and published a paper on it. Possibly you have an idea for extending the work already done or for making a significant modification to previous work on the problem that will substantially improve the solution. If not, then your decision will have to be negative.

If, on the other hand, your search convinces you that your approach is original and your idea is innovative, will meet a need of the agency, and has a potential for commercial application, then proceed. Now you must evaluate your capabilities and background for successfully performing the work. Remember, your firm must actually perform two-thirds of the work to completion of Phase I of the project. This means that your principal investigator must actually be in your employ. You can hire consultants, but you can't have a consultant as the principal investigator. The principal investigator should be a recognized authority in his field. That is to say, he or she must have published a number of papers in the technical journals and be recognized as an authority by the scientific community.

If you have surmounted all these hurdles successfully, you are now ready to decide on the themes, the angles, and the thrust of your proposal that will persuade the evaluator that you deserve to win over all other competitors. In other words, one of the last things you do is strategize your proposal and bounce it around among your technical staff to see how it plays.

And finally, the last item: Can you afford it? This proposal will cost you conservatively between $5,000 and, say, $12,000. It all depends on the cost of your labor, since the other proposal costs are relatively minimal. And remember, you are not reimbursed for the proposal costs. You should also consider the costs of the Phase II proposal effort, because it doesn't make much sense to bid on Phase I unless you are planning on continuing into Phase II. The chances of winning Phase II, by the way, are considerably improved over Phase I—a win ratio of about 2 to 1.

The Criteria for a Winning Proposal

Before getting into the mechanics of preparing a good proposal, let's take a look at just what makes a winning proposal. Of course, technical excellence and innovative ideas are the two most important overriding factors. But consider the most important specific features of a winning proposal:

- Meeting an important need of the agency;
- Meeting a need of other agencies, as well;
- The potential for private sector commercial application;
- The reputation of your principal investigator (PI);
- Your perceived knowledge of the state of the art;
- Past R&D history, especially the PI's experience;
- The quality of your work plan;
- The commitment of private sector funding for follow-on;
- Minority or female ownership of your firm; and
- The availability of adequate facilities and equipment.

Now take the two or three strongest of these features that you can propose and be prepared to weave your themes around them subtly and persuasively into your proposal.

Now you are ready to start preliminary preparations for writing your proposal. First, study carefully the solicitation instructions and then the topic headings provided. These headings should provide the basis for your proposal outline. Use the same headings for your outline.

The Four Steps in Preparing R&D Proposals

Step 1: The Literature Search

You must determine what has already been done in this area. You should have done most of this before making your Bid/No Bid decision. Your literature search should be limited mostly to what has been done in the field in the past two years. You must be able to show how previous research is related to this project. I would recommend that you review at least a dozen reports in your literary search, bearing in mind that you are going to build your work plan around what turns up in the literature search. The results of your literary search should tell you which of four thrusts you should adopt in preparing your proposal:

- You are presenting an entirely new concept.
- Your work will extend an existing theory into new areas.
- Your work will provide a better solution to a problem.
- You are presenting a new approach toward a solution.

Step 2: Organizing the Proposal

Generally, you must follow the outline and format of the solicitation in organizing your proposal. As in any proposal, try to anticipate what evaluation criteria the agency will be applying. Determine what is the key information you will be presenting in your proposal.

Start out by crafting a statement that embodies the thrust of your proposal (one of the four listed in Step 1).

As a guide in gathering your material, your proposal must provide the answers to five questions:

1. How much funding do you need?
2. What do you want to do with it?
3. How will you spend it?
4. What results do you expect to achieve?
5. What qualifications do you have to achieve the results?

It's a good idea to organize all the material you have gathered under these five headings and then apply the answers to the above questions to the appropriate headings in your proposal.

Step 3: The Work Plan

This is a job for your Principal Investigator. This is, of course, the most important part of your proposal, because it outlines the methodology that you propose to apply in proving the feasibility and technical or scientific merit of your idea (Phase I). This section should take up about one-third of your proposal—that is, about seven or eight pages. The work plan must be a detailed, explicit description of your Phase I approach. It will describe the methods by which you plan to achieve each objective or task. It will describe what you plan to do, how it will be done, where it will be done, and when. It will prescribe a schedule of major events, including when the major product will be delivered. And finally, it will describe exactly just what the major deliverable will be. In most cases for Phase I, this will be the final report, but you must detail what you will include in the final report.

The work plan will provide a detailed definition of the problem and a review of the state of the art in solving the problem, including an analysis of existing developed systems. It will describe the design of experimental work for proving the feasibility of your solution and the major R&D tasks. You will need to prepare a statement of work and where applicable, a work breakdown structure.

Mathematical modeling concepts must be described along with flow charts, chemical equations, block diagrams, schematics and whatever else is necessary to inform and persuade the reader that you have a viable approach to an innovative solution of the problem.

I have discussed the preparation of the work plan first, because it should be the first thing you actually draft in preparing your proposal. The reason is that the work plan is the very core of your proposal, and all else flows from that. Drafts of other sections of the proposal can be prepared concurrently, but ultimately everything must be coordinated with the work plan. I recommend that the PI also prepare a first draft of the abstract also, because he or she should have already had a lot of experience in drafting abstracts or he or she wouldn't be a PI. Also, the draft of the abstract should provide a guide to others working on the proposal. However, the final draft must be prepared and approved by management, for reasons which I will explain later.

Step 4: First Draft and Abstract

The first rule, which I have tried to pound into everyone's head from the very beginning of this book is: Follow the directions issued by the agency for whom you are preparing this paper. *Literally.* This is no place for creative, freestyle writing.

You will be provided a document that includes proposal preparation instructions and requirements. They will invariably prescribe a format. The format for most agencies will be roughly as follows:

1. Cover sheet.
2. Project summary. This will include an abstract and, frequently, other requested information.
3. Identification and significance of the problem.
4. Technical objectives.
5. Work plan.
6. Related work.
7. Relationship with future research or R&D.
8. Potential post-applications.
9. Key personnel.
10. Facilities and equipment.
11. Consultants.
12. Prior, current, or pending support.
13. Cost proposal.

First, a few general comments about your writing style for SBIR proposals, then we will look at a few of the headings listed previously, and then you are on your own. Here, even more than for other proposals, your style must be simple, straightforward, and concise. You have a lot of ground to cover in just 25 pages, so you can't waste any words or space. No matter how esoteric the subject may be, you must make the reader understand it the first time. Use words with precise meaning so that you will not have to repeat or rephrase anything a second time. Remember, the evaluators have several other papers to read and, in most agencies, a very limited time in which to read them. Their mission is to eliminate proposals, not to preserve them. Your proposal must stand alone. You can't refer them to other extraneous material to make your point. Everything you say must be carefully organized and flow in a logical train of thought by presenting facts in such a manner that the facts themselves are persuasive. You must sound authoritative and confident, dynamic and decisive. Obviously this will take some editing and reediting by careful, skillful writers. It's much more important here than in most other proposals. If you don't have skillful writers, hire a consultant who is. The preparation of your abstract alone can make or break your proposal.

And that is what we are going to discuss next. Your abstract should run about 200 words. It should be a kind of checklist of your proposal, touching on every main point. You may not want to believe this, but many reviewers freely admit that they never go beyond the abstract in eliminating a proposal. If the abstract does not excite their interest, does not stimulate their anticipation that what follows is going to be a professional presentation of an interesting innovation or advancement in the state of the art, well, they have several other proposals to review, and their time is very limited. So all that work in crafting a superior work plan and all the rest is down the drain!

A good abstract will address all of the following points in the following sequence in approximately one sentence each. If you get to the end and find you have less than 200 words, you might be able to add a sentence where it will do the most good.

1. Define the problem you are going to solve.
2. Tell why it is important to solve this problem.
3. State your approach for solving this problem.
4. Describe your methodology. (In Phase I, you would outline how you are going to prove the technical merit and feasibility of your approach.) Note: Notice how, thus far, this format is almost exactly the same as the one I suggested for starting a proposal input for any other proposal? The thought process is essentially the same.
5. Describe the results you expect to achieve from your work.
6. Describe the quality of your R&D team, especially the PI.
7. Describe your firm's background and related experience.
8. State the commercial viability of the proposed solution and the likelihood of private sector follow-on funding.

In preparing the abstract, it is imperative that the words you use will weave in the thrust of your proposal, the themes, and any angles you may have to distinguish your proposal from all others. Try to use words with impact. No one said this would be easy. That's why I said it requires skillful writers and careful editing and re-editing.

Now, back to some of the other items you will be required to address in your proposal.

Related Work

Here you want to describe the background of your firm in performing other work of this nature, especially as it relates to this project and how the work of your firm is contributing to the advancement of the state of the art in this particular field. Focus on the relationship between the successful completion of this Phase I effort and what is to be achieved in Phase II. Also tell how your work interfaces with other R&D that has been conducted in this area.

Potential Post-Applications

The evaluators want to know how this technology can be applied to (a) use by the Federal Government and (b) use by the private sector. It will help immensely here if you have secured a commitment for follow-on funding in Phase III and can describe the nature of this funding and from whom you will receive it.

Key Personnel

The evaluators are interested mainly in your principal investigator. I recommend you cite at least five technical journal articles authored by your PI if the project is basically research oriented rather than applied research. The more research oriented the project (i.e., basic research) the more emphasis there will be on advanced degrees, publications, association with universities, and so foth. The more involved with applied research it is, the more emphasis on management experience, patents, engineering development achievements, or even technical society or community awards. I recently saw an announcement of a NASA SBIR award for "Enhanced Reality System for Improved Manual Arc Welding." You probably would not need five technical journal articles for that one.

I would allow about one-third of your proposal for these last three items, leaving the last third for such things as the facilities and equipment and your cost proposal. It would be ideal if your firm already had adequate facilities and equipment to support the project, and it would surely win you some points if you have available sophisticated equipment like mass spectrometers, Cray computers, and the like (because it would indicate the high-tech nature of your firm). But all that is really needed is a respectable facility, reasonably equipped to carry out the ordinary type of operations in your field. What you need to do in this case is to delineate exactly what special equipment will be required and be prepared to cost out its use (lease or buy) in your cost proposal.

One word of caution here. Don't try to cut the corners in order to keep the cost down. Your proposal will be judged on realism and on your understanding of the problem. Understating costs may be grounds for rejecting you. (It also might cause the reader to wonder how many other lies you've told.)

Cost Proposal

The solicitation will provide you with a format for estimating your Phase I and Phase II costs. Many agencies, including the DOD (but not the NIH), permit a fee or profit. All winning proposals will be funded under negotiated contracts either cost plus fixed fee (CPFF) or firm fixed price (FFP). The FFP is definitely favored by the government.

You need fill in only those cost items that are applicable to your project. They want only that information that will enable them to understand how you plan to use the requested funds if the contract is awarded. In most cases, you will be required to list all key personnel *by name* and the number of hours of dedicated direct labor by each. You must also show your labor overhead (burdened labor costs);

your G&A; your travel costs, if any; and consultant costs. Remember, consultant or any other nonemployee labor costs are limited to one-third of overall labor cost.

You may also have to use special test equipment or instrumentation to be provided by the government (either lease or buy). If it is to be bought, the title to such property remains with the government. Unless your firm has extensive experience in costing out government contracts, you would be advised to secure the services of an experienced government cost accountant.

Phase II Proposals

The purpose of Phase II is to expand on the results of and further pursue the development of Phase I. Awards are for periods of up to two years in amounts up to $750,000. The Phase II proposal will be much more demanding than Phase I, although the format is generally the same. The work plan, for example, will require double the space used in Phase I. The detailed instructions for preparation of Phase II proposals will be provided to all Phase I winners at time of award. The success of the Phase II proposal will depend largely on two factors: (a) the success of the Phase I effort as evidenced by the Phase I final report and (b) the potential for commercial (either government or private sector) application. If the Phase I final report proves the soundness and technical merit of your approach, and if it proves your firm's capability to continue the project into commercialization, and if the end product will have significant commercial value, the chances of your winning a Phase II award are excellent. Phase II evaluations may include an on-site evaluation of the Phase I project by the government.

Your proposal may show the commercial potential of your project by private sector commitments for funding in both Phase II and Phase III or by your firm's past record in commercializing new products. Or you may present other evidence of commercial potential in your proposal. If you have secured a funding commitment for Phase III, you should submit this with your Phase II proposal, showing specific amounts and when the funds will be available.

In conclusion, I firmly believe there is a very substantial opportunity for every small firm in the country that has any significant innovative capability. The SBIR program was initiated when we were still in the depths of the cold war. With the subsequent downsizing of military requirements and the consequent shift to peaceful products, there is a whole new ballgame out there. Military R&D will continue. The Army budget alone shows research, development, and acquisition projected for $11.3 billion in 1995, $10.2 billion in 1998, and $10.7 billion in 1999. But the future funding of SBIR will likely be expanded to benefit other agencies of the government, to maintain America's dominance in the world of high technology, and to introduce new products which stimulate economic activity.

But here I must reiterate the theme I have preached throughout this book. You cannot expect to win contracts (or grants) without doing a professional job of preparing a proposal that applies all the instruction which has been presented here.

Sadly, some of the efforts I have seen in preparing such proposals (especially grants) looked like the musings of a bunch of laid-back young dilettantes concocted over six beers at the local pub. A document brimming with enthusiasm and naiveté and totally lacking in organization or discipline. Good things happen only through organized, diligent effort.

Chapter 9

What Every Proposal Manager Needs to Know

If you can keep your head when all about you are losing theirs,
If you can trust yourself when all men doubt you,
If you can dream and not make dreams your master,
Yours is the earth and everything [you're after.]
—Kipling

This chapter will be devoted to providing some guidance and assistance to the proposal manager, an individual who has one of the most challenging jobs to be found in the business world—that is, *to do it right.* Actually it is an easy job, if you want to do it wrong; just call frequent meetings, and let everyone know you are the boss and that you expect everyone to work at least 14 hours a day to show your company loyalty. That's the way some proposal managers do it.

Establish the Extent of Your Authority

My first words of wisdom for the eager, conscientious about-to-be proposal manager would be to get a clear and unequivocal understanding of the extent of your authority in managing the proposal. Refer back to Chapter 2. You cannot manage anything unless you have authority commensurate with your responsibility. That means you must have control over the resources it takes to do the job.

Control of Required Resources

The manager of the sponsoring organization has the responsibility to provide you the resources in personnel and materiel and suitable working space. But once the

---

185

proposal process begins, he and everyone else must get out of your way and let you control the operation. You must have total control over these resources without interference, kibbitzing, or unwanted assistance. If management doesn't trust you to handle the job without looking over your shoulder and meddling in the process, then tell them to find someone whom they do trust. I can't emphasize this enough. You cannot manage anything when someone else is meddling in the process. Repeat after me: "Authority must be commensurate with responsibility."

Selection of Key Personnel

Your authority must include a reasonably free hand in selecting the key personnel for the proposal team. No one can write a proposal by him or herself. And that is what you will be doing if they send you a collection of unmotivated cast-offs for your proposal team. Ask yourself this: "Are other managers or supervisors going to *volunteer* you their very best talent? Or will they send you the person they can most easily do without for the next few weeks or months?"

As pointed out earlier, the team leaders of your proposal team should be the key personnel who will make things happen or not happen on your new contract. You, as the proposal manager and the potential manager of the new contract (the ideal situation), are in the best position to evaluate the background of the people who are going to be your key people, and you should be the one to select them.

Corporate Support

You are going to be selecting some people who are now key personnel in someone else's organization. And, you can depend on it, the managers of those organizations are going to cry and whine and howl when you try to take away one of their "indispensable" people. That's why you need to get an understanding from your management on this beforehand. Of course, you have to use some common sense. You can't expect to take more than one of anyone's key people. Spread the burden around.

Second, you must establish the concept that your company has an obligation to provide you backup support commensurate with the importance of winning the contract. First management must back up your authority to control the resources needed to do the job. Then they must provide the resources in materiel and personnel to do an adequate job. The only way you can have some assurance that this backup will actually be provided is to demand that a certain individual be designated in writing to have the primary responsibility of providing this direct support and that a certain named individual in corporate have this same responsibility to provide *corporate* backup support.

As a parting shot on this subject, please be advised that managing a proposal is not the place to practice experiments in democracy or to engage in a popularity contest. You have a difficult job to do and a grave responsibility in spending a lot of your company's money. And you are expected to spend it wisely and effectively.

Your superiors and all the world will hold you accountable if the money is wasted in a sloppy, unproductive effort. And the system is very unforgiving of wasted efforts.

On the other hand, no one can complain if you have conducted the proposal effort in an orderly and systematic manner, employed all your resources to their maximum potential, made all your decisions resolutely and in a timely manner, and produced a proposal worthy of your company. And that is the purpose of this chapter—to help you realize this goal.

By way of summarizing what I have said so far, you must:

- Establish the concept that you will be granted authority commensurate with your responsibility—the authority to exercise complete control over all the resources needed to prepare the proposal. This must include assignment of personnel to the proposal team, selection of key personnel to propose for the contract, a major role in establishing the proposal funding level, an equal voice in determining costing strategy and in major decisions on contract staffing, and freedom from harassment or interference in carrying out your mission.
- Having an official designation, in writing, of the individual who is responsible for providing direct proposal support (normally, the manager of the sponsoring organization) and the individual who is responsible for providing corporate support at the corporate level.

If you can't get a firm commitment on these things, the chances are you are doomed to be a sacrificial goat in a lost cause. My advice in such case would be, as a minimum, to start updating your resume. Then you might consider pleading illness or perhaps *non compos mentes*, because that is probably what you will end up with if you undertake this job without such commitment.

Let us proceed. Your benevolent and enlightened management has enthusiastically bestowed upon you the firm commitments discussed above, so what do you do now?

Do Your Homework

The very first thing you must do is start gathering all the information you can get your hands on regarding this proposal effort. You get hold of those marketing people who have been tracking this opportunity for the past few years or months and pick their brains and read their marketing reports. What? They are too busy on something else now? They haven't prepared any reports? Go to the sponsoring organization manager and start pounding on some desks. You have a written commitment that you will get the proper support to do this job. Right? Suggest that the manager contact corporate and ask them on what basis they made a Bid decision on this effort if they have not gathered any marketing information. And if they do have the information, you want the full cooperation of those marketing cats now, not later. In short, this is a good time to test the system.

It is imperative that you quickly become the most knowledgeable person in your company regarding this proposal effort, because you are going to be asked a thousand questions by your proposal team and management, and you must have the answers. And you must have the knowledge upon which to base a thousand minor and major decisions. And you must make these decisions instantly. Otherwise your proposal team will soon lose confidence in you, and they will start looking elsewhere for the answers.

Organization of the Proposal Team

Concurrently with this information gathering effort, you must start immediately to plan the organization of your proposal team. Presumably, you know enough about this project to determine the nature of the tasks and subtasks that will comprise the subject contract. That's why you are the proposal manager. You should be able to come up with a tentative, rough idea of what the contract organization chart should look like. That is, what the principal line elements (based on the end products of the contract) the principal staff elements are. From this you can envision what kind of people you want for your key personnel to manage the contract and where these personnel will fit in to the organization. These will be the key personnel you will want as team leaders on the proposal. Next, you make a tentative list of names of people who fit the description you have in mind and where you get them (i.e., where they are presently assigned).

The Proposal Plan

Concurrently with this, you must start the preparation of your proposal plan. You will want to get this disseminated at a time well in advance of the release of the RFP, so that all the others involved in the proposal will have adequate prior notice to enable them to begin their own planning. And that time would be as soon as you have gathered enough information and made some of the basic decisions upon which those others can base their planning. Of course, there will be many gaps in your data bank at this time, but you can fill some of those in with intelligent assumptions (labeled as such). (The content of the proposal plan is amply covered in Chapter 7.)

Instructions to the Proposal Team

As soon as possible after selection of all key members of your proposal team, you must convene a meeting of all hands. At this time, you make available all known information and reference material pertaining to the proposal effort: marketing reports, briefing material, correspondence, old proposals, references, and the sources where additional information may be obtained. Then you must carefully outline exactly what you expect of each of the key people, especially the team leaders.

Specific Responsibility of the Team Leaders

Team leaders are chosen for their special expertise in the various disciplines involved in the contract. Therefore, each team leader will be assigned the responsibility for producing an acceptable first draft of the segment of the proposal corresponding to his or her area of expertise. An "acceptable first draft" means that team leaders are responsible for instructing, reviewing, critiquing, rewriting, and correcting this part of the proposal to the point that what they submit to the proposal manager is the very best they (and their subordinates) are capable of doing— that it fulfills all the requirements of the RFP (the proposal instructions, the SOW, and the evaluation criteria) and follows the format dictated by the general outline.

Notice that I say "assign responsibility." You, the proposal manager, cannot *delegate* responsibility. The responsibility for the proposal always remains with you. You can delegate *authority* but not responsibility. And that is why your job is not finished when these first drafts are submitted to you. You have the responsibility to review with a critical eye and critique and return for correction these first drafts, so that the second (and final) draft is as near perfect as you can make it.

The selection and orientation of these team leaders is a critical step in the proposal process. If you can accomplish this step successfully, the remainder of the effort should be immeasurably easier. It's easy to see why the ideal situation is a proposal manager who will be the future contract manager and a selection of team leaders who will be the future key leaders in the new contract. That way, there is an existing chain of command that will continue into the new contract. Without an existing chain of command, there is little motivation for the team leaders to perform their exacting jobs in a diligent manner such as to please the proposal manager. Most technical people hate to write their own part of a proposal, much less review and critique some one else's. But if they are aware that their boss on the proposal will also be their boss on the new contract, they are much more motivated to do a thorough and conscientious job on the proposal.

Before moving on to other things, there is one other point to make on the organization and functioning of proposal teams. And that concerns interfaces. You, the proposal manager, are the single point of contact for any direction coming down the chain of command. The manager of the sponsoring organization is the point of contact for any direction coming from corporate. Likewise for any requests for assistance passing up the chain of command. This procedure is imperative in order for you to control your proposal team and for the manager of the sponsoring organization to control his resources.

But here is where many amateur managers get altogether confused. Each and every member of your proposal team must have a free hand to ignore the chain of command in gathering the information needed to prepare their respective portions of the proposal. They should have an unfettered access to anyone in the corporation for this purpose, because time is of the essence. They have a very limited time in which to accomplish their mission. There is a vast difference between direction and exchange of information. Your team leaders (and others as well) should be *encouraged* to seek out and get information that will help them write the proposal wherever it may be found. And it would be a good idea to document this concept in the proposal plan, so that all the world is aware that top management has authorized these contacts. You must not tolerate any of this "Nobody talks to any of my people without going through me" garbage. I'm making a point of this because it has happened to me, and it will happen to you, too, sooner or later.

Okay, we have selected the proposal team and issued the proposal plan. I have discussed only the team leaders, because the other key members—the proposal coordinator and the editor—have been described elsewhere in this book.

The next thing you may be asking is how best to control this daunting endeavor. There are several well-established devices for ensuring the control and feedback that you need to employ in order to keep this project from getting out of hand. We have already discussed one of them, the proposal plan. It is a control and feedback mechanism because it sets out standards and objectives for the team and instructions for achieving them. It is also a benchmark for you to evaluate progress and performance.

The General Outline

But there are other devices, especially the general outline. You must get this general outline disseminated to the troops within five days or less, because this is where you interpret the proposal instructions and other pertinent parts of the RFP. It constitutes the roadmap for all to follow, and no one can begin to write the first draft without it. And unless you have had some experience in making general outlines, by all means get help from wherever it may be available. But get it, because as I have observed over and over, it is too important a job to be left up to amateurs.

Once you have a general outline, you can assign with precision the various segments of the proposal to your team leaders. For example, "SOW paragraphs 3.7, 4.5, and 4.8 assigned to John Doe." Actually, what you must do is have a large chart made up by your draftsman that lists in one column *every* item in the RFP that needs a response and in another column gives the name of the corresponding writer followed by the calendar days and an indicator of the various milestones. Post this chart in the conference room for all to see; use a color code to indicate the progress of the proposal in such a way that it is clear at a glance who is failing to meet the various deadlines.

Intermediate Deadlines

You must set several intermediate deadlines, the most important of which is the completion of the first draft. If you see someone who is consistently falling behind early on, find out why and take action immediately. Maybe he or she needs help, maybe just a little intimidation, but you can't tolerate missing these deadlines, or your whole proposal effort will suffer in the end.

The best way to avoid this situation is to demand a *detailed* outline within a specified number of days after the general outline is published. And follow this up with a deadline for the *thematic* outlines. These should be critical milestones for you, because they will tell you who is too inept to be allowed to continue on the team, and they will also provide you a good opportunity to make a federal case out of meeting deadlines. If you tackle this problem early on, it will go a long way toward avoiding the panic situations which follow inevitably when the proposal team is allowed to procrastinate in the early stages. And believe me, it *will* happen unless you take aggressive, resolute action early on.

The Organization Chart

An equally important early requirement for you, the proposal manager, is the organization chart, which should also be made available no later than five days after RFP release. Again, no one can start to write anything without it. This, too, must be posted in the conference room for all to see. Besides being the structure upon which the whole proposal concept is built, it also provides you a means of coordinating the activities of the proposal team. It is the basis for establishing all the interfaces involved in the program. It is also the basis upon which all staffing decisions are made.

As in the case with the general outline, this also is too important a step to be left to amateurs. So if you don't understand what you read in Chapter 2, then get some professional assistance. If you did absorb what you read in Chapter 2 and know how to apply it, then proceed with confidence. You will undoubtedly get a ration of unwanted advice from all sides about how to construct an organization chart. (Everybody thinks he or she is an expert on organization charts.) If any of these self-proclaimed experts cannot correctly define for you the distinction between a staff function and a line function, then tell them to buzz off. Don't let them waste your time.

Before we move on, it is imperative that I say a few things about the work breakdown structure (WBS) or the contract work breakdown structure (CWBS). For those of you not already familiar with this, I urge you to study MIL-STD 881A and any implementing documents you can find. The WBS is a very effective management tool for planning and assigning management and technical responsibilities; for exercising control over and reporting of progress and status of engineering and construction projects; and for resource allocation, labor cost estimating, cost tracking, and life cycle cost estimates. Do not confuse the WBS with the contract organization chart. The WBS is a compilation of work packages, having little direct relationship to line or staff function, chain of command, and the like. The main reason I mention it here is to warn you against being bamboozled by an RFP that includes a customer-furnished CWBS. Remember, it is a compilation of work packages. Do not think you have to construct an organization chart to conform to it. Some proposal managers I've seen start assigning a supervisor to every work package they see and really come up with some bizarre results that way.

Sometimes a CWBS is required by an RFP and, in that case, it would be advisable to prepare it in coordination with the costing people, as cost tracking is one of its most useful functions.

In its ultimate application, it is the basis of the cost schedule control system criteria, which is often a requirement in very costly programs, especially system development programs. If you, the proposal manager, see C/SCSC as a requirement or even hear of its possibility appearing in the RFP, take immediate measures to seek assistance, as this is a requirement for specialists with experience in this area.

Meetings

Now a word about meetings. Two general meetings should suffice for the whole proposal process: one after the proposal team has been selected, at which time you distribute the proposal plan, and the other shortly after the RFP has been received. Ideally, at this seond meeting you should be ready to issue the general outline and post the organization chart and the schedule in the conference room. Each of these meetings should be structured. You should have a prepared agenda of exactly what you intend to accomplish. The primary purpose of these meetings should be for you to direct, instruct, and provide information of use to the team. The secondary purpose should be for you to listen to suggestions, complaints, questions, and solicit information. Every meeting should start with you in charge and end with you in charge. It should have a definite purpose and end with action items for certain designated individuals.

An enormous amount of time is wasted in aimless, rambling meetings replete with the musings and irrelevant chatter of unfocused dilettantes intent on wasting everyone's time while they run their mouths. I would wager that the manhours wasted every single day in the conference rooms of America would be equivalent to the number of manhours required to build the Taj Mahal.

Once the RFP is out, you most definitely do not have time to waste. However, you do need feedback devices, so I would suggest you have an informal meeting, never to exceed one hour, at the beginning of each morning and consisting of only the key personnel, for the purpose of brief progress reports and an opportunity to air any unexpected problems that may arise. You should try to limit these meetings to a half hour, but you do need to have them daily in order to be able to take immediate action to avert problems before they arise.

The Costing Effort

So now that you have your proposal team organized, instructed, and sent forth to perform their respective missions, your next concern (and second most important task) is to coordinate the costing effort. True, you are not an accountant, and there are cost accounting experts assigned to perform this function. But you, the proposal manager, are responsible for the whole proposal, and you have a duty both to your company and to yourself to see that there is a proper balance in the decisions that go into the cost proposal.

Coordination with the Bean Counters

You have to remember that there are two conflicting factors at work here. The engineers and business professionals who write the proposal and who will be responsible for managing the contract are primarily interested in the pragmatic considerations of getting the job done, hiring the best people in adequate numbers, getting the best equipment to do the job, and so forth. Costing considerations are just an annoying impediment to them. The bean counters couldn't care less about your technical problems and the state-of-the-art equipment. Their only concern is turning a nice tidy little profit so that their boss will glow with pride at their astute performance and the company president will be able to buy himself a new Mercedes.

So you, the above-it-all proposal manager, must strike a reasonable balance between these two conflicting objectives. First, you must learn the language of bean counters (if you haven't already). You must talk about G&A, cash flow, other direct costs (ODC), fee structure, burden rates, minimizing risks, long-range versus short-range risks, revolving funds, and all that.

That is the only language they understand. Don't talk to them about technical difficulty, software development problems, the ramifications involved with the hardware interfaces, and the like. They are grandiloquently unconcerned with these annoying trivialities. Try to convince them that "we are all in this together" and that you want to work with them to reach a practical consensus in arriving at a realistic cost. My advice is not to try to nail down any concrete agreements with them too early. Wait until the proposal has reached the point of no return in the schedule. At that point they will probably be more amenable to compromises on margin of profit, cash flow, and so on, because there is no turning back then. If all else fails, appeal to your corporate backup for assistance, because it is vitally important to you that the proposal be costed realistically. If not, all your hard work will have gone for naught.

Staffing

When it comes to staffing, you will have the reverse of the previous problem with your team leaders. Their natural tendency is to goldplate the program. This is where your mature experience and good judgment come into play. You should know what it takes to perform a given function. Staff for the bare minimum to support that function and no more. Provide the bare minimum of contractor furnished equipment and no more. After all, you can't expect the competition to be dumb enough to bid more than the RFP required. You may have trouble with your team leaders trying to propose a separate organizational element for every *function* they see in the SOW. You must combine functions wherever it makes sense in order to minimize your supervisory overhead.

If you have done all of the above, at this point you should have your proposal humming along quite well. From here on, it should be a piece of cake. You need to stay on top of everything, put out the fires, and carry on a continuing education program for your proposal team. When the first drafts come in, you must drop everything else and apply yourself conscientiously to this most important task.

Here again is where you apply all the expertise and wisdom of your years of experience and the exercise of good judgment in reviewing and critiquing the proposal inputs. Do not be reticent about correcting your subordinates and sending the inputs back for rewrite. Everyone *wants* to improve his or her proficiency; the writers will appreciate your constructive, helpful comments. But don't ever say something is wrong unless you have a suggestion for making it right. Your approach must never be negative, but always helpful and positive.

But whatever you do, do not start rewriting their stuff for them. Because when you start doing everyone's thinking for them, they cease to do any thinking for themselves. You will soon find yourself immersed in a morass of detail and confusion from which you will never be able to extricate yourself, while one by one your proposal team will silently fold their tents and steal away, leaving you hanging there, slowly twisting in the wind.

In my own experience, I used to look forward to the critique of my work. It was like wanting to know what your grade was on an important test in school. But, sad to say, I was usually disappointed. Too often there was no critique at all. I finally came to the conclusion that no one even read my input. When I did get called in, it would be to tell me something like I should say "broad-based" instead of "vast" in this sentence, or "employ" instead of "utilize" in that sentence. Once I had both a general and an admiral sitting across from me in a management review tell me that my abbreviation for SOP stood for *standard* operating procedure, not *standing* operating procedure. I pulled out a copy of the Pentagon's dictionary of abbreviations and proved them wrong. I thought both of them would have an attack of apoplexy on the spot. Sigh! Such has been my experience with Red Teams[1] and the so-called management reviews, a subject I will get to next.

Red Teams and Management Reviews

In my previous book on the subject of proposals, I came down pretty hard on both management reviews and Red Teams. Well, I don't take back anything I said then except the part where I said, "Fire them all." Up to that time, I had never seen a Red Team that did it right. They were always thrust upon us by top management with little or no notice; none of them having even seen the RFP before; with very limited experience, if any, in the subject matter; and no prior planning for making a comprehensive evaluation of the proposal, just the hubris of an inspection team from higher headquarters, condescendingly bestowing some of their wisdom on us.

However, since writing that book, I have actually seen several Red Teams that had it right. I would like to think that it's because I concluded that chapter of the book by setting out a set of conditions under which these Red Teams should operate, or else face eviction from the premises by order of the proposal manager. Here they are:

- The team members should have thoroughly studied the RFP.
- The team members should have in-depth training and experience in the subject matter of the proposal.
- The team members should have some experience in proposal preparation.
- The team members should be dedicated to the job, not dragged in against their will.
- The team members should be brought in soon after completion of the first draft (after first doing their homework) and be given ample time to complete their work in an orderly manner.
- Reviews or critiques should be presented in person, to the entire proposal team, so that the person making the comments can be cross-examined and thus required to defend his or her comments.
- Criticism should be positive and constructive. If the reviewers believe something is wrong, they should have a suggestion for making it right; if the reviewers don't have a suggestion for making it right, they don't belong there.
- Sarcastic, degrading, or insensitive remarks should not be tolerated and will be grounds for terminating the meeting.

---

1. "Red Team" as used in this book refers to the in-house team of experts appointed by management to review and critique the first draft of the proposal.

- The proposal manager should have total veto power over any recommendation made by the red team. After all, he or she is still responsible for the proposal.

As I said, I have seen a remarkable improvement in the employment and preparation of red teams in the past several years, incorporating most of the conditions listed above. Possibly some influential, pragmatic people out there read my other book and the word got around.

Now as to management reviews. I had pretty much the same opinion of these up until a few years ago. In the past, these reviews would consist of a high-ranking officer from corporate holing himself up for days in an office adjoining the proposal team *at the very last minute,* just before the proposal absolutely, positively had to go to the printer. Then he would emerge like a bear from hibernation and make a few harrumphs and a few growls to the effect that he would have done it better, but it was probably as good as we could expect from such puny talent as we had available. Then we would all breathe a sigh of relief that our long ordeal was finally over.

But actually, what else could he have said, anyhow? By the time the management review was finished, there was no way any substantive changes could be made. And so the Great One would turn over his copy of the proposal, anointed with his usual nit-picking editorial changes like substituting "involve" for "entail" and an occasional exclamation mark in the margin and then plod his weary way back to the executive suite. Nobody ever asked what the exclamation marks in the margin meant.

Of course, we need management reviews. The corporate management has a right and a duty to know exactly what they are contracting to do if they win the contract. But these reviews absolutely must be made in a timely fashion, so that the proper corrective action can be taken, and in an orderly thoughtful manner, not in a panic situation. That is to say, they should be made concurrently with the red team review. Then all the changes can be incorporated at the same time in a coordinated process.

And, second, management reviews should be concerned with top-level management concerns, not with trying to beat a 22-year-old English major out of his or her editingjob. Top-level management should be concerned with how to make money for the corporation, how to manage corporate resources, how to sustain systematic growth, how to develop new markets, how to promote the corporate image, how to manage risk, how to balance the short-term risk against the long-term gain, and so on. More specifically, regarding the proposal, management reviews should be concerned with the pricing strategy, cash flow, financial risk involved, political considerations affecting the contract, availability of facilities and logistical support, availability of management and technical talent, and the general conformity of the proposal to corporate standards and objectives.

Consultants

And now it is time to talk about consultants. Again, I had a lot of uncomplimentary things to say about consultants in my other book, and even though I have now been a consultant for the past nine years, I'm not taking back a thing. Sad to say, this field is crawling with charlatans who have very limited experience or talent for preparing proposals. Most of the worst cases are in the up-front marketing end of the process. And these are the ones who gave us Ill Wind, with its malodorous atmosphere that, sad to say, will linger with us for years.

But I've run across more than a few who pretend to know something about writing and managing proposals. I will say this: If proposals could be prepared and delivered by mouth, most of these people would excel. I talked to one marketing director who was about to hire a consultant when he asked him what he would do to help with the proposal when the RFP came out. His reply was, "Why, I would hang my consultant sign above my door and be prepared to answer questions." Can't you just see him sitting there all day with his feet on the desk waiting for someone to come to the oracle for divine guidance?

The usual "expert witness" type of consultant that I've seen almost never comes prepared with any kind of presentation. They just want to put their feet on the desk (or conference table) and, "Here I am, ask me some questions." And if you ask the right questions, you get answers. One time we had a consultant who came in at a high price and with a bulging brief case. When we asked the right question, he would reach into the brief case and pull out a paper for us. When he left, he still had a bulging brief case, and we all wondered how many more pieces of paper we could have obtained if we had just asked the right questions. We also wondered what he was saving the rest for—our competitors?

One of the companies I worked for hired, over my objections and at great expense, four retired Air Force officers as consultants to come up with a proposal requirement on systems engineering. After a month or so, these four came up with a mishmash of cut-and-paste trash that could have applied to any contract anywhere that involved systems engineering. It read like something out of an Air Force regulation. I suppose all these people had done an adequate job while on active duty involving system engineering, but that didn't qualify them to write a proposal input on the subject. In fact, it didn't qualify them to write anything. Expertise alone is not enough. Experience alone is not enough. The vital ingredients are: having a grasp of the technical subject matter, the ability to apply it to the *specific requirement at hand,* and the capability to *express it fluently on paper.* And this requires some experience in proposal writing, learning how to address specific RFP requirements.

A Practical Set of Rules

The biggest mistakes I've seen in the hiring of consultants are: (a) assuming that because the prospective consultant worked in the area in which you are bidding that he or she is *ipso facto* an expert, and (b) failing to provide any guidelines or specify exactly what you expect from him or her. As to the former, one must realize there are hosts of people out there who show up for work every day and go through the motions of performing a job without any idea of how to articulate what they are doing or why. As to the latter, you really can't expect him or her to read your mind. If you want consultants to give formal presentations, for example, you have to tell them so.

My advice to proposal managers is to find out first whether your prospective consultant is a talker or a writer. Then "calibrate" him by asking some questions that you already know the answer to. If he tries to snow you, show him the door. If he qualifies and he is a talker, tell him to come back at a specified time and be prepared to give a presentation of everything he knows about this procurement to your proposal team and then answer all questions. If he is a writer, give him a small item from the RFP for him to respond to by fax. Either he responds effectively or you write him off. If he shows promise, and only then, you can bring him in to participate with your proposal team.

Now for the positive side of the coin. Consultants, if chosen properly and oriented adequately, can be of immense help in a variety of ways to improve your proposal. They can provide inside information on the target contract and its environment. They can open some doors for you to enable you to glean more information or to give you access to people who might be able to provide you with more information; or they can be extremely useful to you in reviewing and critiquing all or portions of your proposal, especially segments involving arcane fields where they have more experience than you.

Really good consultants can review and critique your proposal and usually find ways of improving it. (However, if they start talking about themes and discriminators and all that jargon, throw them out.) If you can find a consultant who has worked on at least 50 proposals, he or she could be the ideal solution to the situation I have alluded to before. That is where you have a proposal manager (the prospective manager of the program) who has only a little proposal preparation experience. Assign the job of deputy proposal manager to a consultant. But for this to work, you have to give him the backing of your management.

I once had an unhappy experience with that sort of thing. Everything started out well enough for me, having established a good rapport with the putative proposal manager. Then the marketing director (who had hired me) disappeared to work on another project. As seems inevitable in such situations, some self-proclaimed expert came crawling out from under some middle-management rock and started telling me how to manage the proposal. He talked to the customer every day, he said, and therefore he knew better than I what the customer wanted. The customer even told him how he wanted our proposal organized. According to him, the customer wanted us to outline the evaluation criteria instead of following the proposal instructions on formatting our proposal! When I resisted this, he peremptorily changed my outline as soon as my back was turned.

Of course, this guy was also an expert on organization charts, so when I resisted his asinine suggestions on organizing the contract, he loftily informed me *this was the way the customer wanted the program organized.*

The one thing we didn't have an argument about was the costing. And that's because, being a consultant, the very word "costing" was anathema for me. Consultants should actively avoid becoming privy to any company confidential costing strategies or techniques, lest they some day be suspected of giving away any such information to potential competitors. So I remained completely detached from any discussions on costing details, as I always do.

So it was a losing battle, and I eventually bid a not-so-fond farewell to this lugubrious windbag. Funny thing, though, when the contract award was announced, this guy who had been talking to the customer every day and knew exactly what the customer wanted, blah, blah, blah, had overbid the contract by some $37 million! We weren't even in the ballpark!

In summary, here are a few suggested rules on the use of consultants:

1. Hire them for a specific purpose that you are capable of defining in more or less specific terms.
2. Provide them with guidelines and directives to let them know exactly what you expect of them.
3. Select them carefully by checking their capability to do what you expect of them, like talking or writing.
4. Tell them only what they need to know, but tell them everything they need to know.
5. Don't accept everything they tell you on blind faith. Double-check what they tell you until you are sure you can trust them.
6. Bring them in at the earliest possible time—well before the RFP is out if it is for briefing purposes or for writing major segments of the proposal, and immediately after the first draft if it is for review and critiquing purposes.
7. Give them the management backup you would expect for yourself if they are assigned as a deputy proposal manager. Remember, they do not have any official authority at all. Their authority only derives from you.
8. Once they have established that they are competent and experts in their fields, let them do what you hired them to do. More than once I have told clients I am getting paid to do a job, not incessantly arguing over every nitpicking decision I make in doing the job. If you want a seminar, hire someone to conduct a seminar.

The Bidders' Conference and Bidders' Tour

And now for a few loose ends and you proposal managers are on your own. First, the bidders' conference. It behooves you to take a good, hard look at the way these conferences are conducted by the customer. They can be a most enlightening and educational experience for you or they can be a total waste of time.

The last one I attended was a total waste of time. This charade was courtesy of the U.S. Army. Two tired-looking, middle-aged, civil-servant types handled the whole thing for the government—no uniformed personnel in sight. This was for a procurement amounting to several hundred million dollars. Every single thing either of them said was read to us from prepared statements. No questions were allowed at this session. No attempt whatever was made to describe the work to be done. Only a few statements were made describing some of the terms of the proposed contract. (Which I suspect were the only things these two civil servants understood about the program.) We were told we could submit questions in writing, and they would have answers to them if we came back in the afternoon. At this point all but one of us from the company I represented left in disgust. Here were prospective bidders gathered from all over the U.S. at great expense, and not a single thing transpired that couldn't have been handled by mail.

What conclusion can you draw from a performance like this?

Just what I told my clients. You are wasting your time. This procurement office had already had a history of screwed up procurements, at least one of which had been successfully challenged in court and another reversed by order of the GAO.

When you see a performance like this, you can be pretty sure that the customer has already decided whom he is going to select. He is just going through the motions, perfunctorily filling the squares required by the regulations, pretending to make it look honest and according to the book.

I had a similar experience with the Air Force once. While their performance was decidedly more professional—they actually had some field-grade blue suiters there—I noticed that some of the civil service people stumbled over elementary questions that even I could have answered. At other times they were evasive and defensive. In other words, they hadn't prepared themselves for this conference. If you were in their shoes, and you were serious about achieving fair competition in a major procurement, wouldn't you carefully prepare for something as important as the bidders' conference? Again, I advised my client to No Bid this thing, even though we had already expended a sizable effort in preparing for it. And subsequent events proved me right.

Weigh Carefully the Final Bid/No Bid Decision

The first thing you should learn from a bidders' conference is a healthy skepticism about the customer's intentions. A bidders' conference honestly and conscientiously presented will have a high-ranking official from the user community present at least to introduce the procurement key personnel. They will be prepared with audio visual aids to present the background material of the work to be done and then a clear and comprehensive description of the work, along with any idiosyncrasies of the work environment, and so on. Then they should be prepared to answer questions from the bidders. It's all right to insist on written questions beforehand. Some questions do require staffing and research. But the customers should be able to answer the questions extemporaneously without reading the answers. And they should be capable of taking follow-up questions orally for clarification.

After all, what have they got to be afraid of? All questions and answers are eventually published and disseminated to all the bidders, and these written answers, which constitute an amendment to the RFP, *supersede any oral statements*. It seems that if the President of the United States can get up before an adversarial press corps and answer a wide range of oral questions, the answers to which could change the fate of the world, these GS-15s could answer simple questions narrowly limited to their own procurement.

On the other hand, I have seen bidders' conferences conducted in such a manner that they were indeed learning experiences for the bidders, as they were intended to be by the regulations requiring them. You can tell whether the main concern of those in charge is to achieve an honestly competitive procurement by the sincere, straightforward manner in which they conduct the bidders' conference.

Or, on the other hand, does the main thrust seem to be to cover their tracks and fulfill their obligation to comply with the regulations requiring fair competition? If you feel it is the latter, then my advice in general is to walk away from it. Save your B&P money for the honest competitions.

Who Should Attend?

Who should you take with you on these bidders' conferences (and bidders' tours, which are usually conducted in connection therewith)? If you can take only one person, I would recommend that it be the most experienced technical person on your proposal team, provided he or she is alert, observant, and knows how to take notes. The reason I recommend the most experienced technical person is because this person will know what to look for, will know what is important and what isn't. A really knowledgeable person, for instance, can walk through a machine shop and come out with a pretty accurate idea of the capabilities and maximum output of this shop. I can walk through many labs and know just how many and what kind of people it takes to work there and what the output of that lab should be. On the other hand, we once sent two people on a four-day, three-state bidders' tour and they came back with nothing but a hangover.

If you can bring one or two other people, I would recommend the costing specialist and your administrator, business manager. or whatever you choose to call him. (For some reason, the number of people permitted to attend these conferences is usually either four or two.)

What You Should Accomplish

You might be well advised to have a little pep talk with these people before you depart to let them know this is not like going to Disneyland. They have a purpose and a serious one—to gather all the information they can absorb and then return to impart all of this information to the rest of the proposal team. You, as the proposal manager, should have compiled a list of essential elements of information (EEI) by this time, so instruct them that they are expected to come back with the answers or else.

Some procurement offices permit the use of tape recorders. If you do use one, make arrangements to have the tapes transcribed so that you can disseminate the contents thereof to the entire proposal team. It doesn't do anyone any good to have these tapes hidden in someone's desk gathering dust. Actually, I think the most efficient use of time is to have the person who made the tape use it to refresh his or her memory in making notes for a presentation to the key members of the proposal team.

But, I repeat, because this is an item so often neglected, see to it that all the information gathered on the bidders' conference and bidders' tour gets to the proposal team. And give them a chance to pick your brains. Often you will note things you don't think important enough to mention that turn out to be very important to others.

One more thing before we leave the subject of bidders' conferences. Everywhere I go I find people who are extremely reluctant to submit questions at the bidders' conference. This is based on the supposition that the answer to the question would be useful to the competition. But if Bidder A and Bidder B both pass up the opportunity to clarify a sentence in the proposal instructions, they both risk the possibility of being nonresponsive in their proposals. If either had asked the question, then both would have avoided the risk. So how has either A or B gained advantage by not asking? And how about Bidder C, who knew the answer all along and therefore didn't need to ask? If neither A nor B ask, Bidder C will eat their lunch on this proposal.

The lesson is clear. Unless you are 99% sure you know the answer, then ask the question. There are almost always inconsistencies in an RFP. (The right hand not knowing what the left hand did.) *Somebody* has to rectify these errors, and the customer will appreciate your help in pointing them out. In general, then, I would recommend submitting a question on anything that requires clarification or any questionable statement in the RFP, if it is of a substantive nature, unless you are 99% sure you know the answer.

Personally, I don't believe in correcting the customer's nonsubstantive mistakes (like performing his editing function, correcting his punctuation and misspelled words), but if you feel like it, go ahead.

The Orals or Q&A Phase

Next, the orals or Q&A session. This can often be a make-or-break phase if the competition is close and the procurement is honest. This phase has a two-fold purpose: (a) to clarify any ambiguities or possible misunderstandings in your proposal, and (b) to require the bidders to justify or back up what they have promised in the proposal, or, in other words, prove the feasibility of what they proposed.

I might add a third reason for the orals session. It gives the government a good chance to get a good, close-up look at whom they would be working with, to see how you respond under pressure, and to confirm that you didn't just hire some consultant to write your proposal. And conversely, it is an opportunity to show off your whiz kids and your fair-haired boys.

Clarifications and Deficiencies

In almost all cases these days, you will get a letter from the customer listing what he regards as items that need clarification and another list called "deficiencies." Don't be alarmed at the dreary, apocalyptic tone of these letters. This is just a typical example of the turgid, oppressive prose of bureaucrats at work. The clarifications are a minor problem. They can be as innocuous as an arithmetic error in your cost proposal. The deficiencies, on the other hand, are serious matters.

A deficiency is precisely defined in the FAR, and your proposal has failed in one way or another to fulfill the standards by which the SSEB has evaluated it. This is your one and only chance to correct this deficiency and avoid a significant penalty in the grading of your proposal.

Therefore, you must get the person who wrote this section and work with him or her to correct it. Time is always of the essence here. You never have more than barely enough time to respond to these requests, so you must keep a string on all your proposal team, especially the team leaders until after the orals.

The questions you may be asked will range from the ridiculous to the sublime. I have seen on multi-hundred-million-dollar contracts as few as four questions and as many as over 500. The one with only four questions, as you might have guessed, was wired for their favorite bidder. They asked the questions for the sole purpose of filling the squares. Of course, you have already spent your B&P money by that time, so there is nothing you can do about it. Except build your case for a protest, that is. The one that I worked on that involved over 500 questions appeared to be an honest effort. Funny thing, though, the thrust of most of the questions was that we had understaffed the contract. And we were verbally warned that we had to raise our staffing substantially or we were out of it. So we raised our staffing accordingly, and then they awarded the contract to the low bidder!

Another frustrating irritation you may experience is the incompetent SSEB chairman who can't distinguish between a deficiency and a clarification. We once responded to an RFP that included a hypothetical problem that involved a requirement to construct a radar site on a remote, deserted island in the mid-Pacific to meet a national emergency. Problems like this seldom ever provide you all the givens you need to address the solution. So we stipulated some valid assumptions, one of which would be that the transportation to the island would be provided by GFE from Honolulu. I can just see those SSEB cats chortling in glee over this assumption. "Ahah, we've got these guys. What makes them think the government can provide this service. Mark them down for a deficiency."

So it must have ruined their whole day when we came back with a picture of the government-operated landing craft in Honolulu, complete with specifications and the charter under which this boat operated—namely, to support just this kind of operation. You see, we had done our homework. They had not.

A few more words of wisdom about the orals and we will move on to the subject of BAFOs to wind up this chapter. Usually, but not always, after the response to the written questions has been submitted, you will be called into an oral session, the main reasons for which are to explain your answers, to clarify any misunderstandings, justify your approach, to persuade them that your approach is feasible, or all of the above. A really well-planned and executed procurement should definitely include this session.

This is where you bring your well-groomed key personnel, prepared to answer forthrightly and with a minimum of hemming and hawing all the questions propounded by the SSEB and to defend the answers that you have already submitted. And if you have any free spirits on your team who don't own a suit and tie, send them out to buy one.

Choose Your Team with Care

As I said before, this is also an opportunity for the customer to have a good look at the individuals with whom they will be interfacing for maybe the next several years. So it is imperative that these people make a good impression. You might have a few sensitivity sessions with these people beforehand on how to mind their manners and keep their cool. We had a guy on the SSEB once (on a contract now worth over $500 million) whom we called "white socks," because he wore a blue suit and white socks, who needled us unmercifully throughout the morning session. Some of us thought he hated our company. Others thought he was planted by the government to test us. In any case, he didn't show up for the afternoon session, much to our relief. (Maybe, even his colleagues couldn't stand him any longer.) But we kept our cool and we won the contract.

In summary, I would recommend the following preparations for the orals:

1. Assign primary responsibility to a specified individual for each major section of the proposal. This person and his or her designated assistants must be prepared to answer any question within their designated segment of the proposal.
2. Assign review responsibility for specified sections of the proposal to knowledgeable individuals other than those who prepared the respective sections. The idea is to get a fresh perspective here and possibly some ideas that may have been overlooked. But the real purpose is to prepare these individuals to fire questions at the proposal team such as they might expect from the customer during the orals.
3. About two weeks before the anticipated scheduling of the orals, convene a meeting of all individuals mentioned in items 1 and 2 and go over the initial proposal, so that those mentioned in item 2 can simulate the questioning that can be expected at the orals.
4. After this meeting (or concurrently), identify where cost reductions in the proposal would be feasible and determine the possible magnitude and ramifications thereof.
5. About one week before the anticipated orals, convene a meeting between key proposal team members, the proposal cost accountant (bean counter), and the responsible corporate representative (if possible) to determine the minimum acceptable BAFO.
6. The day before departure for the orals, convene a meeting of the entire orals team to provide a briefing on the background of the SSEB members, their peculiarities, biases, predilections, and so forth, as far as is known. (Have your marketing people done their job?) Also you must establish the *modus operandi* for the following:
   - *The agenda.* An opening statement by the proposal manager or (preferably) a high-ranking representative from the corporate headquarters. Introduction of the team to the SSEB,
   - *The protocol.* A clear understanding as to who is responsible for answering a particular question. Who talks and how much. The proposal manager should never try to answer *all* the questions. The idea is to show them this is a *team* of experts, with the proposal manager in charge.
   - *Answering questions.* How to answer questions—directly and crisply, to the point. The truth, the whole truth, and nothing but the truth. And also how to defer an answer to a sensitive question that may require more reflection or research.

One of the things to look for in the questions submitted for the orals is: Are there any hidden messages there? Do they indicate a pattern of doubt as to your staffing levels? Is there an imbalance in the questions about the feasibility of a particular technical approach? Is there an undercurrent of discontent among some or many of your proposed key personnel? We once picked up our questions from the customer, and the very first question was, "What makes you think your program manager is qualified for this position?" I immediately got on the phone and called our company president, "Get rid of this guy; don't even allow him to show up at the orals."

The BAFO

But more important yet are the subliminal hints that should tell you your costing is a little out of kilter. And this is a matter that can and must be corrected in the best and final offer (BAFO). You will get the BAFO announcement from the customer soon after the orals have been completed. That will be the last chance to change anything in your proposal, and such changes are limited to your cost proposal, so you can't change anything in your cost proposal that will have any impact on the rest of your proposal. So that pretty much limits it to your G&A and fee, salary structure, fringe benefits, and ODC. In other words, it is primarily an exercise between the bean counters and top management. You, the proposal manager, will have little to say about it except to object strenuously if they try to cut your salary or that of your key personnel.

Although the hints you get could mean your bid is either too high or too low, I would recommend never raising the bid. You are in the zone of consideration with a competitive bid price or presumably you wouldn't have got this far. So don't take a chance now of bidding yourself out of the competition. The hints you are getting could have been designed to accomplish just that in order to award the contract to their favorite bidder. Get the contract first. You can manage it later.

Just one exception to the previous comments. If you find you have made a gross mistake in your bid (based it on a false assumption, for example), raise your price accordingly. We almost made that mistake once to the tune of $300,000 due to a stupid mistake by the costing specialist. So we raised our bid or we would have been out $300,000.

In conclusion, I would remind you, the proposal manager, once again that managing a proposal is one of the toughest, most challenging jobs you will ever encounter. It involves dealing with a wide variety of people with conflicting interests and organizing and directing the efforts of an *ad hoc* collection of people with diverse talents and expertise into a cohesive, motivated *team* under the most adverse circumstances in an intensive activity and under great pressure to achieve a goal against which the odds of success are not favorable. Can you think of a more daunting endeavor anywhere else in the business world?

The only way to handle this is to remind yourself that no one can expect any more of you than to do your best. To achieve this, first demand the authority and resources to do the job properly. Then do your homework. Prepare yourself by intensive study and analysis of the task and all its ramifications. Then select your proposal team carefully and motivate them to function as a team. Decentralize your authority to team leaders and guide and assist them as necessary. And, above all, stay in control of the operation. If you lose control, it soon degenerates into chaos. If you have faithfully and conscientiously applied the lessons in this chapter, together with the principles and procedures set forth in this book, no one can ask for more.

List of Acronyms

AAA	Agricultural Adjustment Administration
ADP	automatic data processing
AFR	Air Force Regulation
AR	Army Regulation
BAFO	best and final offer
B & P	bid and proposal (funds)
CBD	Commerce Business Daily
CCC	Civilian Conservation Corps
CDL	contract data list
CDRL	contract data requirements list
CFP	customer furnished property
CI	configuration item
CPAF	cost plus award fee
CPCI	computer program configuration item
CPFF	cost plus fixed fee
CPIF	cost plus incentive fee
C/SCSC	cost/schedule control system criteria
CWBS	contract work breakdown structure
DAR	Defense Acquisition Regulations (now FAR)
DCAA	Defense Contract Audit Agency
DID	data item description
DOC	Department of Commerce
DOD	Department of Defense
DOE	Department of Energy

DOT	Department of Transportation
DTIC	Defense Technical Information Center
EEI	Essential Elements of Information
EEO	Equal Employment Opportunity
E-Lab	Electronics Lab
EPA	Environmental Protection Agency
F & A	Finance and Administration
FAR	Federal Acquistion Regulations
FFP	firm fixed price
FOIA	Freedom of Information Act
G-2	intelligence (information on competitors or contracts)
G & A	general and administrtive (costs)
GAO	General Accounting Office
GDP	gross domestic product
GFE	government furnished equipment
GFP	government furnished property
GSA	General Services Administration
GSBCA	General Services Board of Contract Appeals
HHS	Health and Human Services
IFB	invitation for bid
IGCE	independent government cost estimate
MIL-SPEC	Military Specification
MIL-STD	Military Standard
MIS	management information system
NASA	National Aeronautics and Space Agency
NIH	National Institute of Health
NIMH	National Institute of Mental Health
NOAA	National Oceanic and Atmospheric Administration
NRA	National Recovery Administration
NRC	Nuclear Regulatory Commission
NSF	National Science Foundation
ODC	other direct charges (in costing)
O & M	Operation and Maintenance

PCO	purchasing and contracting officer
PI	principal investigator
QA	quality assurance
Q & A	question and answers (session or conference)
QC	quality control
R & D	research and development
RFP	request for proposal
RFQ	request for quote
SBA	Small Business Administration
SBIR	small business innovative research
SOP	standing operating procedure
SOW	statement of work
SSA	Source Selection Authority
SSAC	Source Selection Advisory Committee
SSEB	Source Selection Evaluation Board
TDY	temporary duty
TM	telemetry
WBS	work breakdown structure
WPA	Work Progress Administration

Index